The Working Boerboel:
Fact or Fiction?

Vijai Naidu

First published in 2018 by Sirius Dog Publications (part of Sirius Security Ltd)
London, UK
www.siriuspmas.co.uk
info@siriuspmas.co.uk

© E. Vijai P. Naidu 2018. All rights reserved. No part of this book may be reproduced, stored in a retrieval system, or transmitted in any form or by any means electronic, mechanical or otherwise, without the prior permission of the publisher.

The right of E. Vijai P. Naidu to be identified as the author of this work has been asserted in accordance with the Copyright, Designs and Patents Act 1988. The author asserts their moral rights.

All reasonable attempts have been made to contact copyright owners of images used in this book. If we have overlooked any source, we undertake to correct the omission in any future editions of the book provided that we are informed in writing and the source is verifiable.

Printed and bound by CPI Group (UK) Ltd, Croydon, CR0 4YY

ISBN 978-1-5272-3355-3

Cover photo: collage, 2018. Source: Author.

Table of Contents

Dedication v

Table of Abbreviations... vii

Table of Illustrations.. viii

Chapter 1: Introduction 1

Chapter 2: History of the Boerboel 5

Chapter 3: A Brief History of South African Geography and Politics 25

Chapter 4: The Establishment of the Boerboel 45

Chapter 5: The Importance of the Female.......................................69

Chapter 6: The Importance of Aggression 83

Chapter 7: Of Clubs, Committees and Organisations..................... 99

Chapter 8: The Final Curtain Call: Lessons from History...........127

Chapter 9: Fact or Fiction: The Awakening....................................133

Appendix 185

Bibliography 195

Dedication

In dedication to my wonderful daughter who toiled the muddy wet windy fields day in and day out, to assist and accompany me while training dogs.

For her compassion and empathy, her reaching out to embrace the art of understanding our four-legged companions, forearmed with new found knowledge she too has inherited memories and traditions of dog management that will pass on to the next generation. With all my deepest respect and love I bestow upon her.

Man Meets Dog
by Konrad Lorenz (1953)

> I have a prejudice against people, even very small children who are afraid of dogs. This prejudice is quite unjustified for it is completely normal reaction for a small person, at the first sight of such a large beast of prey, at first to be anxious and careful. But the contrary standpoint, that I love children that show no fear of even big dogs and know how to handle them properly, has its justification, for this can only be done by someone who possesses a certain understanding of nature and our fellow beings.

LUCAS VAN DE MERWE

This book gives special dedication to a man who touched my heart and gave me indelible advice and knowledge. I decided to visit Lucas van de Merwe after many years of phone conversations from London to South Africa. Upon my arrival, the kind generosity and gracious hosting of Lucas compelled me to stay for four nights as his guest and culminated in my being able to fill in many of the blanks in my historical thesis. While many people doubted his words, the truth was always deep within. Born on the 26th October 1931 in Kroonstadt South Africa, Lucas van de Merwe, Lifetime Honorary member of the SABT, Founder of the Historical Boerboel Association of South Africa (HBSA) and the founding member of the SABT and co-founder of this veritable breed, will be remembered for his unbridled passion and dedication to the Boerboel. May you rest in peace good friend. Thank you for all you gave to me and for whom this work could not have been completed with the detail required.

The late Mr Lucas van de Merwe, founding farther of the boerboel breed pictured with the author 2006

Table of Abbreviations

AVD (e.V.)	Alano Verein Deutschland (eingetragener Verein) (Pressa Canario Club of Germany (Court registered association))
AWDF	American Working Dog Federation
BI	Boerboel International
EBBASA	Elite Boerboel Breeders Association of South Africa
FCI	Fédération Cynologique Internationale (International Dog Society)
FH	FartenHund (advanced tracking title)
HBSA	Historical Boerboel Association of South Africa
KUSA	Kennel Union of South Africa
IPO	Internationale Prüfungs-Ordnung (International Trial Rules)
SABBS	South African Boerboel Breeders' Society
SABT/SABBA	South African Boerboel Breeders' Association

Table of Illustrations

Page 21

Bite 1 (Top Left) .... Magda Morarcova, Czech Republic
Bite 2 (Top Right) .... Author, United Kingdom
Bite 3 (Bottom Left) .... Brandon Wilson, Kentucky, USA
Bite 4 (Bottom Right) .... Author, United Kingdom

Page 22

Bite 5 (Top Left) .... Author, South Africa
Bite 6 (Top Right) .... Author, Russia
Bite 7 (Middle Left) .... Alexey Breykin, Russia
Bite 8 (Middle Right) .... Alexey Breykin, Russia
Bite 9 (Bottom Left) .... Author, United Kingdom
Bite 10 (Bottom Left) .... Author, United Kingdom

Page 23

Bite 11 (Top Left) .... Maciej Zaluski, Poland
Bite 12 (Top Right) .... Maciej Zaluski, Poland
Bite 13 (Middle Left) .... Brandon Wilson, Kentucky, USA
Bite 14 (Middle Right) .... Kevin Hartzenburg, South Africa
Bite 15 (Bottom Left) .... Maciej Zaluski, Poland
Bite 16 (Bottom Left) .... Author, Russia

Page 24

Bite A (Top Left) .... Janlo Ungerer, South Africa
Bite AA (Top Right) .... Author, Russia
Bite B (Middle Left) .... Sascha Jirsak, Germany
Bite BB (Middle Right) .... Kevin Hartzenburg, South Africa
Bite C (Bottom Left) .... Janlo Ungerer, South Africa
Bite CC (Bottom Right) .... Author, United Kingdom

Page 80

Jump 1 (Top Left) .... Brandon Wilson, Kentucky, USA
Jump 2 (Top Right) .... Author, United Kingdom
Jump 3 (Middle Left) .... Author, United Kingdom
Jump 4 (Middle Right) ....Sascha Jirsak, Germany
Jump 5 (Bottom Left) ....Sascha Jirsak, Germany
Jump 6 (Bottom Right) .... Brandon Wilson, Kentucky, USA

Page 81

Jump 7 (Top Left) .... Brandon Wilson, USA
Jump 8 (Top Right) .... Dapo Ojaro, Lagos, Nigeria
Jump 9 (Middle Left) .... Dapo Ojaro, Lagos, Nigeria
Jump 10 (Middle Right) .... Magdalena Czechowska, Poland
Jump 11 (Bottom Left) .... Jakub Rutkowski, Poland
Jump 12 (Bottom Right) .... Maciej Zaluski, Poland

Page 85

Prey drive (Bottom Left) .... Maciej Zaluski, Poland
Prey drive (Bottom Right) .... Author, United Kingdom

Pages 97–98

Bark & Hold 1 (Top Left) ....Author, United Kingdom
Bark & Hold 2 (Top Right) ....Author, Germany
Bark & Hold 3 (Bottom Left) .... Brandon Wilson, USA
Bark & Hold 4 (Bottom Right) .... Brandon Wilson, USA
Bark & Hold 5 (Top Left) .... Magda Morarcova, Czech Republic
Bark & Hold 6 (Top Right) .... Author, USA
Bark & Hold 7 (Middle Left) .... Author
Bark & Hold 8 (Middle Right) .... Maciej Zaluski, Poland
Bark & Hold 9 (Bottom Left) .... Maciej Zaluski, Poland

Page 124

Bite 18 (Top Left) .... Author, Germany
Bite 19 (Top Right) .... Sascha Jirsak, Germany
Bite 20 (Middle Left) .... Dapo Ojaro, Lagos, Nigeria
Bite 21 (Middle Right) .... Author, United Kingdom
Bite 21 (Bottom Left) .... Mark Beesley, United Kingdom
Bite 22 (Bottom Right) .... Jenny Wells, United Kingdom

Page 125

Bite 23 (Top Left) .... Dapo Ojaro, Lagos, Nigeria
Bite 24 (Top Right) .... Author, United Kingdom
Bite 24 (Middle Left) .... Sascha Jirsak, Germany
Bite 25 (Middle Right) .... Author, South Africa
Bite 26 (Bottom Left) .... Jonathan Sheldon, United Kingdom
Bite 27 (Bottom Right) .... Magda Morarcova, Czech Republic

Page 126

Bite 28 (Top Left) .... Magda Morarcova, Czech Republic
Bite 29 (Top Right) .... Magda Morarcova, Czech Republic
Bite 29 (Middle Left) .... Maciej Zaluski, Poland
Bite 30 (Middle Right) .... Maciej Zaluski, Poland
Bite 31 (Bottom Left) .... Maciej Zaluski, Poland
Bite 32 (Bottom Right) .... Maciej Zaluski, Poland

Chapter 1
Introduction

The food of our childhood continues to give us such pleasure later in life because of its familiar taste, smell, and touch. These sense-experiences shape us and come to define what we call our comfort zone. The dogs of my childhood were South African dogs, in particular, the fine Rhodesian Ridgebacks (which have a genetic link with the Boerboel). I have such strong, pleasant memories of them being part of our family. And, since the early 1970s to this day I have remained faithful to this familiar comfort blanket.

Late 70s with our fine Ridgebacks

When I first came across the Boerboel in 2002, I spent a huge amount of time in collecting data and information on what bloodlines would best suit my needs as a prospective purchaser. I had then started to travel with my brother up and down the UK to test Boerboels from prospective breeders to see if they held up to the job.

Little was I aware at that time that I had catalysed a series of events which would arm me with great knowledge, or that my journey in both working, testing, and training Boerboels would span the entire globe and would cover many hundreds of thousands of miles over the course of 15 years. During the period of this book's fruition, the amount of changes within the breed have been colossal and difficult to keep pace with; I have also struggled to maintain diplomacy in a breed-enthusiast world fraught with egos and emotions, as a result of which, with great misfortune, we were unable to include many images that would have given you the reader greater insight, from a visual perspective. For the interests of this book, it has been my intention from the start to remain impartial, to not side with the views of any one group or clique of friends, that is to say to not pick which side of the fence my loyalties might lie. The principal reason for what you might call this social courtesy is the desire to not hurt anyone's feelings; but also, by striving to be impartial the book benefits you as a reader and possible consumer.

To be completely transparent about my motives for writing on the subject of the Boerboel, you must understand that I am not a breeder and have no wish to breed dogs for a living, therefore I have no vested nor financial interest in publishing my opinion. Instead, I am doing this in the fundamental belief that education based on the principle of truth is of paramount importance. I wish only to inform you, the reader of the various strands of the Boerboel's history so that you may draw your own conclusions as to the real story.

Truth has no allies, it knows no discrimination and has no loyalty to any friend. It is factual and impartial. In this period of my search for truth, driven by a need to distinguish fact from fiction, I could not have foreseen that I would come to encounter a multitude of prejudice against and even, at times, utter ignorance about the very concept of a dog.

My life as a boy had always involved dogs, an array of which, as we were growing up, were simply not suitable family dogs, but there were others that were true companions. Before my daughter was born, I had decided to go down the path of the Boerboel. Having grown up with Rhodesian Ridgebacks my entire life, I found they lacked the substance I required for an effective home guardian dog and protector of the family, which I had grown up believing was the purpose of having a dog. Me and my siblings had been brought up to understand that everything in life, including dogs, had to have some form of purpose. I never knew as a child that dogs were and are still nowadays primarily kept in the pet dog world as social substitutes for healthy human relationships, particularly so in mega cities like New York, London, Tokyo etc. where society has experienced a substantial shift in its structure as a result of many humans now choosing to remain single, but alas that requires another book. In the meantime, my buddies in cities across the world are working harder than ever to tackle an undesirable niche of problem dogs that has arisen due to this modern phenomenon.

Over the years, I have seen many organisations come and go, while breed registries pop up today and are gone tomorrow; there are more splinter factions in the dog breeding world than in the Indonesian rainforest, more politics and smear campaigns than a US election. And through all this adversity and madness you must retain the ability to focus clearly on your own agenda and goals, and not be sucked into the circus of what some consider a fallacious pantomime of make believe and fairytale romances. The importance of truth goes far beyond the calls of friendships, and truth itself has no prejudice. I have faced great conflict at times, and struggled to remain impartial, to not let my heart and passion rule my head, and more importantly, to allow common sense and facts to prevail. It has been an epic challenge indeed, to say the least, which I admit I have failed to meet on numerous occasions.

While my reasons for owning a dog have not changed over the last 15 years, I have experienced an enlightenment of a kind. Initially, I was used to having dogs that would protect my family, but to fully understand the purported merits of the breed, as described in the breed literature, I followed another path that required self-sacrifices far greater than making phone calls, sending emails and visiting people; it was the path of IPO. This refers to Internationale Prüfungs-Ordnung — German for 'International Trial Rules', which, in its original design, was a breed test (formerly known as Schutzhund) to assess the German Shepherd dog for both police work and acceptability for breeding. Today, it is a breed suitability test as well as a competition sport for all breeds of dog, and now commands huge interest the world over with both professional dog trainers and novices alike.

It was all well and good to train the Boerboel breed to bite, but I discovered alternatives after learning the methods of IPO. This approach to training introduced me to what I now consider to be a more grown-up and intellectual perspective of what constitutes a reliable working dog.

I endured many years of training with this breed, attaining five world firsts for a female of this breed, whose father, Zeb, had been the first male to achieve the accolade of first-ever IPO-titled, AWDF-titled, FH-titled Boerboel in the world. This was an illustrious feat that gave Zeb's owner handler and trainer Brandon Wilson world recognition in this breed and propelled the dog to fame especially after it was featured in *Schutzhund USA* working dog magazine circa 2010.

The results and experience of IPO training opened my eyes to the amount of contradictory and at times even misleading information that is published on the web and by marketing departments, which can wreak havoc in its ability to create falsehoods. Hence the title of this book: *The Working Boerboel: Fact or Fiction?*

Probably the most fascinating observations I have noted on my travels have been those relating to humans: their complex and emotional states; their political, cultural, and geographical dynamics; and their changes in attitude that within dog breeding circles relating to the Boerboel can be as frequent as the great British weather (and yes, they really can be that frequent!). When these factors are considered along with commerce, vested interests, and individual intentions, it is safe to say that the world of the Boerboel is indeed very colourful. But one can also say that at times this world appears very dark, misleading, and at best mercenary. An important note for the reader to bear in mind is that the Boerboel breed from the beginning has been and always will be an evolving species. Caught in the conflict between old tradition and modern expectations, a dichotomy exists in the Boerboel breeding world, with its westernised overseas market and its African heritage in the background. Like all information, this book will inevitably become redundant at some point, but it is hoped that before then it may serve to guide you to a better future with your dog.

This book should act as a guide; its advice is based on my own formative experiences and certainly, the final chapter is formed from my personal opinions. It is up to you to dissect, discard, or take on board both the negative and positive avenues of thought with regard to this breed.

This book was and is designed to embrace working dog people, breeders, and breed enthusiasts, no matter their differences of thought and opinion, and although at times this book will touch your emotional chords, its main purpose is to stimulate thought and debate, and hopefully offer other perspectives as seen through the eyes of a consumer (i.e. myself).

My final thought on this book concerns all the contradictions and scandals that have erupted over this breed and its legitimacy, and the inability of others within this breed to agree on even basic evidence. If I were ever to conclude what has been suggested by notable scholars of dogs, that most individuals involved in the dog world cannot be trusted, then it would be fair to say this book would not ever have come into existence. The material of this book comes from accounts of those mainly old-time Boerboel people who were around when this breed was created. Happy reading.

The authors father with an old type Rhodesian Ridgeback in 1970, the same size as many of the old type Boerboels.

Chapter 2
History of the Boerboel

The importance of evolution

In order to ascertain the true course of history, we have to find evidence, gather witness statements, and inspect historical information. The history of the Boerboel (an Afrikaans word meaning 'Farmer's Boel') is vague, and no vital evidence has ever been documented about the Boerboel as we know it today. The photographic evidence is circumstantial and what is more, we are unable to identify the true type, for the reason that between the time of the Great Trek (c.1835) and the formation of the first Boerboel breed registry South African Boerboel Association (SABT, now called SABBS) in 1983, there was no formally agreed definition of the Boerboel's phenotype.

Thus, this takes us to the question of the evolution of the dog and its purpose as worked out by analysis of historical facts and evidence, and more importantly, scientific logic. We shall need to dig up the history of the Rhodesian Ridgeback, (the officially recognised dog of South Africa), ascertain the strains of dogs used for their breeding programmes, and from there we can move further forward in time. A general background of geographical influences will also be covered, as this will have vital relevance to present day facts. The particular emphasis I have given to the Indian dog will also be relevant to the final chapter of this book and therefore, please do bear with me. It is vital to remain impartial when gathering evidence of historical accounts, so we will examine such evidence with a critical eye.

The origin of the domestic dog can be traced back to some 10 to 15 000 years ago. Since the dawn of our primitive society man and dog have lived as mutual beneficiaries of the environment, helping with hunting, food, companionship, and protection. Such features have been part of an evolutionary progression within this universal culture of man and dog.

Our modern-day dog is pretty much the product of the Indian wolf, and research from the University of Konstanz suggests that all domestic dogs come from one particular, single gene pool. It is also suggested that a large period of isolation occurred in East Asia some 40 000 years ago. The modern-day dog as we know is probably the product of several maternal wolf lines and not four lines as many academics suggest, and now extensive research can reveal through the introduction of mitochondrial DNA testing exactly where the domestic dog began, so that finally, I dare say, we have conclusive evidence, which will indeed support the written recordings of some of the world's finest historians and travellers.

The Mastiffs of Tibet and Asia

We can now move slightly forward in time to the period when the gene pool starts to branch out through migration and other geographical changes. For the purpose of documenting the Boerboel our research has only focused on the Molosser group. The general consensus on the birthplace of the Mastiff is Tibet. Conclusive witness testimonies claim this dog to be of superior size and stature. To quote Andre Guibault in his 1947 book *The Tibetan Venture*, 'They become real wild beasts, capable of tearing a man to pieces'. There are innumerable witness accounts of these dogs and the breed was well documented by various travellers and notified dignitaries of the day.

In circa 1275 Marco Polo described these dogs in greater detail and compared them to the size of a donkey; however, it is imperative to remain objective and realise that the Asian donkey is not of the size associated with the donkeys that children ride on the beaches of Brighton.

The Tibetan Mastiff had lived in virtual isolation for many centuries, although it is true that many dogs would have accompanied Tibetan traders and dignitaries to the lower plains of the Indian Deccan Plateau and farther beyond. Dogs were a great form of trade and were regularly exchanged between humans throughout evolution. What happened to the larger, more powerful Tibetan Mastiff is a mystery, and the breeding of such dogs as of this day of writing remains obscure to me. An interesting article appeared in the *Central Asiatic Journal*, vol. 3 (no. 3), September, 1963 by Robert B. Ekvall, entitled 'Role of the Dog in Tibetan Nomadic Society'. In the absence of historical records, if we were to try and understand the ancient cultures of great gladiator dogs and their masters we can at least look at the nomadic people of Tibet, who due to geographical barriers have preserved centuries-long traditions and attitudes. Ekvall's article is a great achievement for both his observations and understanding of the Tibetan Mastiff within this unique nomadic society. He informs the reader that there are some unexpected aspects of the Tibetan Mastiff, 'which relate to social integration, and to influences affecting the development of personality within a culture.' During a visit to a small encampment of nomadic pastoralists, Ekvall observed that each tent kept at least two watchdogs, called Srung KhyI (guard dogs) or Sgo KhyI (door dogs), with chiefs or wealthy men having up to 20 or more. 'They are two varieties or breeds: the true Tibetan Mastiff – which is somewhat rare – and another equally ferocious and almost equally large mongrel. The latter undoubtedly has, among other strains, more or less Mastiff blood.' At that time, the Mastiffs constituted what Tibetans call a 'bone line' and substantial efforts were made to keep the breed pure. To own one is akin to a status symbol; when Ekvall was writing up his study it was difficult to find one for sale and if indeed found the price was often similar to that of a decent horse. The dogs he saw had 'the typical heavy muzzle, high domed head, hanging lips, the red of the eyelid showing and massive forequarters of the Mastiff breed' and had a long tail lightly feathered which was carried in a loose curl. They were often black and had to be so to be considered pure-bred, although they had 'tan trim on the face, neck and legs, usually some white on the throat and chest, and a tan spot over each eye; from which they get the name Mig bziI Can (four eyed one(s))'. Ekvall even owned a Tibetan Mastiff himself, which he described as weighing 160 pounds. Of great interest is his comment that the breed's 'most distinctive characteristic is an incredibly heavy baying bark much more like the sound of a fog horn than the outcry of any animal'.

Tibetan Mastiffs

Slightly smaller, the mongrel watchdogs were observed in greater numbers than the Mastiffs but were as ferocious. Their bark was reported by Ekvall as being different, not having 'the foghorn quality of tone which distinguishes the true Mastiff'. The mongrel watchdogs were seen in a range of colours, from pure black to a grey wolf colour and even an occasional white one. With a longer pelage than that of the Mastiffs, heads that were wider and flatter with more pointed muzzles, the tails of the mongrel variety were carried in a tight curl over the back. Ekvall reports:

> 'Both varieties are used only as watchdogs and although a dog may occasionally follow the herdsman for the day they are not trained as sheep and cattle dogs to drive and herd livestock. In an incidental fashion they act as scavengers always hungrily on hand when the butchering is being done. Whenever the stock die in unusual numbers from disease or in the heavy snows of late spring the dogs feast to repletion. Their proper function in life, however, is as watchdogs, and as such they are savage and alert. Their mission in life, as defined by the Tibetans, is to 'guard wealth against beasts of prey and thieves' and to the fulfilment of this mission they bring vigilance and ferocity. Indeed, they are so fierce that some of them are castrated to heighten their vigilance but also to lessen their ferocity and make them less likely to charge into a spear point or wildly swinging sword, and get hurt' (Ekvall 1963).

From the *Canis lupus arabs* (the Arabian wolf), descended four new primitive dogs, one of which was the *Canis familiaris inostranzewi*. The latter is the predecessor of the large and powerful Molossers from northern India. The most ancient relic of the modern-day Mastiff that exists in India today is the Sindhi Mastiff, now called the Bully Kutta, and is still in existence partly because of the political and geographical changes that occurred in 1947. This dog has been conclusively proven by witness reports to be a ferocious beast that is not suitable for a family environment, at least not in the modern-day sense. In the tribal regions of Afghanistan and Pakistan these dogs are still used for bull-baiting and dog fighting. The original size of the Sindhi Mastiff would have probably been around 32–40 inches. The dogs are now bred at a smaller size as according to their required function.

Modern-day Bully Kuttas historically descended from the Sindhi mastiffs
Source Tribune Oct 2017 Vicky Ghattu

Further suggestions also propose the larger version of Tibetan Mastiff had come down from the mountain regions and mated with the indigenous dogs of the plains, thus creating the shorter haired Mastiff dogs prevalent today. This information seems to be more or less realistic; we know that in both the wild and with the pariah dogs of the Middle East, Asian and African continents, the scent of a female on heat can attract a male from miles away, so he will travel many miles and overcome many obstacles to mate with the female. The laws of procreation and reproduction are strong, such that environmental pressures can benefit the pariah dog species by exerting a positive influence on natural selection during mating rituals, which ensures a healthy gene selection and reinforces the role of natural selection.

It is also interesting to note that Colonel David Hancock (author of *The Mastiffs: The Big Game Hunters*) believes the Tibetan Mastiff is not a Mastiff at all. He presents this conclusion after considering information on the size and shape of Mastiff skulls, and cautions the reader to beware the assertions of historical translators lazily referring to all large dogs as Mastiffs. The Colonel also leads us to believe that Marco Polo never mentioned the word Mastiff. Historical facts must undergo scientific scrutiny before we can decide what to believe, and so I conclude that since Colonel Hancock has given little reference to scientific proof, I will take his suggestions to be based on old, Victorian romance and fall under the category of Westernised historical rhetoric.

The definition and phenotype of particular breeds of dogs, and if many different breeds existed at all, is a matter for deeper and greater debate than we have either the space or time for here. What is certain and what we can conclude now is that a knowledge of dog breeds was not necessarily of importance to scholars of previous eras, and such knowledge as existed was indeed quite vague and at times misleading. Therefore, it would be wise to remain prudent when reviewing so-called historical facts, although this is by no means an invitation to disregard information without first giving it careful thought, as it may later prove to be important.

So far, we have covered the birth of the Mastiff and its movements across the continent of Asia, but now we need to progress further in time to the spread of the Mastiff to the continent of Europe.

Mastiffs from the Indian to the European continent

We are aware that Marco Polo returned to Europe with these dogs and we are also aware of Alexander the Great returning with these dogs across the Deccan Plateau and over the Himalayas, although whether this was the longer haired version of the Tibetan Mastiff or a cross with the indigenous dogs of the lower plains is open to debate; I am of the belief it is almost certainly the latter. The dogs recorded by Herodotus in his writings of Alexander are Hyrcanian war dogs; at that time the Hyrcanian dogs were a large cattle-killing dog.

Herodotus (c.484–425 BC) the Greek historian mentions in his *Histories* (which were at some later stage split into nine volumes and these appear named after *The Nine Muses* in modern editions) the Indian Mastiffs introduced to Greece by Exerxes I on his long march.

The bas reliefs currently on display at the British Museum are the Nineveh reliefs dating from c.850 BC and display large dogs with substantial bone mass, expressing the phenotype of what can be only considered a modern-day Mastiff; whether these relate to the modern-day Boerboel is but mere speculation. The ancient writings about the dogs of the Cynomones, a tribe from the south of Ethiopia make these a feasible ancestor, however, we are unable to trace any dogs in existence today that resemble the Cynomones' beasts documented in the first accountable records of Europeans (that is to say, in the books and diaries of missionaries, travellers, hunters, diplomats and explorers, listed in the Bibliography). Therefore, I find the historical literature describing the Cynomones' dogs to hold little weight and can almost certainly be dismissed as irrelevant insofar as looking for early influences on the indigenous African dogs. Neither do these sources bear much evidence for the possibility of the Boerboel being descended from the Indian dog, but the trade that took place between the Indian and African continents, and man's migratory patterns, are relevant considerations for such a claim and the link is at least conceivable.

In respect of the Indian dog it is of great interest to note that J. W. McCrindle in his book *Ancient India*, describing its invasion by Alexander the Great, states that a 'breed of dog, large powerful and of untameable ferocity is still found in parts of India'. In McCrindle's book we can also read accounts of dogs written by ancient historians. For example, the famous historian Pliny speaks of the Indian dogs and refers to the description given by Deodoros:

> 'The tiger blood that flows in their veins. These Indians assert that these dogs are begotten from the tiger, for which purposes the bitches, when in heat, are tied up amid the woods. They think that the whelps of the first and second blood are too ferocious, but they rear the third blood.'

The most striking and detailed writing is from Ailtonos, and his writings of Alexander's exploits as follows. Tigers are the offspring of the first and second generation but dogs of the third generation,

> '[T]he dog that boasts of tiger's paternity, disdains to hunt deer or to encounter with a wild boar, but takes sheer delight in assailing a lion as if to show its high pedigree, thus the Indians gave Alexander a proof

of strength by practical demonstration. The Indian who provided the spectacle for the king and whom knew well the dog's capacity of endurance, by casting the dog on to the lion ordered his tail to be cut off. It was accordingly cut off, but the dog did not take the last heed. The Indian then ordered his one leg to be cut off. This was done but the dog held to his grip more tenaciously, as if the dismembered limbs were not his own. The remaining legs and limbs were then cut off in succession, but even then his teeth were seen hanging on to the part he had first gripped, while the head dangled aloft still clinging to the lion, though the original grip no longer existed. Alexander was painfully impressed by what he saw and lost in admiration of the dog giving mettle and perishing in no cowardly fashion, preferring rather to die than let his courage give way. The Indian seeing the king's vexation gave him four dogs, similar to the one that was killed. He was much gratified with the gifts and gave in return a suitable reward' (McCrindle 1927).

Ailtonos further writes in his fourth journal:

'I reckon Indian dogs among wild beasts for they are of surprising strength and ferocity, and are the largest of all dogs. This despises other animals but fights with the lion, withstanding his attack, matches his roaring with baying, and gives him bite for bite. In such an encounter, the dog may be worsted, but not till he has severely galled and wounded the lion. The lion is however at times worsted by the Indian dog and thus killed in chase. If a dog once seizes the lion, he retains his hold so tenaciously that even if the legs are cut off, he will not let go, however severe may be the pain he suffers till death supervening compels him otherwise' (McCrindle 1927).

Of course, the prospect of taking such claims seriously is hardly conceivable today, and while the technical question of whether the cross-breeding of a tiger and a dog is actually feasible is for scientists to explain, it is generally appreciated that in zoological studies such events have rarely if not ever happened between different species. Nevertheless, for the sake of entertainment, I would like to record that Major T. C. Hawley (Hawley 1957) wrote of meeting a lady in Rhodesia who confided to him that the pups presented before him were the great-grandchildren of a lioness.

What is conceivable, however, is the incredibly high drive that the Indian dogs appear to have gone into while in full attack mode; I am sure that many a Pit Bull enthusiast would recognise such a drive.

Now we must cover the story of the prototype, the Bullenbeisser (sometimes referred to as the Barrenbeisser) dog brought to the Cape of Good Hope in 1652 by Jan van Riejbeck and other Dutch colonists. According to my research, the Bullenbeisser was a dog of the central

European countries now encompassing Belgium, the Netherlands, Germany and Poland. How and when these dogs arrived in central Europe is still unclear; they are certainly a culmination of the many war dogs used by attacking armies at times of conflict.

An important piece of information we can retrieve is written by John P. Wagner (1939):

> 'Through comparison of Spanish and French authors of the late 12th to 14th centuries with authentic English and German sources we find that the so-called 'dogge' title was used as a collectivism for all strongly built, short haired chase dogs with large heads, powerfully developed muzzles and triangle like, stubbing and drooping lip, strong bodies and teeth and that the doggen forms of all European countries from the middle ages up to the present day are limited to three types which have in course of time developed in to national breeds, they are the Heavy Bullenbeisser, the large hound, evolved by crossing the Bullenbeisser with the old type wolfhound or deerhound, and the small Bullenbeisser which represents a smaller form of the heavy Bullenbeisser through natural selection' (Wagner 1939).

Another interesting piece of information can be obtained from Hans von Flemming in his book *The Complete Sportsmen* (1719) in which he describes in great detail and at length the bull-baiting dogs of that period:

> 'They are medium sized dogs, heavy in bone. Their chest is wide, the head is broad and short with a short sloping nose. They have erect pointed ears and a double bite, which helps them to hold on more strongly. Nose. Their movement is ponderous, but they are strong, heavy and well-fleshed. Apart from the big 'Danziger Bollbeisser' [bull-baiting dog from Danzig], another type exists in Brabant (a province in the Low Countries). They are also medium sized but most of the time a little smaller than the Danziger. Their limbs are the same and they also are heavily built. These dogs are called 'Brabanter Bullebijters' [bull-baiting dogs from Brabant]. In case of lack of bears these dogs are trained to chase and attack bulls and bullocks, however this sport is more suitable for butchers than for hunters' (Flemming 1719).

Barrenbeisser
Source Reidinger 1698-1769

Typical Bullenbeisser
Image Source John P. Wagner, Published in 1939 By Orange Judd Publishing

An Old Danzing and Brabanter Bullenbijter
Source Ludwig Beckmann, Geschichte Und Beschreibung Der Rassen Des Hundes, 1895,

He continues:

> 'In Brabant I have seen a bull chased by dogs. He was fettered on a long chain while attacked by this type of dogs. They grasped him on the nose and throat, while he was running around in circles. These dogs are also used as watch dogs and bandogs. The very fact [of] looking so ugly makes them appropriate watch dogs. Usually they have a short nose with a black mask and the lower jaw pulls forward. Usually the colour is yellow or brindle. They look vicious and seem to be malicious' (Flemming 1719).

It is quite clear that with these three types of dogs already in existence within central Europe, combined with further cross-breeding as mentioned by M. B. Wynn (Wynn, 2006) of the heavier Mastiff, we arrive at the finished product of today's Boxers and Great Danes. It is of particular interest to mention that some of the finest Boxers I have seen have been of East European working line stock; this is down to political factors restricting certain freedoms such as travel and commerce under communist regimes, which incidentally culminated in close line breeding and a true type. The same can be said of the Rottweiler, and I would go so far as to say the Great Dane as well, in its early days.

Early fine examples of the predecessors of the Bullenbeiser, the Grest Danes or Boerhondes of Germany – Source Unknown

The very fine example of the boxer of early days Source Hutchinsons Dog Encyclopedia Vol 1

Thus, we have now covered the development of the Mastiff, which we can clearly say originates in the Tibetan Mastiff.

The introduction of the De Beers Bullmastiffs

The discovery of diamonds in South Africa in 1867 started an international frenzy for the stakes and mining rights, particularly in the area of Kimberley. Of course, the mines and minerals were then on what comprised a farm, owned by Johannes Nicholas De Beer and his brother Diederuk Arnoldus De Beer.

A few years later, Cecil Rhodes and his brother arrived and purchased all diamond mining rights and arranged the relevant land acquisitions; only the De Beers name was left. Cecil Rhodes formed the new company we now know as the world famous De Beers Mining Company, a name synonymous with luxury across the globe.

Sir Cecil Rhodes and the British government bore a major influence on South Africa where Rhodes was a prominent figure especially in the Boer War.

I have struggled to find in the available data detailed information regarding the particular dogs used by the mining company, and to whom they had dispersed. Despite this, I have been able to unearth some of the history. The first imported Bullmastiff to South Africa was Farcroft Vigil, a bitch, and Farcroft Joe, a brindle male, both of whom arrived in 1925, and imported by a Mrs Heard. The dogs came from the famous kennels of Molesely, but were not KUSA registered, and were followed shortly by John Bull of Damara and Britannia of Damara in 1928 together with a bitch by the name of Trustful Peggy, also an import from the same year, all of whom did become KUSA registered. It was between 1928 and 1935 that De Beers imported Bullmastiffs to South Africa under the kennel name Adamant; of the more notable dogs was a UK champion by the name of Springwell Major, and he is recorded as belonging to the De Beers diamond mines for breeding and guarding stock for the mines. He was imported from the notable breeders Messrs W. & G. K. Richardson in England, he sired Supreme Champion Adamant Baker. In 1948 De Beers stopped using Bullmastiffs and turned their attentions to the German Shepherd dogs.

The first Champions registered with the Kennel Union of South Africa (KUSA) were Ch Castlehill Sally (bitch) and Ch Bullar of Dunmar (dog). A considerable amount of work has been done in establishing the breed in South Africa by Mr O. J. Goddard of Greystoke Kennels, and it is true to say that the Bullmastiff has a heritage of notably British distinction. Mr Goddard started breeding in 1938 and continued into the 1940s. He owned, among others Adamant Quick March (sired by Ch Springwell Major), Supreme SA Champion Adamant Baker which he purchased from Mr A. T. Darke, owner of Adamant Budd, who had originally purchased these dogs from the De Beers Mining Company. Goddard imported Champion Ferdinand of Le Tasyll (Maritime Fearless X Penelope of Le Tasyll), bred by Mrs D. Nash in 1945. This dog went on to win three BIS awards at all-breeds championship shows in the then Union, the first being when the dog was one year old. He was also used extensively at stud and did much to improve the standard of the Bullmastiff in South Africa.

The similarity between the Bullmastiff in South Africa and the Boerboel is evident but details of their cross-breeding are not readily available, and this topic remains a hotly contested one even today.

The Bullmastiffs imported to South Africa between 1925 and 1955 were the finest specimens of their day, having come from the famous Farcroft Kennels, and were bred by the even more renowned S. E. Molesely. These dogs belonged to distinguished individuals, and I find it unlikely that in 1925 (or today) any serious breeder who had gone to the expense of importing the finest champion dogs to South Africa would have considered mating their dog with a farm dog of no pedigree. That is also if we are considering that the Boerboel was a dog of need and shaped from its role of work; the Boerboel, one would have to conclude, prior to 1983 was never a dog of shows or appraisals.

However, one has to be prudent, as pointed out earlier in this chapter, dogs can readily become integral to the identity of a community. So, from my discussions with the Bullmastiff breeders of South Africa I take onboard their staunch denial of ever contemplating cross-breeding their dogs with the Farmer's Boel, although I am at liberty to remain impartial. It is up to you the reader to make your own choice.

There is of course no reason to doubt that the Bullmastiff was used in the creation of the Boerboel, but whether the champion dogs of the Adamant Kennels were used remains to be seen and I remain sceptical of that.

That unlikelihood notwithstanding, from the writings of earlier travellers such as Lawrence Green, Major T. C. Hawley and E. R. Shelley, it is clear that there were Bullmastiffs type dogs readily available in South Africa, which I can only assume (based on my knowledge of the Bullmastiff) bore some relation to the physical make-up of the Boer dog. Additionally, all the initial breeds used to create the Bullmastiff in the start-up of its establishment were readily available in South Africa without any need of importing, hence it is probably the case that some people were creating their own strain of Bullmastiff.

Champion Springwell Major

This is Springwell Major, a Bullmastiff specially selected by De Beers for the improvement of its breeding stock, as documented. Note the size of the muzzle and his athletic build.

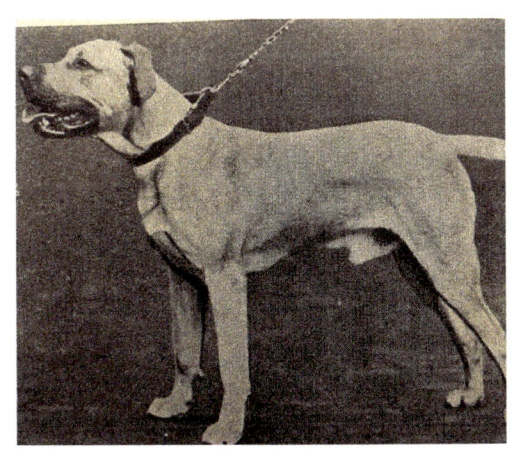

Early type Bullmastiff, note the length of muzzle
Source Hutchinson's Dog Encyclopedia Vols. 1-3, 1930.

I have now covered the creation of the large war dogs, fighting dogs, and the gladiator dogs, genetic machines bred for a reason and for whom death was a way of life. But now we come to the indigenous dogs of Africa and their role in the creation of the Boerboel. I can hear many of you now thinking, 'Why is that important?' and in response to your question there are some significant and important answers; these are the answers which I believe make the Boerboel what it is. I ask you to bear with me as we continue with this history, as it prepares us for what comes in the final chapter, 'Fact or Fiction'.

I have never seen so much injustice done to a dog breed as has been done to indigenous dogs. They are one of the toughest dog types alive and rate among my best pound-for-pound dogs in the world. In addition, nowhere in the world will you see a greater demonstration of the laws of natural selection than with the Pariah/Africanis dogs; these ancient indigenous dogs are the embodiment of Africa and can be considered one of the truest reflections of geographically influenced dogs, in terms of evolutionary processes. The pariah dogs and indigenous dogs of

Africa are born only from natural selection and have developed defences to withstand heat, yellow fever, tick and flea damage, and tsetse fly fever without the need for medications and specialist diets. These dogs are a species well designed by their environment and represent the foundation of the Boerboel. It is of paramount importance that these dogs are included in the history chapter.

The Dogs of the Khoikhoi, San and Zulu

Samuel Daniell, Kora-Khoekhoe preparing to move 1805

It is impossible for me to include a history of every individual indigenous dog breed of Africa; however, in terms of relevance to the Boerboel, the dogs of the Khoikhoi, San and Zulu will be covered.

The Khoikhoi people were pastoralists, arriving in Southern Africa over 2000 years ago and settling in the Cape Province; they had a close and complex relationship with the San of Southern Africa. Dogs were of lesser importance to the Khoikhoi than to the indigenous San. To the San it was of utmost importance to have fast agile dogs with the strength to tackle medium sized prey. This was essential to both the sustainability of the tribe and survival of the dog.

The phenotype of the Khoikhoi dog is quite intriguing and various authors give conflicting views. One thing we do know is the Khoikhoi dog had a peculiar ridge of hair running along its spine, its ears were set quite high, almost pricked and its coat was quite thick. The arrival of settlers from East India and Malabar would have been a source of genetic diversity for both the European stock dogs and the Khoi/San dogs.

South African writer, Lawrence Green commented that:

> 'Dogs are the only tame animals the bushmen [the San] have ever possessed. They have never owned cattle, and thus (unlike the more prosperous Hottentots [the Khoikhoi]) their ideas of numbers are extremely limited. 'One, two, three-many' say the Bushmen. The dogs have been their companions for centuries. Side by side they have travelled through Africa and together they have won many little victories. The finest type of Bushmen hunting dog, a light brown Ridgeback mongrel with a dark stripe and a trace of the greyhound in his appearance, is now verging on extinction. They are without a doubt the finest dogs in the world for the hunter's purpose, lean and savage, ready to keep a wounded leopard at bay until the master finds an opening for his spear. One of the most typical of these dogs I saw stood no more than 14 inches at the shoulder, with a length of body out of proportion to the height. A broad forehead, a sharp muzzle, upright ears and long drooping tail made him anything but a beauty. Yet this is possibly the oldest and most cunning breed of dog in the world.

Typical Africanis – Source John Gallant

> 'A fugitive with his master, the Bushmen dog has learnt the virtue of silence. Some declare this dog never barks; at all events there is no senseless barking to give his master's hiding place away. The dog slinks always behind his master, taking advantage of every patch of shade, reserving his energy for the moment when he is called upon to distract the quarry's attention. Sensing danger, he will give only a warning whine. Between Bushman and dog there is complete trust and understanding.

> 'Many travellers have tried to bribe the bushman with tobacco to part with such dogs, but I have yet to hear of one whom was successful' (Green 1952).

We can with certainty conclude that although Lawrence Green was not aware of this particular trade going on between white European settlers and San, it was however going on quite frequently between the Khoikhoi and the San.

The writer Kolben in his book *Bescrywing van die kaap geode hoop* (1729) sums up in perfect detail the ridged dog as follows:

> 'There is also another kind of domesticated dog, which was in the country in the beginning and which the Hottentots [Khoikhoi], beside employing them for hunting also use for protection; and of which dogs Europeans at the present time make constant use … They have small heads and very sharp muzzles. The coat is ash grey and mouse coloured … The ears are erect and sharp. For the rest they have much in common with the other dogs, being as tractable as the European dogs. They are particularly very faithful when their masters are in danger from lions, tigers (leopards), wolves etc, and for this reason they are valued and sought after by the Europeans as well as the Hottentots [Khoikhoi].'

Bryant, writing in 1881 to 1883, gave an important description of the dog of the Zulu at that particular time:

> 'The commonest Bantu name for dog is imbwa of which the Zulu form is inja. Most of the Bantu dogs are of the jackal pariah type. But besides this the Zulus possessed another entirely different breed, which they called isiQa. This was more suggestive of a small Hyena than a Jackal, smallish in size but stout in build, with shorter, squarer muzzle, short light brown hair, fierce in temperament and carrying a slight mane along the neck and spine.'

In her book, *Dogs of Africa* (2003) Sian Hall puts forward the case that there are two different phenotypes of the same African dog. The variation is thought to be the result of ethnic and geographical diversity in the regions of Southern Africa. One dog is the lighter, smaller, shorter haired Sicha dog and the other is the more robust, heavier dog from the mountainous regions of the Kwala Zulu-Natal Drakensburg region, south of the Tugela river.

Hall mentions the varying colours, stating that any colour is acceptable in the Sicha, with brown, fawn, cream and brindle being the most common. Black dogs are occasionally seen and when encountered, stand out among the predominantly brown shades. Importantly, the IsiQa dog and the Sicha dog referred to by both Hall and Bryant are in fact the same dog but with a different spelling. This motley range also includes blue, liver and pieds, or skewbalds. The dogs I have inspected from the Drakensburg region are the size of a modern-day Ridgeback with the same degree of bone mass and skull definition.

In Hawley (1957) and the *Agricultural Journal of the Cape of Good Hope* (1909) we find descriptions of the Boer hunting dogs, as well as of the cross-breeding of dogs of indigenous origin with the dogs of European settlers. An anonymous contributor to the journal referring to himself as a South African, claims he found a cross between the Mastiff and Bulldog, best for hunting leopards.

Another interesting article also appeared in the *Agricultural Journal*, referring to a dog named Kaffir which was a cross between a Bullmastiff and foxhound, and the owner's other dog called Smoke, a cross between a stag-bloodhound and a Mastiff. He hunted with these dogs for many years and individually they were capable of killing a fully grown male baboon. If this happens to be true, then these must have been exceptional dogs. A baboon is both ferocious and intelligent; I have a first-hand account from a Pit Bull man from the Cape who witnessed his Pit Bull being picked up by the skull and having its skull crunched clean by one of these beasts.

In the 1820s the British Parliament passed an Act to allocate to all British people an amount of £8.00, which in those days was a large amount of money, to secure themselves dogs and thus create a buffer zone for the protection of their livestock in the inhospitable and new land of South Africa. The dogs sent over by the British included the Irish Wolfhound, Scottish Deerhound, and Old English Mastiffs, as well as the short-haired St Bernard. Sian Hall comments that 'the crossing of these dogs created what is now referred to as the frontier dog or the boarhound, these dogs gave rise to the Steekbaard (prickly beard) and the Vuilbaard (dirty beard)' (Hall, 2003). These frontier dogs were the foundation dogs of today's Rhodesian Ridgeback. An interesting and critical point to which we shall return in the concluding chapter, 'Fact or Fiction'.

So there we have it, we have covered the ancestry of dogs from the earliest known facts of their evolution, we have examined the historical literature where we looked at the Indian dog, we have extracted articles relating to the history of the Tibetan Mastiff – the father of all Mastiffs, as well as articles on the background of dogs reared in a degree of geographical isolation. In addition, we have considered the genetic material of the indigenous dogs of Africa, and we have some background as to the arrival of the European stock dogs and the development of the frontier dog. We must point out that at this point the path of the frontier dog splits. In one direction it leads to a refined type of Hound (initially called the Van Royen dog), and then later to be referred to as the lion dog and finally the official name of the Rhodesian Ridgeback and in the other direction the path leads to the development of the dog which eventually many decades later will be referred to as the Boerboel. But, without doubt in my mind, whether bred for hunters or trekkers, it was every bit the same frontier dog at heart. The most valid information we have comes from an unknown south African whom wrote a very detailed article on the Boerhonde, this dog is not to be confused with the German Boerhonde from Germany and also known as the modern-day Great Dane. *Agricultural Journal of the Cape of Good Hope*, Vol. 34, Issue 2, Feb 1909 is a response from a Lady Frere : In Answer to "fanciers" inquiry re Boer Hunting Dog, I remember in 1860 seeing a fine strain on the Thorn river near Cathcart, then a military post known as windvogelberg. But I cannot remember the names of the farmers that owned the dogs. Years after I recognised the strain in the Bedford district, and was told the dogs came from originally Windvogelberg. These dogs were light red in colour, Wiry coat with massive heads, fairly fast and large. They were very viscious. In fact it was dangerous to venture near them without people of the place being present. Later In 1870

I saw some fine Boer dogs, answering the above description excepting that they were darker in colour, in farmlands along Alice and Koonap River Rand. In the 1860s it was not difficult to secure well-bred dogs, as a rule they were to be found on each post, Bloodhounds, Staghounds, Greyhounds, Bulldogs, Terriers and Mastiffs, Pointers and very occasionally Foxhounds. I am of the opinion that the Boer dog was a cross between one or the other of the aforementioned dogs. It was usually in the vicinity of the military posts that the best Boer dogs were to be found. In support to my theory as to the origin of the Boer Hunting Dog I may mention that I owned two dogs, the one named Kafir whose sire was a cross between a Bull and Mastiff and the second named Smoke who was a cross between a Stag and Bloodhound dam and a Mastiff sire. I was often asked frequently by farmers where I acquired these fine Boer dogs. They would often tackle and kill the largest baboon, and badgers. These dogs had all the characteristics of the fine Boer dogs.

The 1909 article in the *Agricultural Journal* gives an account from a South African of his experience using dogs with tiger hunting, which I include here for the interests of both the general reader and for the working dog enthusiast. The passage below gives insight into some of the breeding concepts and the expectations one had of hunting dogs in the days of inhospitable adventure and hunting trips:

> 'When I was a boy fifty-two years ago I often hunted in a company of farmers and others, we hunted Tigers, Baboons, Wolves and Jackals, etc. For hunting game (long range guns were not in use then) we used greyhounds. Foxhounds were not known in this colony, their origin was from Europe. These Hounds were absolutely useless for hunting, or tracking the spoors of a Tigers and Baboons. The very scent of the spoor of a tiger caused the hounds to bolt, I have seen the English and Arabs and pure colonial breeds, which bolted for no apparent reason, when on examination later on a tiger would be seen in a tree or rock, from where the animals bolted. The dogs used for hunting the Tigers and Baboons were a cross between the Mastiff and the Bulldog, the parents coming from Europe. The Boar Hound though big and strong has to fine a skin to withstand the claws of a tiger, the Mastiff though strong and big is to lumpy and no match for the nimble tiger. The cross-breed that combines the Mastiff and the Bulldog combine swiftness and tenacity of the one with the strength of the other, have always proved to be the best for fighting the tiger. (*Agricultural Journal of the Cape of Good Hope*, 1909).'

We shall cover these comments later in Chapter 9 'Fact or Fiction', but it is safe to conclude from our own detailed examination of these vital historical pieces of literature that the dog known as the Boerhonde is also referred to as the frontier dog, i.e. both being of the same strain, and most likely to have been later referred to as the frontier dog due to its likelihood at being both bred and found around the Military frontier posts.

The Boerboel will endure a further 60 years before any well-deserved recognition is given.

However, at this particular point in its history we still need to examine the politico-economic context of South Africa and, later, the end of apartheid. This part of South Africa's history will help us understand why social, economic and political factors have shaped the Boerboel into what it is today.

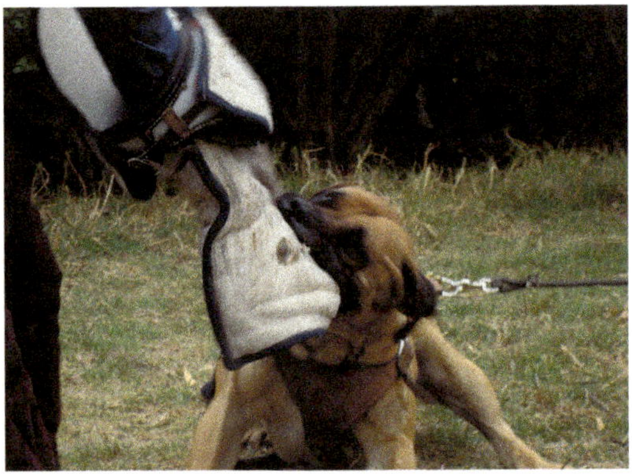
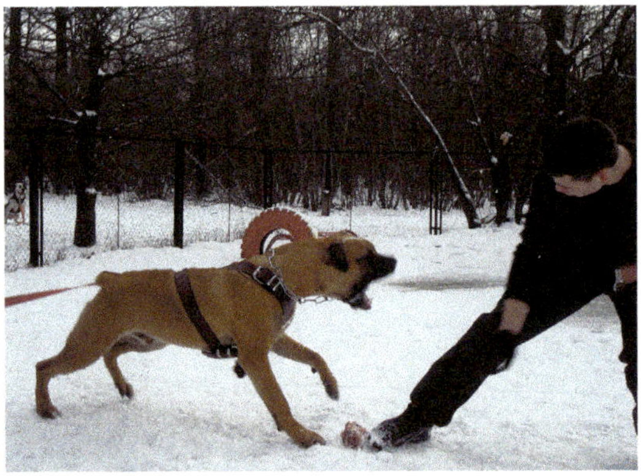
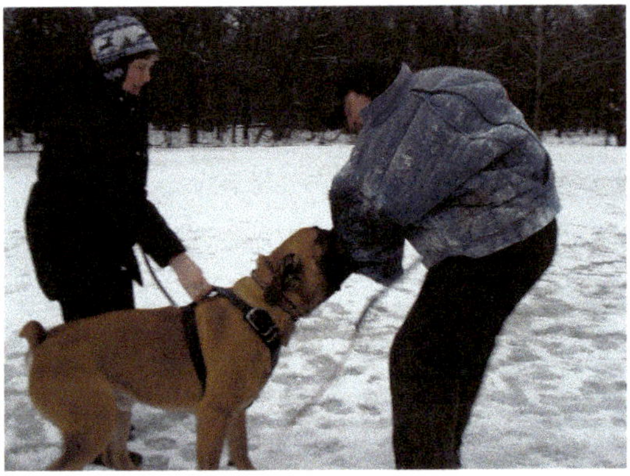
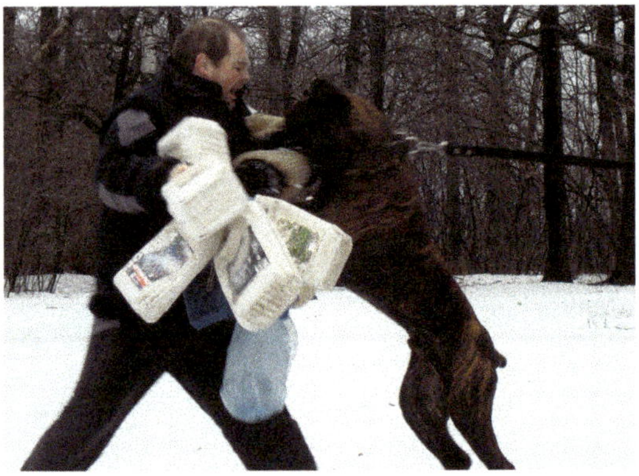
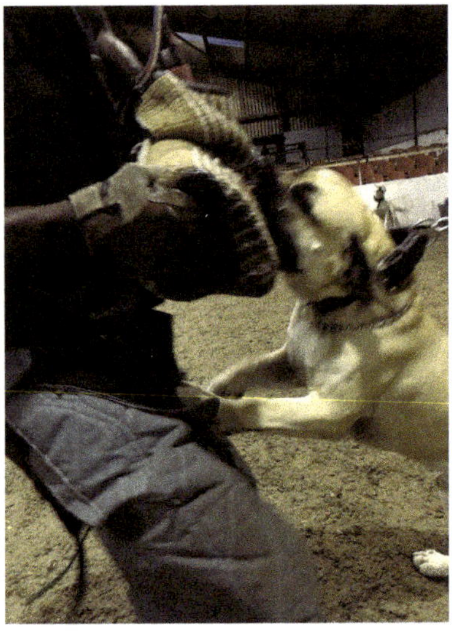
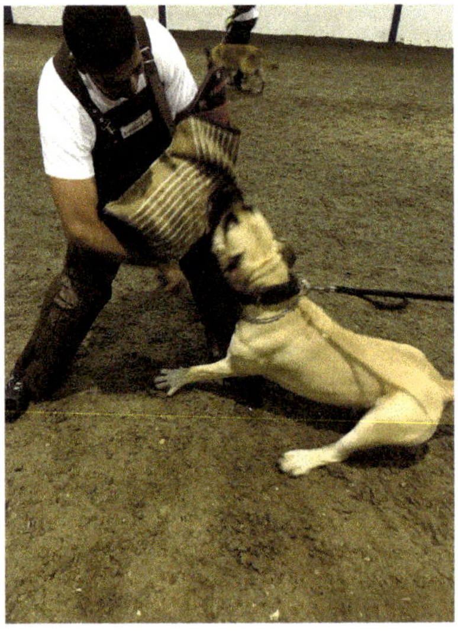

HISTORY OF THE BOERBOEL

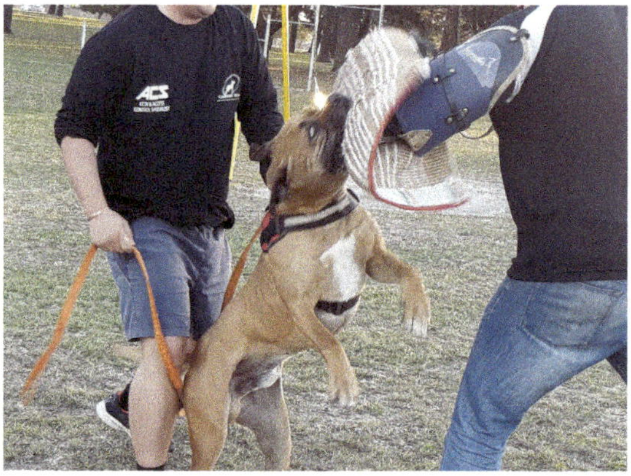
ACS

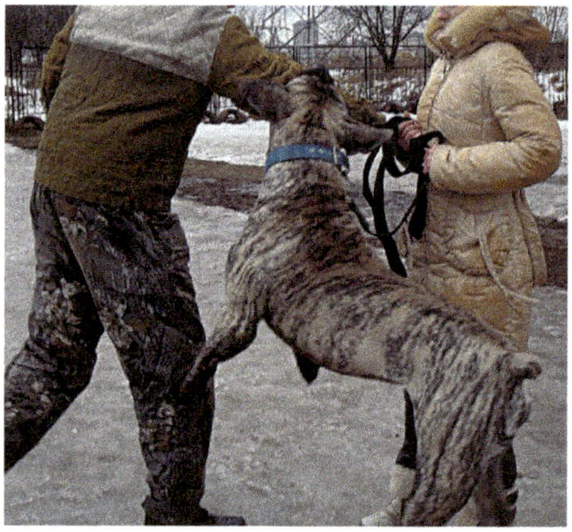

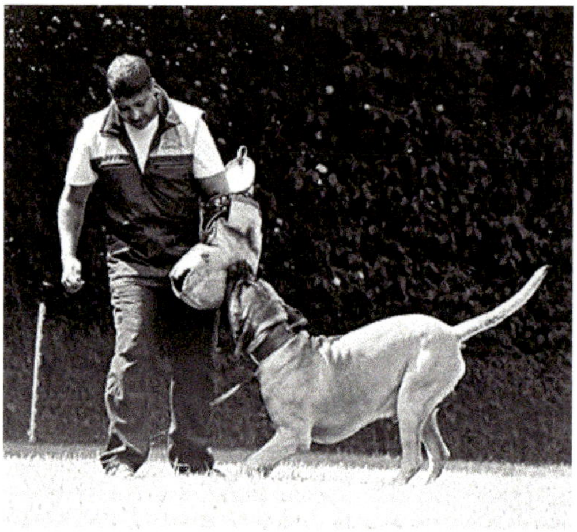

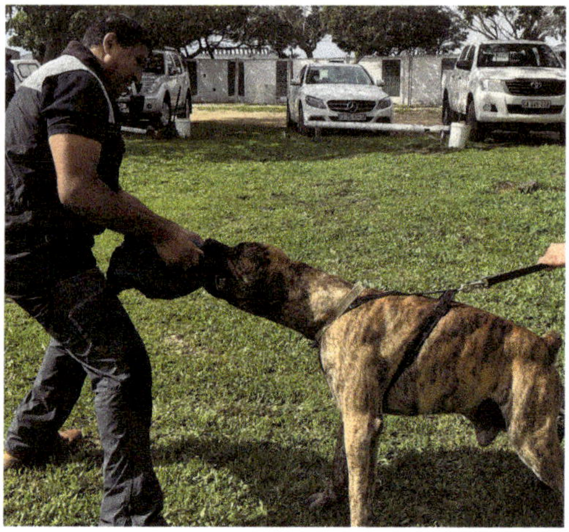

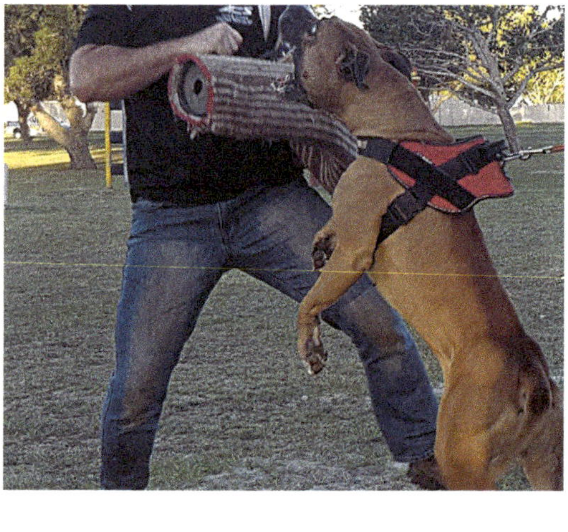

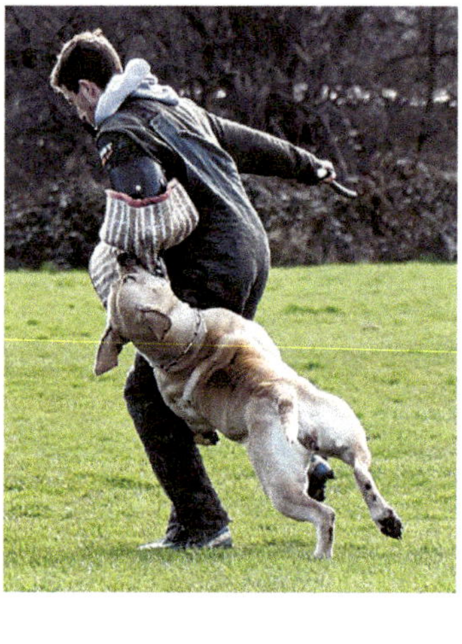

Chapter 3
A Brief History of South African Geography and Politics

The political history of South Africa is significant for the history of the Boerboel. In the concluding chapter we will see how politics changes the dynamics of society, and how this in turn changes both the use and expectations of dog breeds. This is particularly so with the Boerboel, as its social identity has been, and still is, forged by the Afrikaner, and this dog is widely considered to be a mascot of Afrikaner heritage. There is no doubt that this mascot, a reflection of the social identity of its people, will inevitably become either redundant or misused, as the ever-shrinking Afrikaner community slowly declines and the Boerboel's new commercial use is redefined in the twenty-first century. This will lead to the creation of a new, evolving (possibly even deformed) mascot, but the question of the Boerboel's future will no doubt lead us to explore the reality of the role that political infrastructure plays in shaping dog breeds and human social dynamics.

The history of the white settlers

I am now going to briefly summarise the long complex course of four centuries of history in a mere few pages; I apologise in advance that this does not do justice to the interests of those who might be offended by my limited historical knowledge on this matter.

In 1652 Jan Van Reibeck landed at the Cape of Good Hope in the interests of setting up a refreshment station for the ships travelling to and from India and the Caribbean. Of the many settlers were Indians, Malays and Indonesians, and Portuguese to name but a few, as well as the Khoikhoi pastoralists, who had made significant developments before the white settlers arrived, which we shall discuss later. The colony was poor and had few resources. It took a further fifty years before we find a colony approaching a population of 2000. These white settlers were far outnumbered by their coloured servants, whom the settlers were reliant upon for labour. Constituting the white ethnic groups were the French Huguenots, German Protestants, and of course the Dutch Calvinists; the British started settling in large numbers some time later. Van Riejbeck never wanted to be in the Cape, and the resentment he felt against his company was quite evident, as Frank Welsh points out in his book *A History of South Africa* (1998). The new immigrants referred to themselves as the Afrikanders (the people of Africa); their language, a variant of Dutch, is know what we refer to as Afrikaans. The poorest and most aggressively independent of these people were and are better known as the Boers or (trek Boers).

Jan Van Reibeeck 1660s
Source Public Domain

The British government took permanent possession of the country in 1806 at the time of the Napoleonic wars, together with the revenues and wealth of the already then established East India Company; this was a relatively easy acquisition. Despite taking possession of South Africa in 1806, the British had relatively few immigrants residing there. The Boers of the frontiers resisted British rule, the wider implications of which will be explored throughout this chapter (Pakenham, 2006).

In 1834 Britain ordered the abolition of slavery throughout its empire. The actions of Cecil Rhodes, who was a major beneficiary of the British government (it directly supported his diamond mining activities) and key political component in assuring British control of South Africa, played a major part in what can only be considered one of Britain's most brutal and bloodiest wars, which culminated in the first of what we today know as concentration camps.

The Great Trek started in 1835 and lasted until 1837 with no less than 5000 Boers and the same number of coloured servants migrating across the Orange and Vaal rivers and beyond the frontiers of the northeast colonies. Frank Welsh provides interesting insights into the events that took place during the trek (these points will be of value to the closing chapter):

> Although the individual leaders of the Great Trek were brave and often principled, they were usually quite incapable of cooperating with each other. Temporary alliances were followed by often permanent discord. ... Within four years three of the first trekker parties – those of the Reteif, Tregardt and Van Rensburg – had been wiped out, within forty the republics of Natalia, Lyndenburg, Winburg, Utrecht, the Transvaal, Stelland, the land of Goschen, the Orange Free State, and the New Republic had all commemorated Boer divisions and disappointments. None, except the Orange Free State, was viable, the largest, the Transvaal was bankrupt, internecine quarrels at least once

turned into civil war. The only factors preserving the identity of the Afrikaner people from obliteration were the resistance of the blacks they displaced which in turn forced a unity on the individualistic parties, the vacillating incompetence of British Governments, and the discovery of gold in the Transvaal (Welsh 1998, p. 147).

It would be unfair not to include recognition of such notable black chiefs of those times as Moroka and Rolong who had afforded protection to the Afrikaners against the British soldiers together with the Bastaards and a considerably large number of Khoikhoi people whom had fought alongside the Voortrekker.

In 1843 Britain created a second colony by annexing Natal, a predominantly Voortrekker stronghold. In both 1852 and 1854 Britain acknowledged the independence of two new Boer republics, the Orange Free State and Transvaal. Then, in 1877 Britain annexed the Transvaal in an exercise to federate South Africa and this led to the First Boer War on 16 December 1880, which lasted until the later part of 1881. The leader of this first rebellion was Paul Kruger and he successfully led the Boers to the victory of Majuba.

The bulk of De Beers' labour force consisted of convicts contracted to them by the government, the rest of the sorry souls amounted to blacks sent by tribal chiefs, and the Afrikaners. The first workers' trade union was set up in 1882 and successfully resisted the attempts by De Beers to lower their wages. In 1884 the company introduced new strip-search regulations, and six white protestors were shot at the orders of the mine directors. The British government was successful in bringing about solidarity between the blacks and the white Europeans. In 1885 the De Beers mining force changed hands and the mining company started recruiting more skilled miners from England. Their treatment was in stark contrast to both the Europeans and blacks previously employed in the mines and a deep-seated resentment grew within the existing labour force.

In 1870 Kimberley was in a diamond frenzy and the British government was this time on the receiving end of considerable sums of money from Cecil Rhodes' British South Africa Company; their main strategy was to annexe the Orange Free State and Traansvaal. Thus, on 11 October 1899 began the Second Boer War which lasted until 31 May 1902.

Lord Kitchener applied a so-called scorched earth policy during the latter part of the war when the British failed to dominate the Boers on the battlefield. 'This took the form of the destruction of farms in order to prevent the fighting Boers from obtaining food and supplies, and to demoralise them by leaving their women and children homeless and starving in the open fields.' (Wikipedia contributors. 'Herbert Kitchener, 1st Earl Kitchener.' *Wikipedia, The Free Encyclopedia*, 24 Jul. 2018. Web. 28 Jul. 2018.)

It was bloody, and the Boers were outnumbered by alarmingly large proportions of British soldiers, and here we find the origin of concentration camps. Over 26 000 Boers died in these camps, the majority of whom were children. Many people believe today that Hitler created the first concentration camps; there is a lot to be said about the British being the first.

Boer Camp
Source National Army Museum UK

Scorched Earth Policy
Source Unknown

The Union of South Africa 1910–today

Key events in the formation of South Africa are as follows. On 31 May 1910, South Africa became a union under the leadership of Louis Botha. But it was still part of the British Commonwealth. Jan Christian Smuts was elected as president of the Union of South Africa in 1919 and held that office until 1924. Barry Hertzog (James Barry Munnik Hertzog), a Boer general, was President of South Africa from 1924 to 1939. The joining of the National Party and the South African Party occurred on 5 December 1934.

Hertzog was ousted out of government in 1939 due to his non-commitment to the British during WW II. It was then taken over by the highly intelligent and philosophical Field Marshal Jan Smuts, a man whom I personally wish had led the country into the 21st century, (age permitting, of course). It is quite significant to add that it was due to the negotiations of Jan Smuts and the sheer strong mindedness of the Indian middle classes that the voting rights of Indians were allowed.

The United Party of Jan Smuts finally ended in 1948, and Jan Christian Smuts died in 1950.

It is difficult when researching about a country and the diversity and complexity of its people to not be passionately drawn into it, for this reason I would like to draw your attention to the huge and major accomplishments that Jan Christian Smuts had achieved, not just for his country, but for humanity. He helped bring about the implementation of the League of Nations, an organisation that grew from the Paris Peace Conference 1919–1920 and aimed at settling disputes in a diplomatic manner through negotiation and dialogue, which was created on 28 June 1918 and continued until 18 April 1946.

Jan Smuts wrote the opening lines of the Preamble to the United Nations Charter, which would have been similar to the opening lines of the Covenant of the League of Nations. He later went on to address the need for a more internationally focused organisation with military back up. Of course, today we all know this organisation as the United Nations. In addition to his progressive line of thinking it was the far sightedness of Smuts that created the Fagan

Report – an in-depth analysis of the vast and impractical consequences of segregation policies. This report was written in 1948 which was too late to implement and furthermore was not adopted by the succeeding prime minister.

Field Marshall Jan Christian Smuts fought in both WWI and WWII and was a true visionary, setting the standard for the United Nations. Source wikiwand.com

The National Party was elected to power on 4 June 1948 and remained in power until 9 May 1994. On 15 August 1989, Fredrik Willelm De Klerk was elected to power and created the mechanism for a peaceful resolution to end apartheid. In his opening address to Parliament on 2 February 1990, he announced that the ban on different political parties, such as the African National Congress and the South African Communist Party would be lifted and that Nelson Mandela would be released after 27 years in prison. De Klerk further announced that capital punishment would be suspended and that the state of emergency would be lifted. He said that 'the time to negotiate has arrived.' It was under the direct influence of De Klerk that South Africa avoided any major and catastrophic bloodbaths, and we must respect his diplomatic endeavours. He was a man worthy of the Nobel Peace Prize.

The African National Congress was elected as the new government of South Africa on 27 April 1994. The new president was Nelson Mandela, a man who was granted no less than 100 awards for his contributions to humankind. In time we will come to understand the great extent to which the passionate determination of Nelson Mandela bore fruit in the new South Africa.

The right-wing political influence

It is more than enough that you, the reader, have endured this long chapter on the political history of South Africa, without now having to further endure a section relating to the more extreme and right-wing groups. It is even more ridiculous of me to expect you to read such chapters, when all you want to determine is the history of the Boerboel. And it is probable that half of you have completely skipped this part of the book, so why am I writing this section on the right-wing parties?

The reason these histories are vital to understanding the Boerboel will become clear as we continue. There are too many right-wing parties to mention for the purpose of this book, so for the sake of its major relevance to our study we will cite just one, the Herstigte Nasionale Partie ('the HNP'); in English this translates as the Reconstituted National Party.

Formed in 1969 by Albert Hertzog, who was the son of the former Prime Minister General J. B. M. Hertzog, the HNP was created in response to its members' perception of apartheid easing under the National Party Government. Wanting to reinstate a white Dutch Calvinism as the basis for South Africa, the party also advocated a white socialism, complete racial segregation, an independent homeland, and the adoption of Afrikaans as the only official language. Between 1970 and 1989 they contested a number of elections but despite gaining in influence were not able to gain seats in the South African Parliament at a general election. Frank Welsh (Welsh 1998, p. 477) claims that a majority of support for the HNP came from rural communities. We can presume this to include the remote farming communities. By the late 1980s the HNP had effectively become the chief voice of the far-right opposition, which is reflected in the declaration by the Afrikaner Weerstandsbeweging and Boerestaat Party of their support for the HNP's leader in 1989.

To gain an idea of the tensions of the political situation in the mid-1980s, it is essential to consider that 'reactions to the 1984 constitution reflected the confusion in which South Africa found itself':

> After a ferocious struggle eighteen nationalist MPs left to form the new Conservative party, where they were joined by an unrepentant Connie Mulder, a Broderbund faction (another right-wing group) Aksie eie Toekoms (literally meaning) Action for our Future and the neo-NazI 'Afrikaner Weerstands Beweging' (Afrikaner Resistance Movement), led by the unsavoury white supremacist, Eugene Terreblanche. Neither the HNP nor the Conservatives were in a position to challenge the National Party in Parliament, but they were backed by some 20 per cent of all white electorate. The disintegration of Afrikanerdom had begun. (Ibid.)

While violent extremist factions splintered off, the more moderate Afrikaners were loath to be associated with such people and so they began to support the liberals. One of the most significant examples is Anton Rupert, a wealthy tobacco businessman who had formerly worked with Nationalists but who now switched sides and advocated a 'third trek... away from discrimination – towards participation in freedom by all population groups' (Welsh 1998). The Dutch Church were substantial supporters of apartheid but amid the turmoil of the early to mid-1980s, 'even those devoted and ingenious supporters of apartheid, the Dutch Churches were abandoning the cause' (ibid). Only the original and largest church, the NGK, resisted.

> Its western synod, representing the mother church in the Cape, and the theological powerhouse of Stellenbosch University decided in April 1984 that there was no biblical justification for apartheid and

urged its members to confess their participation in apartheid with humility and sorrow. With such a rebuttal coming from the mother church itself, the end of the volk was in sight. Reverting to the fissiparous Boer customs of a hundred years before, new churches and groups sprang up to perpetuate justification for apartheid (Welsh 1998).

We can clearly see that this was a period of tremendous uncertainty and insecurity for those who would have been the targets of apartheid and this sense of fear would have been heightened if one was poor. It is important to observe the number of new political factions that were created during this period by members who lost faith in their group and left to create other organisations. (This tendency of a small number of members belonging to a group to break away from the parent structure to create their own organisation is a point we shall discuss in Chapter 9 'Fact or Fiction'.)

Geographical aspects of evolution: ethnography, wildlife and economy

The beauty within South Africa

To understand the background of the Boerboel it is vital that we first understand both the environmental and the human influences that predetermined the shape of this dog. The indigenous people in South Africa are a vital source of knowledge and hopefully, the section on 'Ethnography' below will shed light on some of the main cultural changes that have occurred in the country. The arrival of white settlers changed the course of evolution across this formidable continent and we shall look at this further below as well.

But why the need to discuss these issues in a book about dogs? Well, our four-legged friend has been by our side from the earliest period of civilisation, he has been shaped by changes to humankind, and by the end of the book all will have become quite clear. To understand how and why the Boerboel is a product of this rather human situation we must first understand the nature of a particular country and the differences of its people. I will begin this section with geographical data as the land is always the basis of all that becomes the beneficiary of it. (This section draws from Wikipedia's entry on South Africa: Wikipedia contributors. 'South Africa.' *Wikipedia, The Free Encyclopedia*, 26 Jul. 2018. Web. 28 Jul. 2018.)

South Africa is located in the southernmost region of Africa, with a coastline that stretches more than 1550 miles across both the Atlantic and Indian oceans. At 470 979 m², South Africa is the world's 25th-largest country. It is comparable in size to Great Britain, France, Belgium, Holland and the Netherlands.

South Africa has a temperate climate, due in part to it being surrounded by the Atlantic and Indian oceans on three sides, by its location in the climatically milder southern hemisphere and due to the average elevation rising steadily towards the north (towards the equator) and further inland. Due to this varied topography and oceanic influence, a vast variety of climatic zones exist.

The climatic zones vary, from the one extreme to another, the arid desert and the subtropical and humid climates, and of course the snow-capped mountains of the Drakensburg region open to skiing at short intervals in the winter season.

The interior of South Africa is a large, vast and open space of land and primarily flat. In contrast, the eastern coastline is lush and well-watered, which produces a climate similar to the tropics. The extreme southwest has a more moderate climate similar to say the south-west of France, with wet winters and hot, dry summers, this area also produces much of South Africa's world famous wines. Further east on the country's south coast, rainfall is distributed more evenly throughout the year, producing a green lush green landscape and a popular destination for driving, otherwise known as the Garden Route.

The Central Free State is particularly flat due to the fact that its positioned quite central on the high plateau. North of the Vaal river, the Highveld becomes better watered and does not experience subtropical extremes of heat. Johannesburg is also positioned in a central point and is within the Highveld at 1740 m and receives an annual rainfall of 760 mm (30 in.) Winters in this region are cold, although you will rarely get the opportunity to build snowmen.

To the north of Johannesburg, the altitude drops beyond the Highveld's escarpment, and turns into the lower lying Bushveld, an area of mixed dry forest and an abundance of wildlife. East of the Highveld, beyond the eastern escarpment, the Lowveld stretches towards the Indian ocean. It has particularly high temperatures and is also the location of extended subtropical agriculture. The mountains of the Barberton Greenstone Belt in the lowerveld are the oldest mountains on Earth, dating back 3.5 billion years. The earliest reliable proof of life (dated 3.2–3.5 billion years old) has been found in these mountains.

The high Drakensburg mountains are home to some of the most beautiful scenery in South Africa and are also rich in history. They form the south-eastern escarpment of the Highveld. Many people think that the coldest place in South Africa is Sutherland in the western

Roggeveld Mountains where midwinter temperatures can reach as low as −15 °C, but in fact, the coldest place is actually Buffelsfontein, which is in the Molteno district of the Eastern Cape. Buffelsfontein recorded a low of −18.6 °C. The deep interior has the hottest temperatures: A temperature of 51.7 °C (125 °F) was recorded in 1948 in the Kalahari (Northern Cape).

South Africa has one territorial possession, the small sub-Antarctic archipelago of the Prince Edward Islands consisting of Marion Island (290 km²/112 mi²) and Prince Edward Island.

South Africa is one of only 17 countries worldwide considered megadiverse. It has more than 20 000 different plants, or about 10 per cent of all the known species of plants on the Earth, making it particularly rich in plant biodiversity. South Africa is the third most biodiverse country in the world and has greater biodiversity than any country of equal or smaller size.

South Africa's most prevalent biome is grassland particularly on the Highveld, where the plant cover is dominated by different grasses. Vegetation becomes even more sparse towards the northwest due to low rainfall. There are several species of water-storing succulents like aloes and euphorbias in the hot and dry Namaqualand area. The grass and thorn savannah turn slowly into a bush savannah towards the north-east of the country, with more dense growth. There are significant numbers of baobab trees in this area, near the northern end of Kruger National park.

While South Africa has a great wealth of flowering plants, it has few forests. Only 1 per cent of South Africa is forest, exclusively in the coastal plain regions. There are even smaller reserves of forests that are out of reach, known as montane forests. Plantations of imported tree species are predominant, particularly the Eucalyptus and pine varieties. South Africa has lost a large area of natural habitat in the last four decades, primarily due to an ever-growing urban environment of sprawling development patterns and, as typically seen throughout growing economies, a mass destruction of trees. South Africa is one of the worst affected countries in the world when it comes to invasion by alien species with many posing a significant threat to the indigenous plant populations, and the already scarce water resources. The original temperate forests that were of abundance within the times of the first European settlers to South Africa was exploited ruthlessly until only small patches remained.

Mpumalanga, previously known as the Eastern Transvaal, has much in the way to offer, from scenery, to ancient history and of course an abundance of big game together with hundreds of species of birds, mammals and reptiles. Of the big game existing in this region, we have the lion, the leopard, the cheetah, blue wildebeest, water buffalo, hyenas, African wild dogs, gembok, impala, hippopotamus, giraffes, zebra, mountain cats, elephants and crocodiles to name but a few.

The economy

The economy of any country is without doubt the most important influencing factor of any land; the economy is so powerful that it has the ability to shape our lives, alter our family structures, impose moral values on us and shape the course of evolution. Therefore, we need to cover this subject, albeit briefly.

According to the UN's classification, South Africa is a middle-income country with an abundant supply of resources, well-developed financial, legal, communications, energy, and transport sectors, a stock exchange that ranks among the ten largest in the world, and a modern infrastructure supporting an efficient distribution of goods to major urban centres throughout Africa with a gross domestic production of over 30 per cent of the entire African continent.

The rand is the world's most actively traded emerging market currency. The South African rand (ZAR) was the best performing currency against the US dollar between 2002 and 2005, according to the Bloomberg Currency Scores. It is rightfully ranked within the 50 wealthiest countries in the world. One-third of all electricity generated throughout the African Continent is produced in South Africa alone.

We must bear in mind that the main focus of such economic growth seems to be centred around Johannesburg, Cape Town, Durban and Port Elizabeth. The government does seem to be readdressing this imbalance by, for example, earmarking future development potential for areas such as, Rustenberg, Bloemfontein, Nelspruit, and Mossel Bay, to name but a few.

With a considerable flood of foreign investment from both America and Germany together with the emerging interest of the Asian superpowers, this newly developed country is moving at an incredibly rapid pace, which in turn can be both daunting and incredibly liberating.

There are some negative influences on the rapidly growing and politically stable government from the immigrant influx, particularly from Zimbabwe, Zambia, Mozambique, Malawi, and Nigeria. Although immigration tends to bring positive change and productive growth to any country, one also has to bear in mind the negative influences, i.e. organised criminal activities, and in a country with a recent history marked by violence, it is likely only a matter of time before the impact of this will become counterproductive.

To help us understand the degree of such crimes, we can look to Anthony Altbecker who comments in his book *A Country at War with Itself* (2007):

> America may have had 50 murders a day in the late 1990s, but it also had seven times more people in its population than we do... there is something about the absolute numbers that makes them more tangible, blunter, than the comparatively detoxified per capita figures. Fifty murder victims a day is about a busload of people. The 19 000 people murdered a year [in South Africa] would be regarded as a big crowd at any of our cricket or soccer stadiums. And the 220 000 deaths [that is] the number of murders in the last ten years in South Africa is four times larger than the death toll over a similar period of Americans in the Vietnam war ... add [this] to the 19 000 murders, the half million or so cases of assault, serious assault and attempted murders recorded by the police every year, the roughly 200 000 robberies and aggravated robberies, and the 55 000 rape cases, to say nothing of the 300 000 burglaries and 85 000 stolen cars and before we even think about the ocean of crimes that go unreported or unrecorded, it is clear that a substantial portion of South Africans are victims of at least one serious crime every year. It is almost no exaggeration to describe ourselves as a country at war with itself.

No doubt the majority of you will consider the above account a powerful and hard-hitting portrait of present-day South Africa (however, compared to the plight of people in Sierra Leone, Mogadishu, and Côte d'Ivoire, these data pale into insignificance). South Africa's rising crime statistics might be an unforeseen consequence of the increasing sophistication of security technologies which by making common theft difficult if not impossible, have increased the numbers of criminals resorting to violent robberies. Consequently, there is an ever larger white population emigrating from South Africa, and the impact of this demographic change on the future of the Boerboel is hard to calculate.

Ethnography

The people of South Africa are the most diverse in the whole of the African continent and I believe that South Africa is on a par with the US in terms of racial diversity, so let us talk about the people. There are the old Arab traders, Dutch, Danish, Germans, Malays, Indians, French Huguenots, Portuguese, English, Mozambiqueans, and Chinese. With a population of over 47 million and a black African majority of over 75 per cent, this country is one of the most tolerant and liberal in Africa.

The racial categories are white, black, Indian, Asian or coloured. Of the black African group there are subdivisions consisting of Zulus, Xhosa, Basotho, Bapedis, the Venda, Tswana, Tsonga, Swazi and Ndebele. But let us not forget the Khokhoi, the meaning of which when translated is 'men of men' (i.e., men par excellence). (The offensive name Hottentot was given by the Dutch and means people who stutter and is no longer used.) Then there is the San who are an indigenous people, persecuted by the Dutch and fought by the Khoikhoi.

At this point, we should make reference to the works of Theal (1919), Dr O. Dapper (1668) as well as the words of Willem Ten Rhijne (1686) and Johannes Guliemus De Grevenbroek (1665), all of whom with the exception of Theal had their historical and scientific notes translated in publications of the Van Riebeck Society in 1933. A cautionary note: the following writings are meant to help us understand the harsh and inhospitable land we know today as South Africa and the precarity, obstacles, and dangers facing its immigrants, as well as the brutality suffered by and suppression of its indigenous populations.

Please bear in mind that the following works were written before we had specific knowledge of genetics and when travel was but a fantasy for the ordinary person. The word 'race' is a nineteenth-century concept, and it is with great relief that today we are able to discredit the ignorant preconceptions of a Victorian society that created the philosophy of race in the name of anthropology. Although crude and ignorant, the writers are nonetheless important sources for us in our attempt to gain a sense of the lands as they were then. I recommend immersing yourself in the following passages to fully absorb the country, and, if possible, try to imagine the dogs of the past and how evolution has brought them through the years into the twenty-first century.

George McCall Theal's The Ethnography of South Africa before 1505 AD (1919)

> 'The land rises from the ocean level in terraces or steps, until a vast interior plain is reached. Deep gorges have been worn by the action of

water, in some places internal forces have caused elevations, in other places depressions, and everywhere along the margins of the terraces distortions may be seen. There are no navigable rivers and the coast is bold and unbroken. The steep fronts of the terraces which from the lower side appear to be mountain ranges, and the abscense [sic] of running water in dry seasons over large surfaces, tended likewise to prevent intercourse between the different parts of the country. The rude people of each section were left to themselves, without that stimulus to improvement which contact with strangers gives. There was very little necessity to exert the mind to provide clothing or habitations, for since the close of the ice period in Europe and the corresponding fluctuations in temperature in the southern hemisphere the climate has been uniformly mild, and even on the elevated plain snow never lies long on the ground. Like the wild animals, man on occasions of severe weather could find some temporary shelter. In this respect a savage is far more callous than a civilised man (Theal 1919).'

Dr O. Dapper's Kaffaria or Land of the Kaffirs (1668)

'One morning in June 1659, after the war had already lasted three months, five Hottentots (including this doman) were overtaken by five of our horsemen as they were running off with two of our cattle which they had stolen from a certain free burgher. A sharp skirmish ensued. The Hottentots, seeing no possible means of a fight, nor desiring any mercy, defended themselves valiantly. They wounded two of the horsemen, one through the arm and under the lower ribs, and the other in the spine. But our countrymen repaid the debt by wounding three of them with the gun and stabbing the other two dead with their own weapons. One of the three shot who were shot was named Eykamma, was taken to the fort on a horse, with his neck pierced, his leg shattered, and a severe wound in the head, but Doman, with the other escaped by jumping over a stream eight feet wide, after which flight proved their best weapon and salvation.

'The wounded Eykamma, brought in to the fort, was asked why his people made war against our countrymen, and tried to cause damage everywhere by killing, plundering and burning. Well nigh overcome by the pain of his severe wounds, he replied by asking why the Dutch had ploughed over the land of the Hottentots and sought to take the bread out of their mouth by sowing corn on the lands to which they had to drive their cattle for pasture, adding that they had other or better grazing grounds. The reason for all their attacks, he continued was nothing else than to revenge themselves for the harm and injustice done to them. Since they not only commanded to keep away from certain of their grazing grounds, which they had always possessed undisturbed and only allowed us at first to use as refreshment station, but they also saw their lands divided out among us without their knowledge by the heads of the settlement, and the boundaries put up within which they might not pasture. He asked finally what we would have done had the same thing happened to us. Moreover, he added, they had observed how we were strengthening ourselves daily with fortifications and bulwarks, which according to their way of thinking could have no other objective than to bring them and all that was theirs under our authority and domination. To this our men replied your people have now once for all lost the land around the Cape through War, and you must accordingly never dwell on the idea of getting it back again through peace or through war. This war in which our countrymen were killed, plundered and robbed by the savages had already lasted eleven months before a dispute was settled (Dapper 1668).'

Speaking of another group of Hottentots, Dapper comments:

'The Heusaquas are rich in cattle ... (none other [than] Hottentots in this country plant or sow the ground) ... Close to the Heusaquas are the Hankumquas, rich in people and cattle. They have never been to our countrymen at the fort. ... The Heusaquas are especially clever in handling young and old lions, which they know how to catch in snares and tame, like dogs, with a collar round the neck. They even set out for war with lions which they have long had and completely tamed, and in this way are able to set the enemy to flight without encountering any resistance. This may seem strange to many readers but is never the less actually the practice among them. ... The favourite and most desired articles for which they are now willing to exchange their cattle are tobacco, brandy, beadwork and copper (Dapper 1668).'

William Ten Rhijne's
An Account of the Cape of Good Hope and the Hottentotes (1686)

'This mountainous desert is a fitter habitation for wild beasts than for men, for here are to be found lions, the cruel enemies of flocks and herds, elephants, rhinoceroses, tigers or rather panthers, wolves, elks, hippopotamuses, wild horses, buffaloes, boars, mountain-bred napes, baboons, porcupines, hedgehogs, lynxes, stags, rabbits, badgers, otters, hares, zebras of a most beautiful colouring, as if [a] furrier had inserted white stripes at regular intervals in a black hide, goats, mountain goats, ibexes, both spotted and ash coloured, springboks, wild cats, shaped like tigers and grey, a species of fox which the Dutch call jackals, and more rarely tamandua-guaca? Differing only in size from the Brazilian variety. In truth an enormous supply of animals must harbour here, for in a brief space of time a few hunters brought the governor several thousands of pounds weight of animals they had taken, chiefly hippopotamuses, elks, ibexes and similar creatures. Hence, we can see into how serious an error Aristotle fell when he says that in Africa (where there is no lack of that beast whose teeth are precious at its death) the boar, the stag, and the wild goat are not to be found. … Among the poisonous creatures snakes are common, differing in shape size and habitat. There are vipers twice as big as I have found in France, Salamanders, Scorpions, Scolopendrae, Lizards, Toads.

…

'Our countrymen have often come off with heavy losses from encounters with the clever tactics of the natives. For the natives have learned from the lions, which here are very common. In rainy weather, which puts our muskets out of action, and damps our strength and spirits, while they depend on cunning for their criminal success, the natives bestow upon themselves in thickets and tough undergrowth, then producing their weapons, they fall upon the enemy, owing their success rather to the rain than to their arms. But in open places, and under a clear sky, they are more prone to raise a cry and take flight, they slip off in all directions in to the neighbouring woods and thorny hillocks, where they must be hunted down before they can be conquered, a formidable task with these wild, woodland creatures whose arrows are so dangerous (Rhijne 1686).'

J. G. Grevenbroek The African Race (1695)
This particular work is a more accurate and significant account than the above. Grevenbroek served with the Dutch East Indian company before retiring, in what is now known as Stellenbosch, as a free burgher.

'This place also produces very hardy oxen, as swift as those found in India near the Ganges. Finally, must be mentioned the very destructive wild dogs, which hunt up and down in packs of ten or twenty, when they come on sheep and calves, with the uptmost savagery they promptly disembowel some and tear the udders and bellies of others with their long sharp teeth. In a moment they destroy a whole flock unless the watchful herds or trusty dogs can keep them off.

'I am astonished that rumour, never bearing a clear report, shoul[d] have acquired such strength in her course and proved so tenacious of falsehood that those half-truths that are spread abroad about our Africans should have reached even your ears. I found this people with one accord in their general daily life living in harmony with natures laws, hospitable to every race of men, open, dependable, lovers of truth and justice, not utterly unacquainted with the worship of some god, endowed, within their own limits, with a rare nimbleness of mother wit, and having minds receptive of instruction.

…

'And for this fault I now seek pardon and sing a palinode; for alas for the disgrace, it is through our countrymen, who have forgotten their ancestral ways, as I now plainly see and recognise, that the natives have been changed for the worse, and have become secretive, suspicious and shut away from us. From us they have learned blasphemy, perjury, strife, quarrelling, drunkenness, trickery, brigandage, theft, ingratitude, unbridled lust for what is not one's own, misdeeds unknown to them before, and among other crimes of deepest die, the accursed lust of gold (Grevenbroek 1695).'

The accounts of these writers are of considerable importance to the discussions in the final chapter, Chapter 9 'Fact or Fiction'.

The hunters' dogs, the dangers and diseases, and their significance

The formidable hunting dogs of the pioneers

The use of dogs in the 1880s and later in the 1930s was primarily to protect the livestock, wagons and inhabitants of the kralls. The hunting of big game was also widespread and large packs of dogs were established for this particular reason. Dogs would bay game quite effectively, they would keep wild dogs and sometimes hyenas away from the prized trophies. There were many occasions when the dogs were expected to hunt for their own food.

The dogs of the Voortrekkers would lie during the hot summer days, under the wagons, seeking what shade could be offered. At night they would be on guard to alert the people of wild animals, and possible human attacks.

In *The Definitive Rhodesian Ridgeback* (1982) David H. Helgesen states beautifully and poignantly the difficulties faced by the trekkers:

> 'At night the dogs would sleep next to the fire inside the kraal, barking at scavengers or predators which came close to the enclosure, or even inside it, they would leap to the attack, snapping and snarling around the beast until it fled or until they or the hunter killed it – unless it was a lion, in that case the odd dog would attack, but most would flee. … Dogs which ventured outside the brush walls at night did not last long. Leopards in particular, it was said, had a taste for dogs. Most observers agreed that dogs were of most value to the hunters at night when they could not see to shoot and when the oxen were most vulnerable to attack by lions. The hunter kralls were little different to the Khoikhoi or other tribes, and the threat of the King of beasts was the same for all.
>
> …
>
> 'When the wagons of other trekkers were encountered, the two packs of dogs would of course investigate each other and probably dispute the road. Dogs from roadside native villages were hotly pursued. The arrival of the hunters wagons at the mission stations, the kings kraal, or lees farm all the usual stopping points was accompanied by much barking and growling, stiff legged pacing, sniffing and occasional full scale brawling by the various packs, if several groups of hunters and their families settled down, with wagons close together for any length of time, for example to spend the whole summer as the Boer families were want to do, new pecking orders had to be established, new territories stalked and new bitches fought over and bred (Helgesen 1982, pp. 36–37).'

This as you have read is vital information and further reinforces the hypothesis of evolution through natural selection.

So, what do we know of the dangers that surround the dogs that entered this harsh and unforgiving country? Well, let us start with the diseases of relevance to humans, malaria, blackwater fever, yellow fever, and a form of disease called sleeping sickness spread quite commonly by the tsetse fly. Oxen, dogs and horses, all three being vital to human movement were not unsusceptible to the tsetse fly or to sleeping sickness and the numerous and varied poisons contained in the plant life, such as distemper and anthrax were common. All these obstacles are evident even before we take into account the large array of animals that were quick to dispose of dogs, be it the individual dog or a full hunting pack.

There are numerous accounts of the different game that challenged the formidable frontier dogs and the same dogs also used by the hunters. Of particular note is a recording by the English artist and explorer Thomas Baines (1820–1875) of a number of events in the gold regions of south-eastern Africa:

> '[W]e had been disturbed all night by skirmishes between wolves and tigers, (hyenas and leopards) and our dogs, and in the morning poor old Vuilbard, Mr Hartley's well proved watchdog, was missing. At first, we thought a tiger had killed him, but the opinion now is he attempted to guard the carcase [sic] of his comrade Camelbuck (Hartley's famous shooting Horse) from crocodiles and that one of these loathsome reptiles seized him. Poor old foulbeard had been for years a valued and privileged companion. He never walked on a journey but, as soon as the cattle were inspanned, would jump up in to the wagon and lie on his master's bed (Baines 1864, p. 531).'

Gemsbock (South African oryx) and various other antelope were quite capable of dispatching dogs, whether the outcome was fatal or non-fatal is irrelevant as there were not the adequate facilities to rescue such dogs from the fate that was awaiting them. Baines describes one of these encounters:

> 'During the morning the dogs brought to bay and killed a sable antelope, but the victory was dearly purchased, for one of Mr Woods, a favourite called Sook, received a sharp horn under the ribs, the point coming out at the opposite shoulder, and lived just long enough to lick the hand of his master, while another was severely wounded, while old Vuilbard (foul beard), Mr Hartley's pet got a scratch just under the eye, this being the third time he has been wounded by this formidable antagonist. Indeed, the zwart wit pens, as this beautiful and formidable animal is termed, is no contemptible antagonist even for a lion. Mr Hartley says that [he] once shot [one] with its skin so torn by teeth and claws as to be utterly valueless, but its sharp sweeping horns were bloody to the base, and it had most probably left the lion dead upon the field of battle (Baines 1864).'

Baines also describes an encounter (one of many in his writings) between the lions and these formidable, courageous dogs:

> Jewell says he was lying asleep in his wagon when the attack took place and, waking at the noise, he caught up his rifle and jumped out, Pickles, who was sleeping with her pups, leaping out and rushing before him, probably in to the very jaws of the lion, she must have been caught by the neck and killed in an instant, for she uttered no cry whatever. Probably the suddenness with which she was waked up and her eagerness to defend her young rendered her less cautious than usual, for she was generally cautious to keep baying him just outside his range (ibid, p. 642).

F. C. Selous in *A Hunter's Wanderings in Africa* (2001) had also written extensively about the magnificent and courageous dogs of the day. He refers to them as old curs or mongrels and he praises these dogs as formidable opponents against most large game. He recounts the story of three dogs challenging a lion near the Umniati River in Mashonaland, where a farmer called Piet Jacobs shot at and missed a lion which had been prowling around the laager. Pursued by Jacobs' three dogs the lion jumped onto a large rock. As Jacobs approached, it charged him, ignoring the dogs; Jacobs got in another shot, but the lion smashed him to the ground and bit him severely. The dogs immediately attacked the lion's hindquarters so tenaciously that the big cat turned to chase them. They continued to avoid and harry it while old Piet made his escape.

The hot baking heat was another problem for the dogs of those days, with its burnt ground and hard stalks, thorny grass and rough and rocky ground. Both E. R. Shelley in *Hunting Big Game with Dogs in Africa* (1924) and Sir Cornwallis Harris mention in their separate writings the problem faced by the European dogs in the lack of hardiness in their foot pads, a problem that was resolved by cross-breeding them with indigenous African dogs.

A further hunter and writer was Roualyn Gordon Cumming who travelled from the Natal to the Limpopo provinces between 1844 and 1848. In his book, *Five Years of a Hunters Life in the Far Interior of South Africa* (1874) he makes special comment on the long-legged bulldogs and greyhounds used by the Afrikaner farmers of the day, pointing out that the dogs were rough, stout, and long legged.

David Helgesen (1982, pp. 10–11) describes a hunter by the name of W. Cotton Oswell who had recorded his journeys of the Transvaal and commented that a tendency to bite and hold would be almost always fatal to the dog. He lost a Bulldog/terrier cross named Tod to a lion for that reason. The terrier temperament was not ideal for the African wilderness. This point was also made by E. R. Shelley in *Hunting Big Game with Dogs in Africa* (1924) where he notes the terrier and Bull type breeds have too much gameness to be effective in making death a quick result. And Oswell left us some invaluable words when he wrote:

> In the times I am writing of I do not think it would have been possible, save with a large number of armed watchers and fires, to have kept your oxen in anything like safety without dogs. You went to sleep in peace as soon as the dog watch was set, and the fires made up for the night (Helgesen 1982, p. 65).

The works of William Charles Baldwin are probably the most detailed accounts we have of the Afrikaner nomadic existence and their agrarian lifestyles, and he had hunted with the most renowned of Afrikaner hunters, such as Joubert and Swartz. But, more importantly for us, he wrote about one particular dog belonging to these trekkers 'he is the best whelp of great promise, Bull and Greyhound, with a dash of pointer, the best breed possible' (Baldwin 1863). The Bull he refers to is of course the long-legged Bulldog. The dog he acquired in March 1858 was from the Bloemfontein Orange Free State.

Conclusion

To recap, you have followed me through a history of the evolution of the dog, and I have discussed the arguments for the proposal of the Tibetan Mastiff as the origin of the Mastiff breed. We have covered the hypothesis that this dog most probably mated with the dogs of the lower plains, thus creating the shorter haired Mastiffs, which we in turn believe to be the same Indian dog referred to by Alexander and various scholars (Chapter 2). More importantly we have examined the evidence for the influence of the South African dogs, of the San and Khoikhoi, and pieced together the historical relevance of the indigenous dogs' influence on the arriving Europeans. There has been a brief paragraph on the influence of the Bullenbijter dog and we have examined the relevance of the Bullmastiff as referred to by many various hypotheses (also Chapter 2). We have dismissed certain theories on the basis there was insufficient credible evidence, and we shall elaborate further on such theories in the final chapter, 'Fact or Fiction'.

More importantly, we have covered the various components within a society that bear direct influence over the evolution of dogs, i.e. the economy, geography, and ethnography. We have also examined various writings from the travellers from the seventeenth to the early twentieth centuries to help us comprehend the situation of South Africa as it was 300 or more years ago.

Now we can begin to look directly at the breeding history of the Boerboel.

Chapter 4
The Establishment of the Boerboel

At this stage, having considered the evolution of the dog from its origins on the Asiatic plains, and having described its journey along Roman and European trade routes, as well as the indigenous African dogs, we can now move on to a discussion of how vital these histories were for the formation of the useful farm, utility, hunting, and catch dog which became the Boerboel.

As early as 1957 the name 'boerbulls' appears in the literature, which indicates that the dog was becoming recognised as a distinct new breed at least 24 years before the first Boerboel association formed. In his book *The Rhodesian Ridgeback*, T. C. Hawley sheds light on the reasons why a standard took so long to be defined for both the Ridgeback and the Boerboel:

> 'The Rhodesian Ridgeback has recaptured favour and vies with 'boerbulls' and the rest as farm dogs. The South African farmer, except for a limited few who are interested in breeding dogs, is content with a useful, reliable dog … Some attempts have been made to standardise this [Boerboel] as a breed, but opinions differ so much that no agreement on a standard has been reached to date–the proverbial multiplicity of cooks spoiling the broth. They vary from anything resembling a small Boxer to a full-sized Bullmastiff' (Hawley 1957, p. 27).

Given that the farmers' principal concerns lay with their dogs being reliable and capable of defending livestock and property, it was no wonder that they made little effort to standardise different breeds of farm dog. It was enough that the dogs they used were capable and loyal. Therefore, Hawley's history gives us an idea of the difficulty the Rhodesian breeders encountered in setting their standard, which is to their credit.

At this point it is relevant to turn to Anemari Pretorius and the recent theories she has put forward in her book, *The Boerboel: South Africa's Own* (2007):

> '[T]hus the European connection of Van Reibeeck with his Bullenbijter now no longer seems to be the only (or most likely) source of origin of the Boerboel – especially if we go back to the mongrels mentioned earlier … In time, various black tribes moved south when they came into contact with the European – naturally their dogs moved with them. A question that arises is whether the 'African' dog with the distinctive v shape on the tail is a descendant of the dogs of Ethiopia. If so, the value of this connection could have far-reaching implications on our current level of knowledge and understanding of the make-up of the Boerboel breed' (Pretorius 2007, pp.4–5).

It could therefore be said that the Boerboel was bred from two main sources of genetic material: the Bullenbijter from Europe, which had genetic roots in Albania and Syria, and the African dog of the black tribes of Africa.

Founder of Cape Town, the Dutch navigator and colonial administrator Jan van Riebeeck (1619–1677) is discussed by several writers. Riebeeck brought a Bullenbijter with him to the Cape. The late Johan Du Preez (originally writing in Afrikaans) describes the early Boer type of Bullmastiff:

> 'About 200 years after Van Riebecks [sic] set foot in South Africa there existed a dog known as the Boerhonde this dog had only a little 'Boel Blood' in it. He was quite muscular had long legges and a long body. Sometimes his ears would stand straight up these dogs were used for hunting purposes. It is said they were even used to kill lions and leopards. They were known for their stamina and fighting qualities. The 'boerhond' was used by the colonists to catch predators. This dog must have been an ancestor to the Rhodesian Ridgeback.'

The Boerhonde type of dog was highly sought after by farmers. The farmers started cross-breeding the two most popular breeds, the Bullmastiff and the Bulldog. The farmers were impressed with these dogs' wit and strength, which they used to master oxen and bulls. Du Preez tells of a trader from the south-east Free State who exchanged one of his oxen for the so-called 'Boele' while he was on his travels.

The Boele dog is also described by Bert Grabbe in *The Boerboels of Southern Africa* (1999) as a large strong dog which reminded one of the Mastiff type of dog. He tells how in 1820 the British settlers brought, among others, the Bulldog and Mastiff types of dog. The UK's Slavery Abolition Act of 1833 had bore certain consequences for South African farmers. The Great Trek began in 1835 and hundreds of farmers left the east Cape to move inland. They had numerous herds of large and small stock that had to be tended by their children after the slaves were freed. South Africa was then a largely unknown country and was rough and empty, posing danger in the shape of predators and other people. The dogs of the trekkers kept the stock safe. Many predators died after an encounter with the 'vlugvoetige Boerhonde' and the 'Boele'.

In 1938 the real Bullmastiff was imported to South Africa by De Beers to guard the diamond mines. It is also known that they imported a champion male dog in 1938. The Boerboel was 'bred from huge, strong dogs with good characteristics. One can become lyrical about these good characteristics. Our ancestors kept their dogs as guardians and friends of their children, as watchdogs and protectors, because [the Boerboel] will flinch from no danger' (Grabbe 1999). As a result of numerous people with varying needs and opinions breeding the dog, the Boele or Boerhonde (interchangeable, but not to be confused with the German Boerhonde) remained quite diverse until the twentieth century. Du Preez writes that after the Anglo Boer War and up to the 1940s:

> Many excellent dogs were bred in the East Free State where I grew up. There were some breeders who bred first class Boerboels among others.

Van Niekerks from Rosendal-Ficksburg, Froemans from Marquard, Fouries from Rosendal and Kommissiepoort and Lamprechts uit Senekal-Steynrus (Du Preez).

In addition, he comments that a lot of exceptional dogs were being bred in the north of the Natal and the east of the Traansvaal. However, through mismanagement and inbreeding the good genes of these dogs were lost. In these regions, owners tried to bring new life to their Boerboels by cross-breeding, notably, with Great Danes and Boxers. This did not bring about the result they had hoped for as the bastard pups were recognisable as such by their heads.

The Boerhonde dog has a varied appearance, possessing at times a wiry coat and at others a smooth, short haired coat, or a thicker, longer haired coat (more prevalent in mountainous regions), and the presentation of different coat colours is one of the unique aspects of the farmer's Boer dog. A further development in appearance was the Steekbaard, or dirty beard, as it is sometimes referred to.

I believe that this one common farm dog (Boerhonde/frontier dog) was the foundation dog for both the Boerboel and the Rhodesian Ridgeback. British hunters used the Dalmation standard to control the Boerhonde's height and bulk and the resulting Boerhonde dog became a mascot for the British hunters. Later, Afrikaners used the Mastiff to add other qualities to the Boerhonde, which resulted in the Boerboel or Farmer's Bull.

The Boerhonde/frontier dog was created to be the ultimate dog for use in the kraals of the Afrikaner farmers, Voortrekkers and British hunters and it was a common sight at most of the military frontier points where you would find fine examples of them. This fine Boerhonde dog was subsequently developed by British hunters and its phenotype redesigned under the influence of the standard of the Dalmatian dog from Croatia. And later, the Boerhonde was used as a working dog by the Afrikaaner, over a much longer period of time than it had been used by the British right up to 1985. During that time, it was developed to enhance its size and increase its bulk, and became the Boerboel or Farmer's Bull.

One would only have to study the striking similarity between a Rhodesian Ridgeback and a Boerboel to see that they are one and the same.

Typical Hound Type Boerboel
Source Author

Typical 1970s Ridgebacks sharing common ancestry
Source Author

I believe that this similarity is not a result of the Rhodesian Ridgeback having been bred back into the Boerboel line at some later stage, but is down to the two breeds sharing an ancestor: the common farm dog, or Boerhonde/frontier dog. The Boerboel and the Rhodesian Ridgeback are in essence the same frontier stock dog, both clearly the product of hunters as well as farmers.

Their tree branches out: one branch goes on to be deliberately influenced by the hound and the other branch to be influenced by the Mastiff. No doubt you will be interested in learning (although some people did not want me to divulge this element of the Boerboel's history) which modern breeds created the Boerboel. When I say modern, I refer to those dogs which I believe were cross-bred with the Boerboel during and after the formation in 1983 of the South African Boerboel Breeders' Society (SABT – initially, now SABBS).

The eminent and successful breeders of the Rhodesian Ridgeback were the first to make us aware of this common farm dog, the Boer hound bearing the influence of heavy, strong dogs, and most certainly influenced by the long-legged Bulldog. We already knew from historic and photographic evidence that some common farm dog type was in existence, albeit variations developed to better suit various environmental conditions as well as the particular stock a farmer kept. These factors would have determined how much importance a farmer gave to possessing a dog with either better running capabilities or protection abilities, for instance, while the thickness of coat would have been a vital consideration for mountainous regions.

What I learned in South Africa

Making a trip to South Africa was important for my professional development as a Boerboel specialist and during the visit I realised that the experience was going to be much more significant than I had expected. Upon my arrival I found that many young breeders were oblivious to the ancestry of their dog. Similarly, I found a number of the old-time Boerboel men wary and suspicious of my questioning, but once they understood that I had done my research they dropped their romantic historical rhetoric and shared some valuable, priceless insights with me.

My trip to South Africa had been planned for a specific reason. I had spent a considerable number of years communicating by telephone to the older generation of Boerboel breeders (they would prove to be a vital source for me when putting the pieces of my puzzle together), but there is only so much information you can gain over the phone. Conversations carried out by remote technologies do not provide the same level of detail as one-to-one meetings. So, I went to meet the breeders in person.

We know from historians and Rhodesian Ridgeback researchers that from the 1920s to the 1950s that the Boerhonde dog was an established farm dog. You might be wondering why the bulk of my research has been dominated by the works of the Ridgeback enthusiasts, and this is a valid and important question that I shall now answer. The credible evidence I have been able to glean from Boerboel historians is vague; there are innumerable contradictions in their reports, not to mention unconfirmed stories. The majority of Afrikaner farmers before the late twentieth century were working class and illiterate, which by no means diminishes the fact they produced incredible dogs, however, the point is, little evidence was published in either

Afrikaans or English on the Boerboel. To understand the development of the Boerboel standard, we have turn to the writings of hunters and travellers whose detailed diaries of their experiences, observations and thoughts reveal a great deal about the culture of dog breeding in South Africa.

It is no coincidence that the majority of those hunters were British. For most of the trekkers, a dog was nothing more than a necessity and was not worth writing about. Those Afrikaners who were educated were likely to be engaged in politics in urban centres, ignorant of everyday life concerns around the kraals, not interested in animal husbandry, and therefore not aware of the importance of the Boerboel breed for South African rural life.

Another reason for the dearth of records is the dominance of an oral tradition. A substantial part of Afrikaner history has been passed down orally, and of course, like all oral histories it has been subjected to exaggeration through the generations. It would be fair to assume that as successive generations of children were told such stories by elders, the details would have become less and less accurate.

However, one of the few people in South Africa who had detailed knowledge of its history was my mentor in Kroonstadt. He told me of his extreme gratitude to the black farm workers who had looked after these fine Boer dogs back from the early 1900s until the Boers returned to their farms years later. This period coincides with the era of the British policy of 'scorched earth', a tactic widely practised across the British Empire to deter civil disobedience and uprisings. Was this also the period when the Boerboel started to be cross-bred with other dogs, as has been speculated by numerous theories online? It is feasible to assume that some form of cross-breeding would have occurred between the Boerboel and the local dogs of the black employees; whether a large number of dogs was involved is virtually impossible to ascertain.

So, we move on to the most significant and detailed part of our investigation.

The formation of South Africa Boerboel Breeders' Association

The South Africa Boerboel Breeders' Association (SABBS) – Die Suid-Afrikaanse Boerboel Telersvereniging in Afrikaans (SABT) – was established in 1983 in a school hostel for boys. The members who formed the organisation that day were Johan De Jager, Johan Du Preez, Lucas Van de Merwe, Dr Andre du Toit, Mrs Owen Read, and of course, the schoolboys eating the freshly baked cakes that were on offer for the occasion. A total number of just two dogs attended (and those belonging to Johan Du Preez, which never ventured out of his pick-up truck throughout the meeting). What happened at the meeting that crisp high veldt morning is of vital significance.

The impact of decisions made that day continues to be felt. Even today there are severe consequences for those individuals who inherit the modern legacy of this breed. The first Annual General Meeting (AGM) took place one year later in 1984 and a total of not exceeding 30 dogs was present. The venue was held at Kameeldrift in Pretoria. The size of those dogs has been stated as not exceeding 24–28 inches, a size that would be almost dwarfed by the standard required of today's Boerboel enthusiasts.

Two tours (to document Boerboels around the country) commenced after the first SABT meeting in 1983 (although I have been unable to identify the details of the putative second tour). The first took place in August 1990 and covered a total of 5500 km, which was carried out by Lucas Van de Merwve and Jannie Bouwer, together with Lucas's wife at the time, Anneke. A total of 250 dogs were inspected and only 70 or so selected, although, this is only a rough estimate. My source has led me to the conclusion that there were no more than 41 dogs selected within the formative years of the SABT and it was these dogs that made up the bulk of the foundation dogs for creating and legitimising this breed. This information is somewhat contrary to the history I once read many years ago on the Boerboel claiming that there were 71 dogs used as foundation dogs. However, we have to take into account the fact that the development register for this breed remained open. The members whose names appear in the list of the first 50 breeders of the SABT do not correspond to the first foundation dogs used and this was partly due to the fact that many people who had joined the SABT back in 1983 and 1984 had failed to actually contribute dogs to the breeding programme. As you will see from the list of foundation dogs I provide below, many dogs were registered under a kennel name, due to the fact that they did not have breeders or kennels associated with them. Therefore, you will find blank space where the details of the dogs' owners and kennels ought to be. A typical example is the Volksrust lines: they were dogs found on the 1990 tour that did correspond with the definition of Boerboel and to whom their town of inspection was given as their name. I would like to point out at this stage that even though it has been only 29 years since a legitimate effort was made to standardise this breed, it is yet a breed of 15 dog generations. This is plenty of time in which to formalise a definitive type for the breed and participate in a continuous dialogue to agree on a means of sticking to a breed standard.

Having looked at the details of the dogs used as foundation specimens and which provinces they came from, we can now turn to the most significant evidence, which is photographic evidence. Finally, I hear you say, after all the previous pages of speculation and theories, we can finally start pinning down the migration and evolution of this fine Boer dog!

My source in South Africa tells me that when the first SABT AGM took place, many dogs were brought, of varying contrasts, displaying an abundance of diversity. It was a similar event as the first meeting of the Rhodesian Ridgeback society that appeared in June 1925, following a request by a Mr Francis Richard Barnes. A total number exceeding a little over 20 dogs appeared that day and a real diversity was also on show. There were Bull Terrier types, Great Dane types, Bullmastiff types and every colour conceivable, including black and brindles. The type was formulated a few days later by B. W. Durham and was based on the conformation of the Dalmation. You might be wondering why the Dalmation, I want you to bear in mind I said conformation only, no such dogs were used in the breeding of the Rhodesian Ridgeback. The Dalmation was a dog of great movement, it was a versatile utility dog initially used as a watchdog, ratting dog and hunting dog, and especially for trotting alongside carriage horses for very prolonged periods of time. Its form was designed by its work and use: this was important.

To understand the dogs of those days and their instinctive behaviour, most of which has been lost in the dogs bred today, we first need to understand the importance of inherited instinct. In *The Definitive Rhodesian Ridgeback* (1982), David H. Helgesen presents a report from a local newspaper on the event of the first show of the The Rhodesian Ridgeback Club, held Thursday 9 July 1925:

'The Rhodesian Ridgeback (Lion Dog) Club held their first show in conjunction with the Agricultural show in Bulawayo with results which must be highly satisfactory to the officials. Twenty-four representatives of this old African hunting breed, which now seems likely to meet the recognition it deserves under a specialist club, came before a judge of long experience. … Notwithstanding a large notice warning visitors that these dogs were dangerous, several had narrow escapes in attempting to handle exhibits. Dogs of this breed will not as a rule allow strangers to touch them and it would be well for everyone to remember this as the officials cannot always be on the spot to give words of caution' (Helgesen, 1982).

The above description sounds like the Ridgebacks I was familiar with, unfortunately this is no longer seen in the majority of such dogs today.

The black Boerboel

A typical Black Frontier Boerhonde dog, 1928 and long before the formation of an official recognition for the Boerboel breed spread across many voortrekker camps, this is a common example
Source Linda Costa, Rhodesian Ridgeback Pioneers

Why are there no black Boerboels today? There are a few possible explanations. Breeders were concerned about individuals who might use Rottweilers to cross-breed with the Boerboel. In my time in South Africa, particularly in Johannesburg and Pretoria, there was a widespread belief that the black Boerboel was a myth. However, I did meet a gentleman from Bloemfontein, a board member of the SABT, who stated he had a clear recollection of fine black Boerboels being bred in the small town of Dealsville in central Free State over 40 years ago. Similarly, an honorary life member of the SABT has confirmed the black Boerboel's existence and legitimacy. Perhaps of relevance is that some black communities in South Africa hold superstitious beliefs about black dogs; there is great fear of and prejudice associated with a black dog. My Afrikaner friends in England confirmed that this is a widespread belief and informed me that their parents had kept black dogs as a deterrent against trespass from black people. Another interesting point is made by Helgesen on the Ridgeback (Helgesen 1982, p. 73), when Trooper Ockes' conversation with Cornelius Van Rooyen informs him that the establishment of the breed, i.e. the lion dog was strictly the result of the importation of two bitches, both of which were a grey/black colour, obtained from Fredrick C. Selous, a hunter and writer (Selous 2001 [1881]). These were crossed to Selous's Boerhond. As well as attesting to the possibility of a black Boerboel, this history also supports my theory that the Boerboel and the Rhodesian Ridgeback descended from the same ancestors and that the trading of hunting and frontier dogs was a common occurrence. Another point worth mentioning comes from William S. Rosenthal whose thesis *The Black and Tan Rhodesian Ridgeback Genetic Issues and Possible Solutions* (Rosenthal 2005) describes how 'In some quarters of the Ridgeback community there seems to be this irrational belief that black and tans are a scourge, only recently visited upon the breed. Both the history of the breed and the genetics of dog colour argue against that view.' How succinctly put.

Of paramount importance is the fact that the French Night Dog which accompanied the French Huguenots to South Africa was predominantly black in colour. Despite the dynamics of political disenfranchisement and Huguenot suppression under Dutch control, the Huguenots would have contributed to the creation of the modern-day Boerboel. In fact, I could be brave and state in no uncertain terms that the likelihood of the Huguenot Night Dog having contributed to the modern Boerboel is equal if not greater than that of the Bullenbijter.

A French Mastiff, note the colour could indeed range from black to brindle.
Source Charwynne Dog Features

It is clear that black farm dogs did exist, and since all farm dogs that belonged to the Afrikaner farmer were considered Boerbul then it is safe to deduce that, prior to 1983 and the birth of the SABT, black dogs were given the same status as wheaten Boerboels in both name and value by Afrikaner farmers.

Columella, writing in the first century AD puts forward the opinion that the guard dog, used to guard the farms and property and flocks, should be black because this colour blends in with the dark (Columella was translated into English by Harrison Boyd Ash, E. S. Forster, and Edward H. Heffner and published by Harvard University Press in 1968). Today, a lot of controversy surrounds the legitimacy of this colour for the Boerboel and as with all such debates, the facts often get mixed with propaganda. The consensus is that other breeds have been introduced within the last 10 years and the Cane Corso appears to be one of the names mentioned. Both the Bullenbijter and the French Mastiff (or Nightdog) had black as a solid colour accompanied by other colours, including brindle, pied and red, so if the theory of Van Riebeeck's famous prodigal Boerboel is true, then we must consider whether his Bullenbijter was a black dog. Please be aware that, as noted by Dapper, since the time of Van Riebeeck the history of the French Huguenots and Afrikaners has been turbulent, so much so that the writings of Dapper, published by the Van Riebeeck Society, state that 200 French migrants were separated by order of a Dutch general to prevent them from promoting the French language, thus keeping Dutch as the official language of the migrants. Bearing this in mind, then we have to also consider whether it was possible that the French Mastiff was taken on board ships to South Africa? If so, we could say that the black French Mastiff is probably an additional contributor to the Boerboel.

But, let us set aside this discussion of black or very dark coloured dogs being frequent in both Afrikaner and British communities, and let us go straight back to 1983 and the establishment of a breed that clearly excluded the colour black.

Some of the most famous original black dogs of today have a history that goes back to the Helibron district and a famous breeder who lived there, who was a major exporter of the Boerboel breed across the world and one of the first prominent breeders of black Boerboels within the breed community. It is rightfully argued that because the black Boerboel was not part of the original breed standard decided the day in 1983 when the SABT was established, the black Boerboel no longer has any claim to be an original Boerboel. The black Boerboel was rejected due to the possibility it would be bred to the Rottweiler.

A typical example of the old-style Black Boerboel 2006

Although I have a duty to remain impartial to these debates (which seem to have destroyed many people along the way), it does seem rather odd that the piebald Boerboel which was clearly bred by numerous breeders at the time of the establishment of SABT was eventually accepted in to the current breed standard while the black Boerboel was not. Another quite strong and valid article was published online on various social media platforms some time back when the issue of the black Boerboel was under question. ('The Dark Side of the Moon' *Tuebor Boerboels*, online at https://www.tueborboerboels.com/en/boerboel/bbb/. Accessed 29 July 2018.) The article was written by a scholarly and knowledgeable woman by the name of Alla Fridman, currently residing in Russia and with whom I had the pleasure of meeting over 10 years ago. Her views on the creation of the black Boerboel might have merit and I have no reason to doubt her sincerity on this subject. When it comes to the question of the black Boerboel we need to look beyond the standard that was approved in 1983. Black dogs existed within the Afrikaner farming and the hunters' communities alike. We know that the frontier dog presented with black colouring as well as many others, so if the frontier dog is the foundation of the modern-day Boerboel, as I argue, then it must be admitted that black Boerboels did and still do exist, whether or not they are part of the standard today.

The Muller Brothers and their alchemy

The author with Bokkie Muller

During my recent trip to South Africa in August 2017 I was fortunate enough to arrange a meeting with the Muller Brothers whose name has become a prefix to some of the foundation stock of black Boerboels today. Some of the foundation stock of the black Boerboels of today were founded on the Muller Kennel name. It is important to point out that there is an alternative story that contradicts the theory that black dogs originated from Bokkie Muller and this story has only recently changed rhetoric and states that the Muller Kennel prefix was named after Jan Muller the former judge of the HBSA. I have my own theories; you the reader can form your own opinions.

Bokkie and Fritz Muller were brothers born and raised in the Free State. Sadly, Fritz died some time ago. I had met with Bokkie, an avid hunter and for me one of the few authentic and sincere dog men left in South Africa today. Today, almost 50 years after the demise of the illustrious frontier dog, I was able to witness first-hand the ability of an 80-year-old man doing alchemy with his dogs that reflected functional ability over standard. Observing Bokkie with his dogs was like, I imagined, stepping back in time to the days when both hunters and Boer trekkers alike trained the dogs for farm work. It seemed to me that genetics is like a river of coded history travelling through time, manifest visually in the body and made evident by the soul.

Bokkie discussed the black dog and its use. He mentioned a black Great Dane and Boerboel cross being used by the then Kremetat Boerboel Kennels of the Limpopo Province. He discussed the purchase of numerous puppies of this sort, such as the red puppies from these litters that were purchased by Deer De Plessis in the early 1990s. Bokkie told me he knew that the original Boerboels in the Free State were a white and brown colour which corresponds to what I have established so far in this book. He gave a description of the Boerboel as being an average of 70 cm tall with narrow chests, the heads smaller and the beaks (as he put it) were longer but still quite broad. He said the black Boerboel puppies he had were all much smaller in size to the red siblings of the same litters. But the most significant piece of information he supplied was that they could all run.

So, how did the formation of the black Muller dogs start? Well, according to Bokkie, it started with a black Pitbull Terrier his son had brought and kept at Bokkie's house. The dog was mated to his brown Boerboel female and the pups were given to neighbours and some sold.

A direct breeding dog from Bokkie Muller's farm and placed with a neighbour – Source Author

A more vivid picture of this dog's colour Source Author

One of the sold pups was taken by a man named Stephan Vassels from the Clocolan area and then sold to Adam Vessels from the Vesselbron district over 150 km away. Now comes the most significant part of this tale, Vessels sold the dog to the prominent breeder in the Helibron district who took a trip back to Bokkie Muller to enquire if there were any more of these dogs available and upon arriving had informed him that they needed to be larger, with bigger bone. Bokkie Muller denies that he had any direct dealing with the breeder from the Helibron district and stated quite categorically that to this day he is completely unaware of how and why Adam Vessels, an avid Boerwindhonde breeder, had decided to purchase and sell the dog to a prominent Boerboel breeder. But I shall leave you the reader with the final words of a genuine true dog man and a man whom for me simply cared very little about either the people or politics of this breed: 'The Boerboel I see today is not the Boerboel I used and worked.'

Below is a recent photograph of a phenomenal working-type Boerboel. Pictured in 2018, this dog displayed an immense surge of prey drive. The river of DNA always reminds us of our past: the resemblance of this dog to the Pit Bull Terrier of Bokkie Muller's foundation dogs is certainly striking (after all, we are the living history of our ancestors).

Source Magdalena Czechowska

The piebald Boerboel

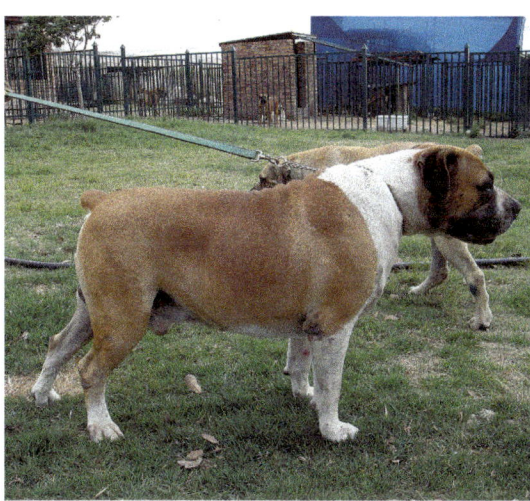

Source Stoffel Bloom *Source Author*

A piebald coat is one of white irregular shapes on a brown (tan, red), fawn or brindle dog. According to the SABBS breed standard, a piebald Boerboel is a brown (tan, red), fawn or brindle dog with a white blaze, which is a white chest that can extend to a white collar and white feet and legs.

Like black, piebald is another coat colour that has presented in dogs on South African soil since time immemorial. The piebald Boerboel probably arises from old hunting types having been bred with the wheaten Boerboel. The Rhodesian Ridgeback historians and E. R. Shelley document the huge numbers of hunting dogs, Pointers and curs brought to South Africa, initially by American hunters, which laid the foundations for the development of frontier dogs. Later, the short-haired St Bernard was introduced to the frontier dogs and in the mid-1980s influenced the modern phenomenon we know as the Boerboel.

The piebald Boerboel was a favoured type of the breed in certain sections of the Boer community, particularly in the cold mountainous climates of the Kestell and the Harrismith districts. There, these dogs were prolific where they served as both a hunting and flock guardian type dog. Initially, the piebald Boerboel was dismissed in the breed standard owing to the opinion of Johan Du Preez, one of the founding members of SABT, who said at the meeting that he had grown up with piebald dogs and was bored to have them in the new official Boerboel breed standard. In this way the piebald suffered a similar fate as the black Boerboel. However, a great many 19 years later in early 2002 this colour became part of the accepted standard by the founding breed registry, much to the benefit of the Boerboel community. My historical source in South Africa stated that the decision to not include the piebald coat colour was based purely on the personal preference of one of the founder members of the Boerboel association who had been raised with piebald Boerboels and wanted a new outlook for the breed. Whether this decision was the right choice is not the question, but the fact that the piebald was recognised at that time as being a Boerboel is the point to be considered. An influential member of the board of the then HBSA commented that in the Northern Transvaal and eastern free states there existed some significant piebald dogs that had the appearance of a smooth-haired St Bernard with docked tails. He further writes that the head resembled that of a St Bernard, which explains the success of piebald Boerboels as flock guardians. The current recognition of the piebald coat colour is in contrast to the views of a notable member of the HBSA who stated that the piebald Boerboels of old were predominantly white.

Dr P. Les Milstein a then board member of the HBSA was quoted in an article he had published on behalf of the HBSA:

> 'The fuss over the Boerboel is boring, exaggerated and involves hidden agendas. From the early days of formal Boerboel breeding, two unusual Boerboel populations were known, and are still largely present. One local concentration is in the eastern Free State and another in the north-western Traansvaal. In both cases the colouration was unbelievably constant. White with large plain orange blotches, and the white skin was almost without exception pigmented. In fact they looked exactly like smooth coated St Bernards with docked tails. They also possessed excellent temperaments and fine heads like St Bernards. No selection against this characteristic pattern and colouration apparently took place here by these like-minded dog owners, and these large pied dogs were considered to be the norm locally. Luckily we have a few breeders with foresight that have saved the piebald colour from vanishing from the plains and mountains of South Africa' (Historical Boerboel Association Newsletter 2001).

At this point we have to consider that the pied coat had been the norm prior to the formation of SABT and form and function was the number one prerequisite for keeping dogs in those days. Interestingly, it has been noted that the short haired St Bernard played a substantial role in the exaggeration of bone density, height, and loose excessive skin developed in the English Mastiff and other Mastiff breeds. In *The History of the Mastiff* (2006 [1886]), M. B. Wynn discusses descriptions in the literature: 'I have seen several specimens of this alpine breed, their size equal to that of a Mastiff, the muzzle deep and ears pendulous'. He says that between 1800 and 1850 thoroughly typical specimens of the Mastiff were repeatedly brought from the monastery of St Bernard and the Alps:

Old Short-Haired St Bernards – Source Joseph Vuyet

> Our English Mastiff has been more or less alloyed with the blood of these two varieties, producing greater size, coarser and more porous bone, accompanied with often inferior loins and general muscular development (Wynn 2006 [1886]).

In fact, a large majority of Mastiff writers from the 1800s onward wrote of the detrimental influence that the cross-breeding of alpine dogs with the Mastiffs of that period had on the original Mastiff types.

Enough of SABT and its meetings for now. Let us move onto the popular topic of cross-breeding. This topic is referred to in nearly every book and website about Boerboels and the general consensus goes somewhat like this – much harm was done to the Boerboel during the years of depression when agricultural exports lost value and large numbers of Afrikaner farmers migrated to urban centres to work in factories, leaving behind their dogs which were cross-bred by farm workers with their own dogs. This being but a rumour, it is of paramount importance for us to decipher exactly which dogs were cross-bred with the Boerboel and when.

So here it goes, the following list specifies the dogs I believe were cross-bred with the Boerboel, perhaps not before but certainly after the formation of SABT and I propose that the cross-breeding was carried out by senior members of SABT to enhance their dogs' aesthetic values. The short-haired St Bernard was used to enhance the Boerboel's size, bone density and hardiness, to cope with the terrain in mountainous regions. The other dogs include: the Boxer, Pitbull Terrier, Pyrenees Mountain dog, Bloodhound, Great Dane, and the Bull Terrier. This list will be of no surprise to the Boerboel men of old. Indeed, I imagine a few of those men number among the guilty who created this mongrel phenomenon; that is, if we ever considered the Boerboel to be a pure breed in the first place.

Some of my knowledge about the dogs used in breeding programmes of that time in the mid-1980s (and which continues to the present day) comes from my observations of the people I met and interviewed, but a lot of what I have learned about the practices of Boerboel crossbreeding comes from people telling me about the dogs of other breeders. Of course, this could be construed to mean that the people I interviewed were trying to sabotage the good work of other prominent breeders, so I decided to check for myself. I inspected photographs of the old Boerboels belonging to those breeders accused of bad practices. And there was a significant resemblance between the old Boerboels and the dogs mentioned. Upon considering the photographic evidence, I came to the conclusion that certain lines of Boerboel will carry particular characteristics of the breeds mentioned above, in their physical attributes and, more importantly, their mental attributes. I was not alone in thinking this. One of the good people I had the pleasure of meeting in South Africa said to me, 'Vijai, if this Boerboel looks like this dog, that's because it probably is this dog somewhere along the line'. This was aptly put! I will return to this matter in Chapter 9, 'Fact or Fiction'.

The Boerboel rewritten: A hypothesis from a non-Afrikaner

Old Deerhounds taken in large numbers, a vital contributor to the hardy frontier stock

Old English Mastiff
Source Hutchinson's Dog Encyclopedia Vols 1-3

Champion Farcroft
Bullmastiff Stock

The Archetypal Hinks Bull Terrier
Source Wikipedia

THE ESTABLISHMENT OF THE BOERBOEL

Old Longer Legged Bulldog Type
Source Hutchinson's Dog Encyclopedia Vols 1-3

Old Short-Haired St Bernard
Source Hutchinson's Dog Encyclopedia Vols 1-3

In truth, the Boerboel is a hard-as-nails farm dog, a large broad-skulled hound that has its origins in the various types brought to the region by Dutch, German, French and British settlers and Portuguese colonists. It was *the* frontier dog – the definitive Boerboel, which we hear so much of in the romantic rhetoric used to market the dog to international consumers. (It is my own opinion that the Boerboel has a greater Bulldog and Mastiff influence than its cousin the Ridgeback, which, as we know, had a clear and stringent breed standard applied from a much earlier date.) During the latter part of the nineteenth century this veritable frontier dog was influenced by geographical conditions as well as its use in Boer trekker work, as it was defined by each clan. The Boerboel was a mixture of various breeds, the old type varieties of the smooth/wire-haired Deerhounds and Wolfhounds, long-legged Bulldog, Old English Mastiff, Bullmastiff and short-haired St Bernard, the latter particularly within (but not exclusive to) the more mountainous regions of South Africa, and most significantly of all, the indigenous Africanis dogs, which formed the most substantial contribution.

Today, many dog historians would attribute this mix to the frontier dog. The frontier dog was most certainly the Boerboel we refer to today, but the frontier phenotype could only be attributed to a dog hardy enough to run, to dispel immense body heat rapidly, have the right length of muzzle and a bone density durable enough to incur prolonged shock absorption. Today the Boerboel has improved rapidly in terms of one phenotype, but to what expense?

A more modern example
Source Author

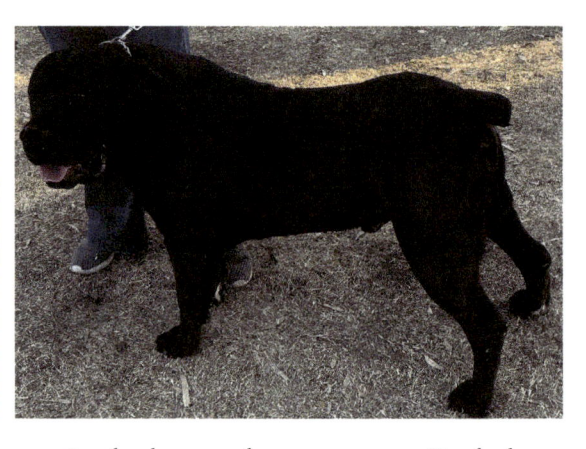

Another heavy modern consumer type Boerboel.
Source Author

Is the Boerboel you see today the same Boerboel that the literature of the early scholars refers to? Are the Boerboels we see today the same as those that survived on the farms and across the Great Treks? You have inspected photographic evidence and read the writings of eminent travellers. You have gained an insight into the different theories of many a renowned Boerboel specialist. You have been subjected to boring (at times, painfully so) issues that are not directly linked to the Boerboel, and a considerable number of you will have questioned the relevance of such material. The works discussed above, written by European travellers, British hunters and missionaries of the day have tremendously helped us to reach a substantial conclusion on the history of the Boerboel.

Foundation dogs

Here I list those dogs, along with their kennel names, that I believe formed the initial foundation dogs of the Boerboel. Please bear in mind there might be spelling errors. The names of owners are correct to the best of my knowledge at the time of writing. Some dogs that appear here will be claimed as having belonged to a number of individuals rather than one alone, and most dogs probably did. My inadequacies in finding out the exact location of particular owners must be attributed to a lack of formal records. To assist in creating an accurate record, I warmly welcome my readers to help fill in the blanks or correct any errors.

DOG'S NAME	BREEDER'S NAME	DISTRICT
Amsa Pote	Mrs A. M. Botha	Eastern Transvaal
Bobbas Bella	Francoisse Du Plessis	Northern Transvaal
Bosveld Prins & Tessa	Bert Grabbe	Northern Transvaal
Bothma Les	Mrs Rina Bothma	Standerton
Craddock Moaner	Jan Bouwer	Bedford
Christina Lena	Steyn Opperman	Lesotho
Dendon Jasper	Mrs Botha	Central Transvaal
De Beer Nikitha	Chris De Beer	Pretoria
Die Minste Ounooi	Wf Uys	Rensburg
Donkerhoek Kalpoot & Donkerhoek Waakssam	Gert Leibenberg	Northern Natal
Dopper Oubass	Rev J. C. Buys Parys	Driefontein
Dogs Unknown		
Elandskloof Boerboels	Sakkie Vorster	Middleburg
Freidenheim Erica, Freidenheim Leeuw, Freidenheim Mosadi, Freidenheim Duiwel	Johan Du Preez	Senekal
Geelbos Bless	Nick Van Der Linde	Standerton
Gretchen	Magriet Greyling	Carolina
Hofni Ounooi	De La Rey Schoeman	Utrecht
Jan Su Sansa	Jan & Susan Bouwer	Bedford
Jan Su Dante Donderbos	Lucas Van De Merwe	Kroonstadt
Jaarsveld Vanger	D. J. Van Jaarsveld	Unknown
Lady Ficksburg	Steyn Opperman	Lesotho
Lategan Ranger	Louis Stemmet	Lesotho

DOG'S NAME	BREEDER'S NAME	DISTRICT
Ounooi & Spike		
Leonard Oubass	Leon Riekert	Pretoria
Lourina Stud	Andreas & Lourina Louw	Northern Traansvaal
Mervander Sweepslag	Jan Ellis	Pretoria
Mizpah Plestiek **Mizpah Flenters**	Lucas Van De Merwe Kobus Rust	Kroonstadt
Moormoel Boerboels	The Nel Family	Ficksburg
Oppibult Tolla	Lucas Van De Merwe	Kroonstadt
Paarl Vallei Boerboels	Dr Andre Du Toit	Paarl
Pienaar Haagar	Marianne Chamberlain?	
Ravata Baby	Babs Bosman	Douglas
Rhabe Tia Tia	Unknown	Standerton
Remille Meerai		
Rustverwacht Koera	Johan De Jager	Utrecht
Slamat Bella	Walter Hodder	Kroonstadt
Smit Tessa	Piet Smit	Jacobsdaal
Venterspaad Boerboels	Mrs Owen Read	Warden
Waterval Boelie	Ella Louw	Volksrust
Wakkasam Klaryn	Schalk Louwrens	Eastern Traansvaal
Ysterberg	Bella Klaas Van Waveren	Pietsburg

On the following page is a small sample of photos of the Boerboels of yesteryear. Some of these dogs were the foundation dogs that bore the predominant influence on the Boerboel of today. I will conclude in the final chapter (Chapter 9, 'Fact or Fiction') whether this was a positive influence or detrimental to the progress of this breed.

THE ESTABLISHMENT OF THE BOERBOEL

Amsa Xena

Bankfontein Maybe

Cormabuks

Donkerhook Kalpoot

Dopper Oubass
Source Rev Buys

Dopper Dominique
Source Marietha Pietriese

Jan Su Dantie Donderbos

Dopper Hitler

Mervander_sweepslag

Ysterberggogga

Cabaret Kelin Buks

Roenardmartiens

Conclusion

I shall now sum up this definitive Boerboel history. When you consider the migration pattern of the dog's ancestor in Tibet, the Mastiff, which was taken to the lower plains where a short-haired Mastiff was developed, and later entered Europe, the event of the Boerboel's ancestors entering South Africa centuries later can only be attributed to the immigration of European travellers. We have also studied the Indian dog, and the varying hypotheses for its migration to Africa via Ethiopia, however, I have not found an account of this that was made after the 1500s and therefore, we can only assume that either the ethnographical or geographical influences did not favour this type of dog, and its subsequent use became determined by the laws of natural selection, which in turn disproves this romantic concept. It is on this basis we can clarify that the Indian dog or dog of the Cynonomes had no relevance to the Boerboel you know today, and probably no relevance to the African dogs of South Africa.

Neither has the Bullenbijter any great predominance in terms of influencing the genetic make-up of the Boerboel. The diaries of the Dutch travellers, which are scant, contain no reference to Bullenbijters, and furthermore, the probability of this breed being the dog of choice for farmers and trekkers is remote.

The long-legged Bulldog, the lightly built Mastiffs, the Staghounds, Deerhounds and hunting-type dogs were the breeds which contributed to the real Boerboel – that is to say, the frontier dog/Boerhonde. The voortekkers' historical oral tradition has passed down many tales of these wonderful dogs over the generations. They certainly were a major, significant genetic component that went on to influence the majority of Vuilbaards and Steekbards for trekkers and farmers, which ultimately created what we know as the frontier dog.

Although the Bullmastiff has some influence over the Boerboel, which we know from material presented in earlier chapters and from articles which refer to Bullmastiff crosses, that there is a considerable difference between the phenotype of the Bullmastiff described in historical articles and the Bullmastiff of today. There is no real evidence available (or no individual has come forward to present such) to support this theory from 1940 till present. Since there is no evidence to prove otherwise, it is safe to assume that, unlike the Bullmastiff, no Boerboel entered a direct breeding programme at Adamant Kennels (owned by the De Beers Mining Company) and I have still not found any evidence to support the various theories that claim Ch Springwell Major was used for the breeding of Boerboels (see Chapter 2).

Other influences – mostly undesirable, in my opinion – that have shaped the Boerboel over time can be found in the human world. After the introduction of mechanical farm machinery, the function of being a working dog was stripped from the psyche of the Boerboel. Mass urbanisation has also affected the breed consequent to increasing numbers of the urban population choosing to keep a Boerboel in their city residences. Another regrettable influence on the breed has been the super kennels that produce hundreds of puppies a year, which alas, I believe, have created a new genotype.

In essence, Johan Du Preez was correct to say that 'the Boerboel was a dog of no definitive phenotype' (Du Preez). This dog was bred by farmers from various districts to meet their own requirements; the individual preferences a farmer or group of trekkers particularly liked would have influenced the looks of these dogs. The work required of these dogs also would have created a distinct phenotype, and therefore, while many farmers utilised their dogs for a particular job, some would have utilised them for other tasks, thus creating a separate phenotype.

It is most certainly prudent to point out the very detailed breeding records of Klaus Van Waveren of the famous Ysterberg kennels, whose detailed notes have long been a mystery, with the most deepest gratitude I have been supplied with these for the printing of my works, and as you can see Bull Terrier and various other breeds have been included going back to the 1950s, a massive recognition must be given to Stoffel Bloom whom has inherited his uncle's legacy and is currently breeding under the name Mouzer Mastiff, if Stoffel can find the way to introduce fresh blood into this breed from pherhaps more dominant Bull breeds then it can only enhance the gene pool of this breed.

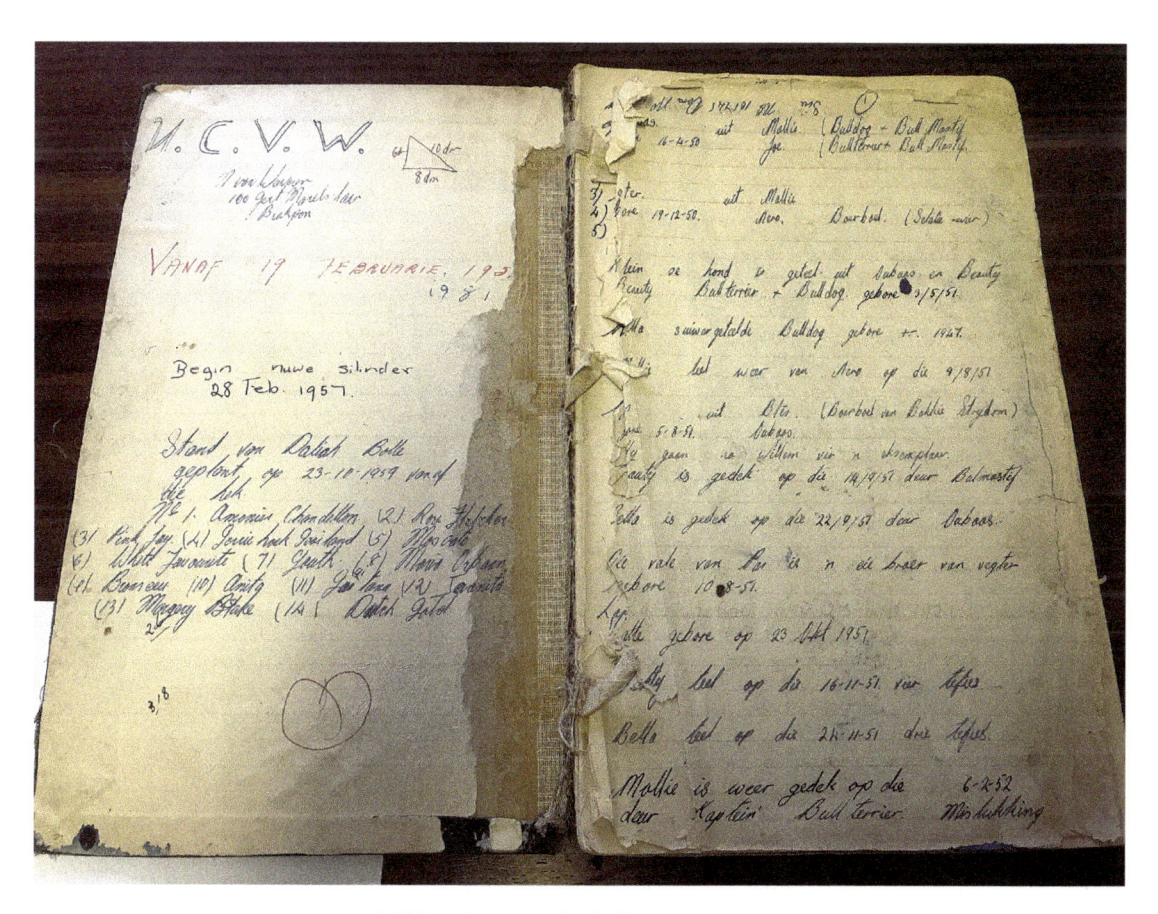

Old breeding records of Klaus Van Waveren
Source Stoffle Bloom

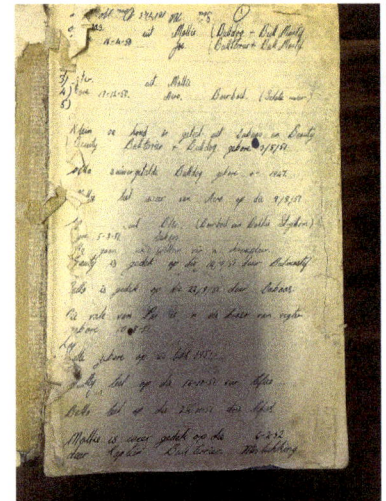

Source Stoffle Bloom 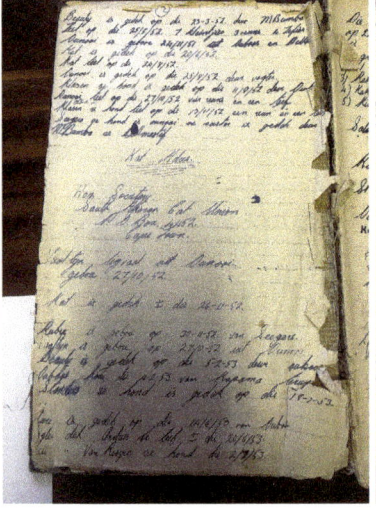   *Source Stoffle Bloom* 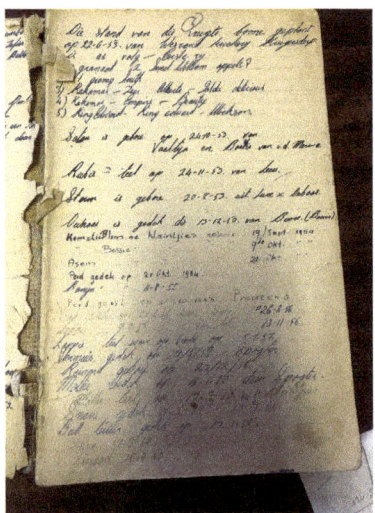   *Source Stoffle Bloom*

And finally, the African dogs provided the most significant chromosome – they were the real mechanism that created the Boerboel. It is important to remember that without the inclusion of African dogs there would be no Boerboel today. The unique African dog's gene, selfish in its willingness to fight and adapt, was without doubt the most crucial and significant addition to the Boerboel.

The various hypotheses of the history of the Boerboel have been passed from one individual to the next over the course of several decades and have suffered from exaggeration. I have tried to disentangle fact from fiction. Conducting my research has not been easy. I have sifted through the evidence and anecdotes, and weighed them against my own opinion, informed by a lifetime's work with Boerboels and the Boerboel breeder community, to arrive at the conclusions I present in this book.

We have reached the end of a long history which has spanned many centuries. Now we move on to a new Chapter, one which will emphasise the cultural and religious significance of the Boerboel's identity, which has predetermined its evolutionary course and its achieving international status. But more, it is related to the dismantling of the apartheid system and free world trade. All such influences have compelling, powerful yet subtle consequences for the future of this breed. I would like to now introduce you the reader to the importance of the female, a subject that has created a new movement, but it is the transition from old thoughts to new and the historical conflict of religious faith versus economical progression that will fundamentally redress the common and sometimes perverse ignorance of our own species.

Chapter 5
The Importance of the Female

I had never thought when documenting my research that I would need to write this Chapter. Like many of you, I am sure, I took for granted the basic values and morals I grew up with; that is, until I came across an alarming and destructive cultural practice. I am concerned that the material in this Chapter might be offensive to women. Please know that this is not my intention. On the contrary, my aim is to expose exploitative treatment of the female dog and to protect its interest, for it impacts significantly on the future type that the Boerboel will evolve into.

This Chapter looks at the importance of a healthy and happy female dog – especially for breeding purposes. We will look at how historic Dutch Calvinist attitudes have influenced contemporary welfare and selection practices in breeding the Boerboel. By the end of this Chapter, it is hoped that you will understand why the worst of these practices has catastrophically degenerated the female sex of the breed to a deleterious level of submissiveness and neoteny (that is to say the retention of juvenile characteristics into adulthood). Such poor treatment of the female dog reflects the ignorance of its breeders and is rooted in an archaic misogyny that has pervaded human society since time immemorial.

No doubt, many of you will be wondering why I would write about a subject most people would agree is beyond question. Why on earth would anyone in their right mind want to question the validity of the female? This is not a study on the sum total of differences between the male and female sexes, but an account that deals with the insignificance of those differences in respect of choosing the most desirable and stable female for artificial selection purposes.

In the earlier days of breeding Boerboels, a lack of knowledge about the female led to certain practices becoming established. These practices set a precedent in the breeding community that has been damaging to the Boerboel. The principal problem is the prevailing attitude that gives disproportionate importance to the role of the stud male. I cannot understand this philosophy and remain shocked at the results of its irresponsible methods. This Chapter will push out the boat in respect of biological science; this is in order to give you, the reader, strong, credible evidence for my point of view. I hope that by reading this Chapter, it might be at least possible to change the outlook of one if not a few breeders out there. Parallels to humans will be considered, as, of course, understanding one's self is far easier than understanding another species, but do not for once consider that the genetic differences between humans and our four-legged friends vary very much, as we shall demonstrate. I shall delve into the paradox of what I refer to as 'super kennel syndrome', and for this Chapter we shall only delve into it as much as is required to discuss the role of the female dog in breeding practices.

Most comments I had the displeasure of hearing were along the lines of:

> 'Well, she does not look much, but she will throw out good pups?'

> 'She is not the best, but I am using an exceptional male.'

'We always pick up a good male stud, as he will be the more dominant gene.'

'We don't temperament test our females because they are used for breeding.'

'We don't use our females for the protection work because they are not the same as the males.'

'The males tend to be much stronger and have more drive than the female dogs.'

These are only a few of the numerous ignorant and uneducated comments I have had the displeasure of being subjected to. I shall now attempt to dismiss such ludicrous and preposterous claims, and furthermore, explain to you why your mother was so much more important than your father.

My mummy gave me mitochondria

This section deals with the importance of mitochondrial DNA in terms of the title of this chapter.

The one unique ancestry all humans and almost all species have in common is our mitochondrial DNA. These mitochondria are important in genetically inherited diseases, and mutations of mitochondria are also influential to this theory. This view runs contrary to the Mendelian theory, which assumes that 50/50 inheritance is contributed from each parent. However, it is clear from scientific studies that mitochondrial inheritance comes solely from the mother.

Before my life began, 'I' was nothing more than an unfertilised egg; at this stage my father had already been programmed by 'nature' to inseminate my mother. Let us assume this programming was nothing more than a biological impulse built into his genetic fabric: the need to replicate one's genes.

I received 50 per cent of my genetic mapping from him and 50 per cent from my mother. This would make them equal contributors to my new cell or my zygote. This is where Mother Nature steps in to determine her selfish rights and assert her dominance. She has given me something far more sacred than inherited genes – the matter derived from her egg's mitochondrial DNA. Since paternal mitochondria is now known to be destroyed by the egg cell after the event of fertilisation, we know that mitochondrial DNA is passed down the generations exclusively by the female. This means I carry my maternal grandmother's mitochondrial DNA. Interestingly, the Jewish faith is and always has been matrilineal, so that Jewish descent is traced through the mother, who passes on her Jewish identity to her child. I do not know if Judaism had access to knowledge of molecular biology in the creation of its faith, however, I do know that the mitochondria determine our family trees and origins. The controversial African Eve is another compelling phenomenon in our growing knowledge of our lineage as traced through the female.

At this stage in my embryological development I have inherited my family tree programme and my father and mother's programmes, so I start to divide and my cells start to rapidly multiply. The next significant phase of development is gastrulation. This stage of development is when the germ layers and the embryo form a cup shape. There is much contortion of cells in sheet-like form. The cells have quadrupled and multiplied by thousands and millions and the embryonic stage is now in development. My DNA is encoding my amino acids which in turn are forming my proteins, or tiny building blocks, that will constitute a predominant amount of my body. During the 4th to 5th week of pregnancy my brain is slowly starting to develop, and if the process has completed positively, we finally reach the finished product, which is me, or in the case of dogs, lots of little bundles of fur.

During the above process, for not one minute has it been an easy task for any part of the body involved. It is only for the sake of a straightforward narrative that this example far over-simplifies the intricate and detailed chemical reactions being produced within my mother's womb. We have not included a discussion of the various forms of protein or the specific details of this biological miracle, as to include this would necessitate a new and entirely separate book.

Each of my parents passed on their DNA to me in equal contributions and between what my mother and father gave me, my chromosomes begin to pair off. My phenotype will be determined according to which parent I have inherited the more dominant gene from. In my case, my mother's genes won and my chromosome replicated her gene for (short) height. Unfortunate as the case may be, the different reproductive process that produced my brother resulted in him benefitting from my father's chromosome for taller height, the result being that my brother was influenced by my father's phenotype, thus he is taller and better looking.

The really significant question is who won this battle of chromosomes? Which sex is the ultimate victor in this creation? In order to answer this question, I shall move onto another topic – the placenta. As you are well aware, the placenta was neither controlled nor contributed by my father.

My mother had direct influence on me when I was in her uterus. Fortunately for me, she was allowing a healthy inflow of oxygen, regulating her diet, refraining from harmful toxin intake and taking the right nutrients and supplements. My mother was safe and comfortable, happy and relaxed. I will not try and support my theories with the popular myth of maternal impression, which is clearly an outdated and controversial concept, and was a common belief even among the educated classes in the eighteenth century. But to briefly introduce you to this, it was a belief of certain members of medical institutions that considered emotional stimuli acting on a pregnant woman to bear physical repercussions on the unborn foetus. The famous elephant man John Merrick was believed to be a product of this phenomenon in as much as he claimed his mother had been frightened of an elephant during her pregnancy with him. Other extreme cases lead us to Mary Toft in 1762 who claimed to have given birth to a litter of rabbits due to her fondness for rabbit meat. In the world of animal husbandry, cow breeders would keep white female cows in stalls with black cows in the sincere belief that they would give birth to midnight-black cows. This primitive belief is evident in the Book of Genesis in the story of Jacob who quite alarmingly used it against his tricky father-in-law. The idea of maternal impression was a perfect template for eugenics. To give my conclusion more credibility I shall stick to mainstream and confirmed medical studies, although the ideas I will discuss do bear some similarity to the maternal impression hypothesis.

You have seen how well my mother was during her pregnancy, well, this allowed for her bloodstream to be consistent, there were no significant increases of hormonal activity that would have affected her bloodstream and thus affected the placenta which I was gaining my nutrients from. This in turn helped to form the brain I possess today. My neurological development was determined by my mother, my nervous system was determined by my mother, my risk of developing a whole multitude of disorders was determined, once again by my mother.

Mummy, me and the crack pipe

I suspect I have not yet convinced you, so I will elaborate along a different tack. In this scenario, my mother is a crack cocaine addict, her bouts without crack are supplemented by a large amount of cheap alcohol. My father is doing really well for a living, he is self-employed and is now an entrepreneur. Many people might refer to him as a pimp. They are dependent on each other for all the destructive negative reasons they got together, and me, well, I am still the unfortunate foetus.

So, my mother is taking the crack pipe and alcohol. Well, of course, you know what will happen now to the unborn foetus, but *how* it happens is the crucial question. It is all down to her placenta, for it is this that has determined my fate. The placenta receives oxygen, antibodies and hormones from my mother's blood, and passes out waste. It acts as a protective water bag which filters out certain substances that could harm myself, the foetus. Of course, the placenta will not allow for the mixing of both mine and my mother's blood types and they will remain completely separate for the duration of the gastrulation period. My mother's sudden fears and anxieties are felt deep within me as and when she is threatened with various forms of violence; her glucose levels start to rise as her muscles become pumped with blood, and her adrenaline levels rise as well. Abnormal levels of androgen (the main component of testosterone) are being produced. There are high levels of various hormones being secreted into my water bag and these are now beginning to create a chemical reaction. These chemicals are not being filtered out and are hindering my state of wellbeing. An activity known as metabolic activity is now affecting me as my mother's irresponsible actions start to manifest in my biology. I am not receiving the nutrients I require for healthy development and I now start to suffer biologically within my mother's womb.

My mother's pituitary gland together with her nuclei brain stem has directly and indirectly controlled my brain and nervous system development. Hormones, incoming sensory information, and cognitive processing performed by the brain determine the brain's state. Stimulus from any source can turn on various receptors in my mother's brain which in turn will directly affect my development.

Other factors are also playing a vital part at this stage within my brain's development. The sounds and noises of external factors together with my mother's sense of fear are influencing my development; I am now going through a subconscious change in personality. You can conclude, therefore, that the neuro-hormonal changes within my mother as a direct influence of her social stimuli and behaviour have led to severe consequences for me and contributed to both my poor physical and mental state.

So, what about dogs? Well, a dog, you might argue, does not smoke crack, and we are all aware that male dogs do not pimp out their bitches. But, they are subject to other factors which correspond to the human scenario outlined above. We shall now move on to the question of how nature has defined male and female.

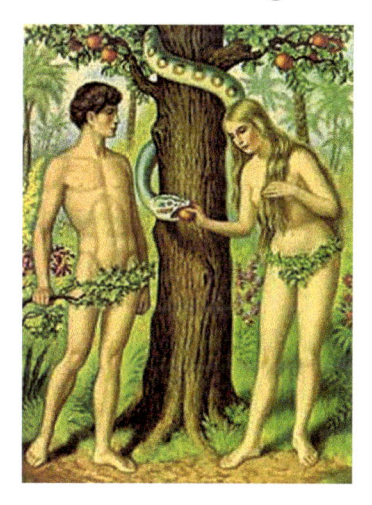

The World According to Adam

I sincerely promise you that this book is most certainly about dogs! However, in the introduction to this chapter I explained in order to fully comprehend what we are doing certain tangents will have to be covered, for this I ask you to bear with me.

It is the general consensus, at least in the biblical sense that the world started with Adam and Eve, but how many Adams and Eves is a question I most certainly do not have the answer to. Since men can have far more children than women, and can also reproduce longer in to their lives, I am going to suggest there were more Eves than Adams.

An interesting point to remember is the fact that women carry a double XX chromosome. This is evidence enough for me to conclude that nature prefers the female sex. My reasoning is that for nature to produce a male, the genes need to instruct a further chemical to be produced, that of androgen, which is more work for nature. This means that the female of the species would have been more dominant in numbers. We might ask ourselves why is it that through a period of thousands of years we lived in a society which privileged the male? Thankfully, at this point in human evolution, the ideal of a patriarchal society has lost favour. Society is changing as the status of the female begins to gain ground, at least in Western societies. It seems to be the case that humankind is slowly starting to evolve into a monogamous species, when we most certainly are not. This is a very important point and will be covered at the end of this chapter.

At the start of this chapter I informed you of some of the statements I heard made by various Boerboel men on the validity of breeding more feminine females and the debate of male versus female strength. I hope by the end of this Chapter you will understand the emphasis I am trying to put across.

Woman athletes are exceeding men in long distance endurance sports, they achieve an almost insignificant difference in running times and are even excelling men in certain other activities, for example, in swimming. Women are capable of appreciable improvements in muscle strength without displaying increases in muscle bulk at the early stages of weight training as a result of improved neuromuscular recruitment. Neuromuscular recruitment is the capacity to recruit motor units simultaneously and is created when the neuron receptors work in conjunction with muscle, thus creating what is referred to as muscle memory. With repetition this becomes a motor pattern and with consistency the muscle becomes conditioned and strong without excessive size development. In general, however, muscle strength is equivalent in both sexes when comparing the same cross-sectional area of muscle.

The effect of power and aerobic training results in physical adaptation whereby the differences between male and female trained athletes are far less than those between sedentary men and women. There are no studies to date that confirm that the menstrual period affects the performance of women in the pursuit of physical sports, so it is likely a myth (and one which is stubbornly resistant to scientific evidence). Further, there is absolutely no evidence to confirm a reduction in time laps in female athletes as a result of the menstruation cycle, and there has been no evidence of menstrual dysfunction caused by competing in sports, in particular at international competition levels.

Females can and do compete in full contact sports, this has, however, always been in controlled separate sex competitions. In the world of boxing, when sparring, female boxers have done favourably in having male sparring partners. There is a size difference between the sexes which is usually around 10 per cent to 20 per cent, with men being the larger of the species. This is the general pattern, but some women can be much taller than most men, they may be broader, more aggressive, and may be more readily conditioned to physical competitions, as we have mentioned above.

Racial stratification plays a role in how it provides different physical characteristics to different female populations depending on their geographical location (historically and in the present). It also plays a key role in defining body size, but does this mean that any one woman is any less a female than the other females, just because she is a different shape and size?

The Conclusion

As mentioned earlier in this Chapter, I have not written this thesis on the basis that the male and female of any species are the same. Although very different in biology, the male and female differ very little in terms of either performance or mental capacity. While I have discussed their differences, I have not tried to draw favouritism to my own sex. On the contrary, part of the beauty of all species is the biological differences of each sex; nonetheless it is critical to fully understand those differences and the degrees of difference, and here I shall try and convince you.

We have seen the scientific explanations of how genetic influences are passed down by the female, which receive my full and conclusive support. So, let us recapitulate. My mother was responsible for my development in her womb, and her neuro-hormonal activity had direct consequences for my wellbeing. The mitochondria I have inherited from her is also a key player in facilitating any known mitochondrial genetic mutation I might later develop or hopefully not develop. It is certain that my sister will carry any such mutation, and should this mutation not develop within her, then most probably she will be a recessive carrier, and her progeny will be as well. This single fact alone can vouch for the importance of the female. But, there are additional factors to add weight to my argument. We have discussed the physical differences of the male and the female of our species, or rather their lack of differences, but how does all this relate to the dog? And, more importantly, to my tale of the crack head mother?

The crack head mother scenario was partly used to grab your attention, so that you did not flick past that page. However, the real reason I included that illustration is for its parallel with a specific real scenario concerning the breeding of the female dog, where the dog is kept in a so-called 'super kennel'. My definition of a super kennel is that which houses more than 10 dogs.

A breeding female, born and raised in these super kennels, kept there over many generations of litter, is subject to spending the duration of her natural life housed within a kennel, mostly isolated from other dogs. Consequently, she becomes duller and duller, the neural networks inside her brain stop functioning properly and her body conforms to the small little kennel space she has been allocated. The body starts to change and adapt to the environment she is exposed to and the millions of genes in her DNA start to alter in order to accommodate this new environment and prolong their status in replicating and multiplying. This is not a change in the phenotypical sense but in the genotypical sense, however, like anything genotypical, the process is gradual and perhaps takes several generations before the ramifications become readily observable.

In this super kennel, the female is given no positive stimulus, and her whole survival mechanism is based on being fed by her kennel hand, with very little or no work to do in order to get her food. There is no alertness apparent, for the need to protect or have purpose has become non-existent. There are no dangers for this female in terms of competition or threat, no recourse to allow the natural fluctuation of hormonal fluids, a lack of opportunity to exercise her body and instincts. The breeder is the man or woman who will expose her to the numerous studs he or she has selected, and whom is directly responsible for her degeneration.

Their selection is based on nothing more than synthetic appraisal scores. It is quite possible, or even probable, that the super studs exposed to this poor unfortunate female are also victim of super kennel syndrome. It is quite evident that isolation for any species causes stress which, together with lack of social and mental stimulation, (consider again my hypothesis on the interlinked value of physical and mental stimulation) cause the neuro-hormonal changes of a female dog to become evident. Her diet and welfare conditions act indirectly upon her placenta to cause her great stress and anxiety. These influences create a new generation of genotypically modified puppies. Hyperactivity, nervousness and skittishness, as well as perversions against her own puppies are but a few of the isolated side effects. The parallel of this stressful situation is seen in the crack head mother story. The violent and confrontational events that took place within my mother the crack head draw similarities with the isolation, purposeless and emotionally deficient situation of the super kennel. Despite my desire to push this parallel I need to be quite clear that there is a huge difference between the dog and human on sociological grounds.

It is abundantly clear in today's world no decent human in their right mind would subject their unborn child to the stimulation of crack cocaine addiction, but it is important for me to explain that I chose an extreme example to help you understand the principle. Had my hypothetical crackhead mother not been carrying me but my sister, then the repercussions would have been even greater. Androgen secretion in a female foetus can cause a female to become overly aggressive and replicate a male. The oestrogen levels normally associated with calm and submissiveness are overtaken, and androgen secretion affects the neurological development of the female foetus, creating the above behavioural traits. Once neurological influences are determined in foetal development they cannot be undone at any stage during the adulthood of any species. This was shown clearly in multiple experiments and is now a widely accepted conclusion. You may now point out that the female Boerboel dog would have been exposed to violence and poisonous substances during the Great Trek, and would have certainly attracted the attention of various males and even other animals, perhaps which would have been hostile, or detrimental to the preservation of her genes. In fact, referring back to the history of the Boerboel in Chapter 2, we can safely assume that this was not so much probably as certainly the scenario.

Considering the evidence before me, that, due to both social and mental stimulation at the time of the Great Trek, and throughout the period thereafter up to the advent of farm machinery, female dogs were already evolved to cope with the stresses and dangers of the formidable African lands, their genes had developed successfully to counteract any sort of damaging influence. This successful evolution was partly due to the keeping of dogs in packs, a philosophy I greatly respect and propagate. In packs, the dogs were able to satisfy their need for interaction and continuously find both physical and mental stimulation. The dogs' desire for human interaction was less, as the dogs did not suffer confinement then, which they do today as pets in the home or in a kennel. The keeping of dogs in packs and exposing them to human social activity required a dog to observe and think, to solve problems, and did not produce hyperactive, exaggerated behaviours which are a result of mental and social neglect. The dogs of the past were not a financial commodity; they were raised in both human society and dog packs and were not confined to cages like battery chickens.

Let us agree that due to political, geographical and ethnographical influences the Boerboel had evolved sophisticated and effective neurotransmitters and healthy genes enabling it to cope with occasional stressful and life-threatening situations without its body needing to secrete abnormal levels of androgen and various other hormonal chemicals to protect it. Any unborn male and female foetuses would not have been subjected to abnormal hormonal influences.

So, we have to wonder why the female Boerboel today displays a typical and strange behaviour. I believe this is due to the effect of severe hormonal imbalances being produced within the female of the species. Is this a new phase in the development of this breed that has been caused by super kennel syndrome? Is it due to an inability of the genes to adapt rapidly to the varying possible hormonal reactions occurring during the gastrulation period? Consider the fact that oestrogen creates sensory perception and the ability to sense threat. Super kennel syndrome removes this. Occurring since the birth of the super kennel in the mid-1990s up to the present, I believe the ongoing isolation of the dog and the removal of its social stimuli have extinguished all possible threats and knocked out certain receptors in the brain that control oestrogen levels in the pregnant females.

In humans, women who have low oestrogen levels and high androgen levels may have congenital adrenal hyperplasia (CAH), a condition which affects 1 in every 100,000 people. Following recent research, if we are to assume that a mother's hormones affect her unborn foetus, it would be reasonable to suggest that women with CAH who are able to bear children might produce female children that have typically male attributes, because of the potential effects of high androgen levels on their foetus. Women with CAH have been shown to display the same behavioural patterns as healthy men, and to test this, studies were carried out on mice, which revealed a lack of maternal instinct displayed by the mice who were exposed to high levels of androgen. Conversely, other studies show the existence of a natural, protective mechanism in pregnant women (even those with CAH) which protects their foetus from overexposure to androgen during embryonic development (Lo, Schwitzgebel, Tyrrell et al 1999). Keeping abreast of this line of research should be one of the breeder's priorities. After all, to him or her breeding is a business and like all businesses, they need to be invested in. If you are breeding dogs for a living then this research is for you to carry out and take action on, not the prospective purchaser.

Now that we have considered the social stimuli ('My Mother the Crack Head'; the super kennel syndrome), let us look at the parallels between humans and dogs from the physical sense. For those of you out there who work dogs, you will probably be able to tell me that you have not seen such large differences of aptitude between your males and females from a physical standpoint, and for those who do agitation, decoy work and Schutzhund, I have been informed that in these areas the dog workers are unable to differentiate or discriminate the sexes based solely on the dogs' abilities. When I spoke to these people I asked if they knew of any of their females having problems in breeding, or perhaps abnormal maternal instinct? The questions were all returned back to me with a 'no problems' answer. My friend in South Africa who I mentioned in earlier chapters (the blunt, honest man), told me that the hardest-hitting Boerboel he had come across was a female of no more than 90 lb. This supports the theory that claims that the overall muscle strength of a male and female in a cross-section of the muscles is equal. Another fact to add to this discussion is the second hardest-hitting Boerboel in Russia was a female and managed to successfully knock out two ribs of her agitator, a remarkable feat indeed.

This female shows her strength and speed can out manouvere most 70 kg male boerboels with ease
Source Author

One of the fastest and hardest hitting females, old Avontuur lines in Russia 2008
Source Author

You may be wondering whether the female menstruation cycle is a hindrance to the dog's ability to function. Well, once again by considering the parallel with the human, and the fact that there is absolutely no scientific evidence to support this theory, we can safely obliterate this doubt. Some might say, 'But my female is used for breeding'. This is the attitude that the bulk of this Chapter has dealt with. In truth, if breeding healthy dogs is your priority then that is the most important reason to exercise the female dog. In pregnancy women can and do train regularly; if controlled to a safe level, fitness training does no harm to the foetus at any stage. Many of the world's top athletes have trained, and at times quite rigorously, during pregnancy. Furthermore, biological studies carried out in female athletes have all shown rapid recovery times for females, no adverse effects on training, and no ill effects on performance levels. So it is safe to say this is no less the case for a dog.

It is vital to include the fact that the oestrogen hormones of a female are what modulate her sensory perception. This facet of the female has been displayed time and time again, for example in female watchdogs, who are far superior in this work than the male of their species.

Perhaps you still need me to convince you, so I shall look for a new perspective on my point. As humans we have become smarter and taller, we have adapted to our ever-changing society. However, it is not strictly 'us' who have adapted, but our genes, for they have reacted to changing circumstances without us even being conscious of our body's genetic activity. You may be asking yourselves why our genes react and change. Well, they need to survive, and should it be shown that the indigenous Africans had developed long legs to run, or that the facial features of Caucasians developed due to the geographical influences, then such logic extends to female dog genes developing in ways that accommodate her environment. For example, the super kennel. The dog's bone structure will modify to accommodate the lack of space, sensory perception will also become modified, the lack of social stimuli will dampen the growth of dendrites (or nerve endings in the brain), this in turn once again modifies the brain and creates further genetic modification to be passed onto the offspring of that female for her progeny to survive. In fact, everything the healthy genes do will be done to survive.

You may believe that you have not bred any dogs that have visible genotypical differences, but you would be wrong. We must remember that this process is gradual. It is quite right to say that phenotype can be resolved quite rapidly, however, genotype change is a gradual evolutionary process.

So why do breeders have these preconceived ideas and where did they stem from? The various possible answers to that question would require another book to explore fully, and unfortunately, we cannot accommodate them here. However, to sum it up in as brief a context as I possibly can, they are ideas born of a sociological imprint, and are the very ideas we were brought up with, this belief is also the manufacture of female Boerboel breeders and is not a prejudice exclusive to men. Our beliefs and our religions, despite our education and broad mindedness, are inevitably the foundation of our identity, they are our safety blanket. When you try to remove this safety blanket, people tend to have all manner of reactions. Some people enter into a state of complete denial whereas others might display signs of aggression, at least in the verbal sense. But perhaps the real reason we have laid down our various sets of values and traditions, some would go so far as to say cultural theories, is that men are unable to produce the most powerful and meaningful reason for our very existence, that is to say creating life, so in its place men create values and traditions. Nature starts with women and ends with women. As far as science has informed us, there are three crucial senses in which it can be said that nature begins and ends with women: first, all embryos are female unless imprinted with male sex hormones; secondly, only women can give birth; and thirdly, given the current stage of technological development, if women did not exist there would be no means to reproduce humans.

I sincerely hope that at least one of you might be convinced to look in retrospect at the significance of the role you have played so far in the developing role of the female Boerboel, and that in time you will better understand the implications of your inability to safeguard the functional qualities of the breed. It is only by preserving and endorsing the importance of the female that I believe we shall see positive results in the future welfare of this dog.

I once asked a female breeder in South Africa, whose breeding programmes I had been closely following over a period of five years, how she had managed to obtain such consistent phenotype in her dogs. Her answer to me was that she will only ever select the right female. I am not aware to this day if she knew exactly how right she was.

THE WORKING BOERBOEL

THE IMPORTANCE OF THE FEMALE

Chapter 6
The Importance of Aggression

Source Author

Source Author

Source Author

Source James Brennan

When I first mentioned the title of this Chapter to the individuals who had displayed an interest in my writings, I was advised to avoid using the word aggression. They suggested different titles, like, 'The Boerboel (Guarding Abilities)' or even 'The Importance of Protection Work'. However, this Chapter concerns exactly what it refers to. I can imagine that you, the reader, might agree with the advice of my acquaintances, since the word aggression readily conjures up images of harm, violence and hate. But, there are other meanings and contexts for the word which are relevant to dog breeding and this Chapter will guide us through this contentious subject.

Although I acknowledge that harm, violence and hate are a by-product of what is perceived as aggressiveness, it must be emphasised they are in fact inhibited by the properly handled mechanics of aggression. It is of fundamental importance to stress that I have felt the need to educate a large proportion of individuals (the breeders I have met and the readers of this book) in the importance of aggression and this book is a dedication and tribute to the very meaning of aggression. You could even consider this Chapter a celebration of aggression, of my unequivocal support for aggression, of my wish to see the Boerboel being bred from pure unadulterated aggression. This is very much a subject I can relate to through my professional experience, and although at times this Chapter may be passionate, it is controlled, and written from an objective perspective. To illustrate my theories on aggression I shall draw parallels between different species of higher intelligence, including, most importantly, *Homo sapiens*. It is also in this particular Chapter where we shall elaborate further some of the different tangents you were thrown into in previous chapters.

The desecration of sophisticated ancient civilisations was the by-product of violence and not aggression. Murder, war and genocide are but a few examples of the result of our evolutionary process. We possess the most advanced intelligence of all species and yet some of our most destructive actions stem from that intelligence, especially our exceptional ability to gather and create knowledge. Perhaps you are wondering where I am going with this pessimistic approach to the human genome. Well, with all the knowledge and wisdom we as a species have accumulated through instinct and nurturing, trial and error, and curiosity, man has begun within the last 20 or more years to degenerate his very own best friend. It is unfortunate and dangerous to the welfare and future preservation of this breed, so unique in its development, that a number of ill-advised and misinformed individuals are the perpetrators of this venerable breed's decline.

The dog has helped and protected man, given him warmth on a cold night, alerted him of dangers ahead and protected his progeny. We will explore the less than generous gift that we have given to the dog, because we as a species have defined what we consider to be a correct temperament and we have imposed our inherited, human values on a species which is quite content to adapt, as regrettable as that may be.

Thus, I shall try and convince you of the errors of believing the absurd statements that I so often have come across when discussing the subject of biddability, created by ill-advised humans and which is in my opinion the evil of all evils in the dog world. I shall elaborate on the sometimes sanguinary reactions of dominant dogs kept in human confines, and the complex reasons for this quite understandable behaviour. More importantly we shall discuss the different drives of the dog, and why in particular my findings support the importance of aggression for a dog's constitution, particularly for the Boerboel.

I have discovered a great deal of conflict in the observations of numerous individuals who discuss their theories of the dog's drives, or what I shall refer to as the evolutionary stability programme, the mechanisms of which have evolved over many carefully programmed generations – and have been selected or deselected for by humans who breed this dog and are therefore highly artificial. I will show you that this artificial selection process in Boerboels displays today in such a manner that we could only conclude that the breeders' selection choices have been detrimental to our four-legged friends. The consumer market has opted for submissive, docile dogs. By breeding for this quality, breeding programmes have removed the dog's ability to think independently. The research I shall refer to has obviously been selected to support the ideas I believe in, but it can be countered by numerous experiments, so it will be important to discuss the different schools of thought on matters pertinent to the subject of aggression.

I can only hope to convince you, the reader, of my views on this subject so that you might concede the fact that the mechanism of aggression is of fundamental importance to the dog. I understand that not every point I make will be relevant to your particular end goals, however, it is my aim to furnish you with sound reasons and arguments supporting my view. If by reading this book many of you would-be purchasers looking for a pet are put off by the possibility of inherited aggression in the genome of the Boerboel, then I have succeeded in averting you from buying a dog best not suited to your causes. Similarly, for those who wish to pursue a solid, more consistent animal for the purpose of work, I wish to give you evidence for both sides of the debate on whether the Boerboel really is the working dog legend it is reputed to be.

For the interests of this Chapter I shall focus on the two most significant drives in a dog that I would personally look for and explain the logic behind these drives. We shall start with the prey drive followed by the defence drive. The latter for me is of greater significance of the two, as this is an inherited drive which tends to be more heightened in all Bull breeds and Mastiff type dogs, and at times can appear exaggerated.

The prey drive

Source Author

Probably the most fundamental drive seen in the dog, and inherited from ancestors through both evolutionary as well as man-made processes (animal husbandry), the prey drive belongs to a set of predatory behaviours which include eye, stalk, chase, bite, kill, dissect and eat, as noted by Raymond and Lorna Coppinger (Coppinger 2001). The very word 'prey' conjures up images of the ancestors of dogs stalking and pack driving towards an unsuspecting creature; we can all certainly imagine a hungry pack of wolves closing in on a young fawn.

This drive has undergone development across thousands of generations and is an important factor in the survival mechanism of the dog. Without this drive the pack would most certainly have died out, but as we have shown earlier, the gene is not programmed to die, indeed it is programmed to do everything within its power to survive. The fact that wolves hunt in packs is evidence enough that the genetic make-up of this species, like many other species has been selectively programmed, like a complex computer programme, to promote the sociological patterns of altruistic behaviour.

We shall discuss the matter of altruistic behaviour further on in this Chapter under the heading 'The Importance of Pack-Keeping', but for now we shall cover the more specific mechanism of the prey drive.

In order for any species to activate this drive it is imperative that it be triggered by some form of stimuli. The repercussions of this activation are dependent on the species concerned and more importantly the breed of dog concerned.

A working terrier will have an abundance of this drive and the results of this will leave a large majority of its prey lifeless. I have fond memories of learning this when, as young boys, me and my friends would spend our Sundays in a desolate run-down farm we called the 'Pig Alleys'. There we found under the garbage and debris a whole army of rats. This was my first exciting glimpse at watching the predatory motor patterns of the Jack Russell we had, he displayed the whole river of DNA that had been programmed over many generations; it played out like a carefully orchestrated symphony of eye, stalk, chase, shake, bite and kill. Border Collies will have this drive too, however, it will be inhibited by a mechanism that does not allow for the end result, i.e. the kill, dissect and eat patterns.

The Mallinois has this mechanism but has absolutely no inhibition to withhold its ultimate purpose, i.e. the bite and shake. Flock-guarding breeds have this drive, but it is extinguished during the critical stages of the puppyhood period. But what of the Mastiff, in particular the Boerboel?

Lurchers, Fox Terriers, sheep-herding dogs and Hounds all have an abundance of this drive, however, within each specific breed there will be a variation in the degree to which they demonstrate it. One can learn a lot about this by asking the committed German Shepherd and Mallinois men about the gradual split between working and non-working ethos in dog breeding and training practices.

The prey drive is fun, aggressive in a competitive way, one could call it the game. There is no malice about it. This drive is inherent in all living species, playing tennis, football and boxing are but a few examples of how the prey drive manifests itself in humans. Species of advanced intelligence, especially *Homo sapiens*, have gradually evolved over time to focus the prey drive onto any number of objects or rewards. Please do not for one minute assume that this drive which the human genome strives to replicate is in any way different to the drive of our four-legged friend. Both have a goal, a focus and an aim, and more importantly the most aggressive will succeed in obtaining that goal. The dog with the greatest degree of prey drive will under normal physiological conditions outrun or shake harder at the object of attention than its other counterparts. Perhaps you are wondering why? Aggression is the mechanism.

It is important to note that my interpretation of the word aggression as used to define the Chapter and in discussion of the prey drive should be used in the right context. Later we will discuss the word aggression in relation to the defence drive where the same meaning will apply but will be rationalised with a slightly different twist.

Aggression in prey mode is always non-hating, although the results will culminate in violence when the animal is set on obtaining food sources. Lions are happy to chase, kill, dissect and eat their food as much as any other successful predator. Observations of various species have shown their tails wagging in excitement and exhilaration at the thought of bagging the trophy. We will define aggression in this context as competitive aggression, and not aggressiveness (the act itself) as defined by other behavioural scientists. The reason being is that the act itself in modern human evolution is given very negative connotations. An aggressive act is considered anti-human, immoral and primitive and conflicts with that part of the human brain that is programmed to feel empathy. The experience of empathy is not exclusive to humans and is seen in most species with advanced intelligence. We know from the history of our ancestors that we have displayed the prey drive – that results in a violent act – and yet today we call violence by another word, namely, aggression. I am giving importance to the interpretations of words as in the twenty-first century they have been used to contort and play with human emotion. An interesting point to note is that experiments done with lab animals and dogs which have been socialised with other animals normally considered a source of food show the socialised dog to be able to discriminate between friend and prey.

This result shows what a masterpiece the prey drive is. The ability to bite, shake, kill and dissect a potential food source becomes extinguished by exposing dogs and other predators during their early stages of behavioural development to other animals. Flock herding (flock guardian dogs in particular), foxhounds and other hunting dogs are socialised and exhaustively introduced from an early age to the pastoral and domestic animals that they will protect, or encounter in the course of hunting other animals, before the onset of certain motor patterns, and during the phase that those motor patterns create a sense of novelty and play.

The prey drive is captured and developed through training with great frequency by working German Shepherd and Mallinois men the world over. In French Ring, KNPV (Royal Dutch Police Dog Sport), Mondioring, in nearly all the dog sports in fact, people will start to promote prey behaviours in puppies as soon as they acquire them. But when asked, a small minority of people will know neither the reason this behaviour has evolved and is still developing, nor the reason they themselves so militantly reinforce this behaviour. My own studies of the past litters I bred, as a hobby breeder, showed me the nature of prey behaviour in Boerboel puppies. Yes indeed, despite the indiscriminate breeding of the Boerboel they still have and do display this drive. Young cats do this too and will play by self-stimulation. After this evolutionary information becomes a blueprint for the adult cat, one day it surprises you by bringing into the house a mouse, proudly dangling from its mouth. So what exactly is this behaviour that these dogs are displaying, and why do they independently play to develop it? Why is it that my Mallinois friends and German Shepherd colleagues promote prey drive so thoroughly? Well, for training purposes we know it as the ball drive, which motivates dogs to work for reward and play, and assists in the transition of training for competitions, but for the young puppy it is most certainly an innate behaviour programmed through many natural and man-made circumstances to promote the hunting drive. The prey drive is innate behaviour that will favour its survival, its ability to eat and to survive. So why is the prey drive so critical for promotion? Well, if it is not reinforced in domestic dogs it will start to diminish. And this is certainly the case with the Boerboel. We have seen from our own experiences that within a litter of young Boerboel puppies this behaviour becomes quickly extinguished because the promotion of such has not been militantly reinforced. And in sport work and modern training, the prey drive has so much use that it is vulnerable to an abundance of possible manipulation. The prey drive is associated with play in young puppies and is the foundation for adult hunting skills.

Now this Chapter on the prey drive leads us to a fascinating discovery and one that sets out some significant points that we will return to in the concluding Chapter. Raymond and Lorna Coppinger have noted the predatory motor patterns of dogs. They make substantial reference to the flock guardian breeds in the weak display of predatory patterns. 'The very best livestock guarding dogs never develop any predatory patterns. The less than the best (which is practically all of them) display one or two predatory motor patterns (most likely chase and grab-bite, but very weakly' (Coppinger 2001, p. 116). I have no doubt that Raymond and Lorna Coppinger, after having dedicated many years of hard work to the study of guardian breed dogs, would feel disappointed by those people who market flock guardian breeds as suitable for security purposes, or indeed for anything other than working with sheep and livestock.

In this final note on the prey drive, it would be rude not to mention the works of Helmut Raiser in his book *Der Schutzhund* (1996) in which he states that the prey drive is part of a dog's food-gathering behaviour. In predatory animals that means the prey drive governs hunting and killing techniques, i.e. chasing, flushing, pouncing, biting and shaking to death and is exactly the point made by both Raymond and Lorna Coppinger. But there is a difference between the prey drive of the herding breeds and of the Boerboel as a result of differing prey-selection pressures. The Mallinois has been shaped over 40 generations during which time its excellent predatory behaviours of chase, shake and bite have been consistently, artificially (man-made) selected for. In comparison, Boerboels have been bred to retain docile, juvenile behaviours to satisfy the consumer demand for overly large cumbersome and docile dogs, and so the Boerboel experiences a very flat predatory pattern from puppyhood. From an international perspective, this difference bears huge consequences for service people who are to work with and assess working dogs.

The Belyaev experiment

Dmitry K Belyaev
Source Sputnik_alamy.

In 1959 in Novosibirsk at the Siberian branch of the USSR Academy of Sciences a ten-year experiment was created by the Russian geneticist Dmitry K. Belyaev. Under Belyaev's directorship, the Academy of Science, now the Russian Institute of Science, became the centre of basic and applied science and centre for modern molecular genetics (Wikipedia contributors, 'Dmitry Belyaev (zoologist)', *Wikipedia, The Free Encyclopedia*, 26 Jul. 2018. Web. 30 Jul. 2018).

The aim of the experiment was to establish if and if so, how, domestication affects the physical characteristics of an animal. Taking the wild fox as his subject for the experiment, Belyaev's studies looked at changing a single behavioural trait to see if it correspondingly altered any physical (i.e. morphological) ones. Belyaev selected the silver fox because it had never been domesticated and was closely related to the domestic dog, which would allow for comparisons.

Upon publication, Charles Darwin's *On the Origin of Species* (1859) was highly controversial and, like all great individuals who think out of the box, Darwin was lambasted by public opinion. Yet 160 years later his work is accepted as fact. He noted that 'Not a single domestic animal can be named which in some country has drooping ears' – a feature not found in any wild animal except the elephant. Belyaev was influenced by Darwin's ideas and believed that selecting tameness in the most biddable and submissive foxes would bring about corresponding physical changes.

Belyaev's theories were rewarded some forty years later when the results surprisingly showed piebald foxes; selecting for tameness and biddability had produced curled tails. The embryonic development changed and resulted in larger litters albeit very slightly so, the vocal calls changed to that of a dog's bark, and the skull sizes of the domestic foxes became smaller, particularly in the males. The words used in the thesis were 'feminised morphology'. In fact, some of the foxes bred in the late 1990s resembled modern Border Collies.

Particular emphasis has to be made as to the neurochemical transformation of Belyaev's domesticated foxes: there were huge changes to the serotonin levels of his tame foxes; the adrenal cortex responded less sharply compared to the wilder, less-tamed foxes; the serotonin levels, which are inversely proportionate to the level of aggressiveness, had significantly increased; and the length of muzzle became much shorter. Another important behavioural phenomenon which was associated with tameness was that the tamest foxes selected would cannibalise their pups, it is known in the ethology world as the destabilising factor.

Belyaev dedicated his life to the understanding of how genetics correlates with physiology and morphology, and the direct consequences they have which influence behaviour and tameness in domesticated animals. He died in 1985 and his work was diligently carried out with ever-reducing government funding by Lyudmila N. Trut.

The defence drive

Source Author

Source Dapo Ojaro Lagos

This word is exactly what it refers to, A defence of one's self. In the old days and even up to a few decades ago within many UK police forces a dog was selected by testing it on its ability to protect itself. Its ability to fight for survival. Today we approach the selection and testing process differently and survival is no longer used as the sole barometer of assessing a working dog. Whether I agree with this or not is not important for this discussion, but nonetheless one wonders if modern training methods have led to a decrease in the standard of grading and if we have become puppets to a politically left agenda? This agenda has pushed us towards becoming a society that does not recognise that we exist in correlation with other species of nature; instead, we have risen above nature like demigods, and have imposed our own thought processes and ideals upon dogs, which were designed to do work.

All animals have a defence drive, it comes from exactly the same place as fear, and from it come the fight or flight responses. There are of course theories that hold that the fight response is another drive – entirely distinct from the defence drive; other theories claim a pack drive exists. In fact, if we get stuck in the classroom of theories we would never get out in the field to practice at least one or two of these ideas, which would allow us to draw our own conclusions. So, for the sake of progression, and with the greatest respect to the theorists of pack, hunt, and fight drives, I will only discuss the two drives that all other drives stem from: the prey and defence drives.

In the literature on the defence drive we come across the word 'aggression' again and again where the general argument goes that the dog shows aggressive behaviour to extinguish the threat or concern at hand. Indeed, aggression, as discussed earlier in the section 'The Prey Drive', can be defined as the intention to neutralise the stimulus that is creating concern or fear, through the use of violence. Like hunting to catch prey, aggression is important – only the aggressive succeed, they possess greater motivation and desire, but most importantly and most significantly, greater hope that they will succeed. Aggression is not violence per se. The act of harming, damaging or disfiguring is violence, the desire to rip and tear flesh is violence, but that is a human interpretation, it is a human emotion projected on an animal, as in anthropomorphism. I am for the most part guilty in having on numerous occasions projected my emotions onto my dogs. There is no morality involved, as far as I am aware, in a dog's mental state. I am not sure there is any conclusive scientific study that reveals dogs have a conscience.

But let us discuss the word 'flight'. Well, flight is used in this Chapter in the sense following the description given by the late Walter Bradford Cannon, a Harvard student, who discovered the fight or flight concept and published it in his book *Bodily Changes in Pain, Hunger, Fear and Rage* (1929). He used the term to mean the physiological change in a given species forming part of an evolutionary protective process that can results in an increased blood flow, which either increases bowel inhibition or can cause relaxation, can create complete stillness, regulates the cortisol levels in the brain, increases the amount of adrenaline issued to the muscle tissue and leads to the ability to escape or fight. For the purpose of working dogs, we will conclude that the act of violence is exactly what we both desire and expect, nonetheless we can also accept that flight is also a perfectly acceptable defence behaviour as the ability of an animal to protect its DNA is the measure of success. But one thing we do know, dogs bred for and selected for tameness – as in Belayev's experiment on the fox – display a prolonged response. The fight or flight syndrome had already been carefully manipulated by artificial selection, so the response times in the tame foxes were far slower than in the wild foxes. When we consider the German Shepherd, which is closer to wildness than either the Bull or Mastiff breeds (in my opinion it is Darwin's perfect dog) and yet is loyal, devoted and far from behaving wildly, and understand how far off it is from modern non-working dog breeds, then how can we learn from it to help the cause of the Boerboel? How distant is the Boerboel from what nature had intended?

The defence drive will always work simultaneously with the prey drive, never are they mutually exclusive of each other. It is why doing protection training can be so rewarding, as we are able to manipulate both drives simultaneously, training the dog to switch its attitude from *prey* to *defence* to *prey* within a split second. Occurring so quickly, the transitions can be practically invisible to the naked eye yet the shift in attitude is so powerful a change for the dog.

The importance of pack-keeping

Modern-day pack keeping, a dying art of animal husbandry with one of the last left breeders of this principle Coomore Boerboels
Source James Brennan

Source James Brennan

The noted and renowned Klaus van Waveren, an old fashioned art of animal husbandry, when the Boerboel was bred for the real Boer.
Source Stoffel Bloom

One must never forget that the Boerboel breed was founded by pack dogs. The wide range of Southern Africa's dog breeds is built upon the social group of 'the pack'. From the hunting dogs to the dogs of the settlers, from the wild Africanis dogs to those that followed the caravans and trekkers throughout inhospitable lands, from the formation of a frontier dog (which should rightfully be considered as a legitimate entity) to the Boerboel, each type of dog owed its existence to the influence of natural selection occurring in the context of social grouping by pack.

Many years ago I saw the importance of pack-keeping in South Africa and although there is no doubt that pack-keeping has its fair share of dog vs dog attack, the reality is that careful and considerate keeping of the Boerboel in packs clearly regulates the hierarchy from the ultra-dominance dog to the least dominant, so that the pack develops a self-preserving harmony that most individuals find difficult to maintain with their dogs. The pack without doubt provides a fundamentally important measure of understanding the true nature of our dogs and the temperaments they possess; it is a very clear barometer useful for selective breeding based on the dynamics within the pack. One might ask why I do not differentiate the Boerboel from other breeds? First, this book is primarily about the Boerboel, and secondly, it sets out to determine whether the Boerboel has any proven merit as a working dog, hence the title *Working Boerboel: Fact or Fiction?* The German Shepherd community, the Mallinois community, the Presa Canario community and the American Bulldog community (to a small extent) all have a series of tests and evaluations to assess the working and historical attributes of their breeds. However, with great misfortune there is no such established evaluation of the Boerboel. The importance of pack-keeping and the destruction of super kennel syndrome (discussed in Chapter 5 'The Importance of the Female') have to be, in my opinion, implemented sooner rather than later, but regrettably, there is also the need to have transparent, honest and genuine breeders whom can be held accountable for their breedings, and to put in place policies that ensure the survival of the fittest, most self-assured, dominant Boerboel.

In *Man Meets Dog* (2002) Konrad Lorenz writes on the merits of observations he made in his own, dominant, dog:

> 'All the higher domesticated dogs, in which Jackal blood is predominant, remain all their lives as dependent on their masters as young wild dogs are on older animals of their own species: but this is not the only youthful characteristic which, in contrast to the wild dog, they retain all their lives: the shorthair, curly tail, and hanging ears of many breeds, above all the shortening of the muzzle and doming of the skull which we have already seen in the turf dog are points that characterise only the young animal on the wild form, but which continue at all ages in the domestic dog' (Lorenz 2002, p. 22).

One of the most innate displays of natural dominance I have ever seen, a South African import, and put dead by authorities for his dominant tendency, a huge waste of good breeding stock

Konrad Lorenz explains that juvenile features in an adult dog (what scientists refer to as neoteny) are seen in its degree of domestic biddability and can be either a merit or a defect. Neoteny can be a defect in a dog because the retention of juvenile behaviours into adulthood can be unhealthy if the degree of neoteny is great. It results in biddability, passiveness, docility and even unintelligent thinking. While a certain level of docility can be desirable in dogs intended to be house pets, too much docility is abnormal. In contrast, dogs lacking in neoteny are highly independent and self-confident, and consequently do not bring their master much pleasure; such dogs as they get older, Lorenz says, become increasingly dangerous as they think nothing of biting and shaking their owner as they would another dog. Lorenz then expands on this point by stating that although dominant and independent, a dog lacking neoteny does not lack loyalty to or friendliness for their master but remains on an almost equal footing in a mutual relationship dynamic. The importance of selection for dominance in a working Boerboel will be discussed further in the final Chapter.

Interestingly, not only was Konrad Lorenz an amazing ethologist and scientist, he was also an avid dog owner and spent many decades understanding the sanguinary behaviour of his four-legged friends whom he also classed as a higher-thinking species.

And finally, the penny drops. Thanks must be given to the ethologists for debunking the twenty-first century myth that aggression in domesticated dogs is undesirable. This myth created by a modern society has led to the projection of the human values of compassion, compliance and submissiveness onto animals – which is cruel. The same society that formulates conveniently safe niches for biddable humans to work till they get old, then retire and die, having never enjoyed the fruits of youth. You might be wondering why this Chapter has digressed from the discussion of the importance of pack-keeping. The reason I have chosen to include this point in a Chapter titled 'The Importance of Aggression' is that it brings home for me a vital fact about intraspecific aggression. Konrad Lorenz, Richard Dawkins and many modern behaviourists and ethologists in the twenty-first century have commented that the common patterns of violence and aggression in certain species are related to behaviours which are designed to limit and neutralise damage to oneself. In all species, including humans, the alpha males very rarely engage in actual direct combat (in the case of humans, one exception to the rule might be a staged sport match) since they are prevented from doing so by the genetics of self-preservation. Competition within a pack leads to hierarchy in domestic dogs, it allows for a window of opportunity to view the battle for food aggression and territorial aggression. It is absolutely vital to bring back the purpose of dominant dogs within the genome of the Boerboel breed, for we can safely say that dominance can manifest in the ability to take opportunity, to increase pleasant feelings, to rise the dog's rank within the pack. The sanguinary repercussions of this in the pet community can be displayed with acts of violence usually directed to inhibit or suppress those who might object to the source of its goal. The growing pet industry in combination with the decline of the working dog/service industry certainly points to a huge modern-day conflict for the role of the dominant dog in modern society. This will bring about a momentous disappearance of the innate aggression that is naturally inherent in dominance. It is quite possible that dominant behaviours are reinforced in the early stages of a dog's life, however, with truly ultra-dominant dogs this behaviour must always be considered as both acceptable and necessary. It is the responsibility of the working enthusiast to manage these dogs' motivation to enforce the dog's position through violence and aggressive means: this is both perfectly acceptable and necessary for the benefit of the breed.

In my years of training the Boerboel, nearly all problem dogs just so happened to be males reaching maturity around the 20-month mark, as the testosterone was starting to take effect. It is beyond doubt that nearly all the cases were not displays of true ultra-dominance, but were, for the most part, the fault of a learned behaviour somewhere in the chain of its nurturing process. But in a small number of cases (which I had first and direct contact with) I have seen Boerboels display ultra-dominance with the result being severe attacks on their pet owners and the dogs being euthanised forthwith. As Konrad Lorenz points out, truly independent dogs have the capacity to do this, the dog's ultimate desire is for its self-preservation by improving its position. True ultra-dominance can be quite evident in pack-keeping breeder's dogs and in their small pups. Studies have shown, for example in the eminent studies of James Serpell and the Coppingers, that dominant behaviour in young puppies can be observed at a very young age and although a peak can move both up and down for a small dominant puppy, there was a strong likelihood of its dominance remaining intact during its adult life.

Another important point to note is that promoting pack-keeping allows for the interaction of puppies with the stud father. In some cases, as part of the pup-rearing process, very strong alpha fathers expose their young offspring to tough behaviours that promote aggressive and competitive behaviour at later stages, and this also allows the puppies to learn the benefits of aggression. Pack-keeping also promotes the basis of altruistic behaviours. From the minute the pups are weaned from their mother they will most certainly never miss an opportunity to work together with her, and pin her down, albeit briefly. Should they succeed they will have had the great fortune to have received a new 'programme' mapping for their tiny brains: the teamwork 'programme'. When promoted this will have huge benefits for working Boerboel enthusiasts who, like all working dog people the world over, require a canine friend to work as part of a team network.

Promoting pack-keeping within the Boerboel breed has so much significance and there is a great need for it. Pack-keeping stimulates the creation of a multitude of nerve connections during the most critical three- to ten-week period; the sounds, smells, sights and most importantly the pack order are imprinted during this stage and can serve as a fundamental head-start for prospective owners. Pack-keeping promotes hunting skills, it teaches a harder school of raising with exposure to alpha males and to the others in the pack, it promotes competition and intraspecific aggression and so much more.

The breed has no direction as of this day and therefore every effort to preserve old customs of animal husbandry in the infancy of this breed is critical for its development.

Conclusion on prey and defence drives

A drive is a form of energy within the animal, it is the internal engine, the driving force to get to the desired target of its motivation, and it is the ability to neutralise threat with forward-fight response. Herein lies the truth about the defence drive. In the selection process for breeding, we select for dominance, super-confidence and not the submissive neoteny that Bull breed dogs in this post-pet world have now been selected (submissive juvenile behaviour, i.e. flight syndrome).

The importance of aggression is that it drives the will to succeed and the motivation of its desire is a self-preserving force that surpasses the learned behaviour to please the handler. Aggression is a force so strong it will override all external conflict and go over and beyond what is necessary to extinguish competition and protect its resources and food sources. True ultra-dominance has at times (and most certainly within less socialised dogs) high territorial values. Aggression is the mark of true ultra-dominance and is not the right selection criteria for the average pet home or pet breeder, as they simply cannot provide the environment and other conditions required to reveal the wonderful working attributes of these dogs and the potential they can attain.

Aggression is also the ability to *neutralise* violence, be it intraspecific or human and it is the ability to dominate. Dominating behaviour is innate and also epigenetic (genetics and epigenetics work in harmony). It starts at birth and can fluctuate, but inevitably remains an internal genetic force right through to adulthood. Dominance in the domestic dog is a far more exaggerated behaviour than is found in its wild cousins. Dominance in the domestically bred dog is most certainly fashioned through a procedure of selection which, over the centuries, has created a fundamental use to working handlers. Today in modern dog training we are able to readily manipulate the flight syndrome that is part of the defence drive. The true ultra-dominant dogs as discussed earlier have a natural innate tendency to be super confident, hence displaying behaviours indicating an intention to cause violence. Submissive weak dogs have the natural desire to flee, but training can create the illusion of ultra-dominance and is very easily achieved in the higher echelons of the dog training world. Thus, not only in the Boerboel world, but also in the Pressa Canario and Bulldog worlds, the practice of training dogs for breed surveys and breed-specific Protection of Handler tests, it is not uncommon to find weak submissive dogs being trained all year round to compete in tests that require nothing more than two bites on a sleeve or suit.

It is common to hear, particularly in the sport arena and within the GSD community, discussions of what constitutes a hard dog. But very few who I had discussed this with really understood what that means; some described aggression (or what I call the internal driving force of success) as hardness. So, it is safe to assume that aggression to succeed above all external conflict is the precursor to what they understood as hard. I reiterate that my definition of aggression can be compared to the definition used by many successful entrepreneurs of today: the ability of a human to succeed despite external problems and conflicts. It is their internal aggression that is at play. Never have I known humans to sit back and analyse their emotions when they are aggressively pursuing a particular goal, this comes after the fact, when we are able to put events into perspective, then the situation becomes so evidently clear. It is quite simply an aggressive approach to their task that makes them succeed. That complete tunnel vision, the vision we see with the game-bred Pitbull Terrier, or the Mallinois that will get into a pit of broken bottles for its ball, or the German Shepherd who resource-guards his toy or food or shows a violent vocal response while searching for its ball, now that is what a really good trainer should dream of. The dog you cannot train is the dog you want to train, because quite simply it is the most fundamentally reliable, the safest, and the strongest in its behaviour and action, the intention it shows is pure unadulterated aggression. And fundamentally that is the only dog worth its salt and certainly the only dog I would trust to be a protector to my own child. Aggression is fact, it is truth and it is self-preservation, it is the ability to neutralise sexual competition in order to procreate, food source competition and territorial competition, it is the eternal life force for breeding what many refer to as a hard dog.

So where does the Boerboel fit into this, you might ask? Well, finally you will reach the final Chapter here and this is where all the different tangents you have been thrown across finally tie together, like the strands of DNA that flow through your body as a carefully orchestrated opera. In the end it all makes perfect sense.

98 THE WORKING BOERBOEL

Chapter 7
Of Clubs, Committees and Organisations

Introduction

This Chapter presents the breed standards set out by the following Boerboel organisations, not all of which are active today, but each deserves to be accounted for if we wish to see a comprehensive record of the groups that have worked hard on establishing a standard. These clubs, committees and organisations are: South African Boerboel Breeders' Society (SABBS), Boerboel International, Historical Boerboel Association of South Africa (HBSA), Elite Boerboel Breeders' Association of South Africa (EBBASA) and Kennel Union of South Africa (KUSA).

It is with considerable caution that I have chosen to write about these particular organisations. But in the interests of any particular fancier of this breed, there is a need to address the legitimacy and function of these groups. I have always been sceptical of clubs and organisations; I imagine this is partly due to my rebellious side, my inability to conform to the norm, or follow the crowd, and my constant striving to be something different, for these are my inadequacies, and accordingly I have given the benefit of the doubt to the particular organisations I had the privilege of meeting with.

My reason for giving credit or, indeed, dedicating a portion of my book to the above organisations is a need and desire to encompass all the various bodies that exist today, in a hope that they will all at some point in the future merge into one body, and that some form of solidarity be maintained. It is not startling to find that the one common denominator that relates these separate bodies is their willingness to embrace the one thing they share a passion for: the Boerboel. Of course, if one was to be negative about it, one might easily interpret that passion as a yearning for power; but me, I am a born optimist.

Another phenomenon which gives considerable weight to the conduct of clubs and organisations is most certainly the internet, especially its quasi-chatrooms with their visitors' ability to misconstrue the principles of the particular organisation they might favour having a huge effect on the decisions that these very organisations make. Although, I have found at times there to be an anthropomorphic tendency of the members of these chat rooms, in the way in which they humanise their dogs. This phenomenon is not new. In the most primitive societies, people worshipped the elements, earth, wind and fire, and later, through the effects of evolution human thought processes became more articulate and it was at this time the elements took on the form of mythical creatures and began to be translated to human form. It is, after all, no surprise that individuals of the human species, who have considerable adoration for their dogs, start to subconsciously translate these feelings to represent their dogs as humans with feelings of a human nature. I feel troubled to find such intelligent individuals wasting life's precious time to chat about matters relating to dogs, unless of course the debate bears considerable financial gain to any one individual. So, what to make of chat rooms? They are a curse in the sense that they can easily influence new or novice members or spectators to believe in false propaganda, and the social pressure exerted by being part of a collective or group makes the novice more likely to support the loudest opinion than not. In Chapter 9 'Fact or Fiction' I will discuss the relevance of internet social media platforms to the Boerboel's cause.

So, what is my definition of a club? I can say with certainty, it is a group or organisation of like-minded individuals who conform to certain rules and regulations, most hopefully being voted upon. It is a group of people with common goals and a shared vision, who meet and support one another, who share experiences and knowledge and are able to give unprejudiced advice.

A club or organisation dedicated to a particular subject should be able to accept all interested people who apply for membership and actively invite others who also share in the common purpose to work together on improving the future welfare of their chosen special interest.

A club or organisation should be both democratic and, more importantly, open to inspection, it should be transparent and allow for freedom of speech, encouraging the viewpoints of its individual members, and allowing for the open and constructive criticism from those who are merely spectators. It must have the ability to control and promote in a positive and influential manner the breed standard. Clubs and organisations have a duty to both their members and their longevity to promote their cause and create a stronger and more unified body.

In the period since the emergence of the South African Boerboel Breeders' Association (SABT/SABBA) back in 1983 to this day of writing, many other organisations have sprung up. This troubles me considerably, and I cannot help asking myself why. There are, of course, many theories. I observed in my meetings with numerous people in the Boerboel fraternity that they had formed some conclusion that the SABT had disintegrated into some form of oligarchy. But then, could not the same be said of the EBBASA, the brain child of Perte Sprinkhuizen? Considering that the Boerboel is a relatively new breed, why does a conflict of interest abound? Do we really need yet another organisation or club? And can one organisation serve the interests of its individual members better than any other?

I need you to bear in mind that this book is not the *National Enquirer*, and my aim is to be both methodical and unbiased in discussing this subject. My criticisms should only be construed as constructive and it is not for the aims of this book to highlight any one particular individual, as this will be both negative and pointless. I have refrained from joining any one particular organisation or club; this has always been a conscious decision of mine in order to remain completely impartial to any given philosophy.

Therefore, you might be the potential new member or you might be an existing member of a club and no doubt you can make your own decisions on what the best organisation is to serve your particular interests. For those who are members of any of the above committees, I should explain that I have taken this voyeuristic approach as an exercise in minimising bias when examining any possible shortcomings in the clubs. Shortcomings will be quite transparent to those who have high expectations from an organisation. After all, I am nothing more than a possible candidate looking for an organisation to join. And my conclusion is nothing more than an independent observation.

South African Boerboel Breeders' Society (SABBS)

This organisation is currently the largest and most mainstream organisation for the Boerboel in the world, being the only legal registry officially appointed within South Africa to preserve and oversee the development of the breed. Over the years this registry has undergone both name and board changes, the latter is changed on a regular interval by vote. This ensures that breeders that serve on the board do not maintain too much of a grip on decisions, or hold a monopoly on promoting prevailing fashions for the breed, or allow favouritism of their own breedings to dominate matters. Currently (at the time of writing this being 2018), no evaluation of the temperament test is carried out, however, talks are under way for a constructive and open dialogue for this to be considered as part of the appraisal system. Should this materialise and the present multitude of cooks be reduced, then they have a credible future to pursue (certainly within the small percentage of working purists). SABBS has a database and also a methodical information system capturing DNA and pedigree data to assist the breeders of this generation to enhance existing and improve future litters and kennels.

The following text has been reproduced from the breed standard published in the SABBS constitution, available publicly online at: https://sabbs.org/6-subscription-and-fees/56-about-sabbs/constitution/94-constitution-3-boerboel-breed-standard [accessed: 29 June 2018] © SABBS 2018.

1. SOCIETY NAME
The correct name of the Society is the South African Boerboel Breeders' Society (SABBS), subsequently referred to as the Society, which was registered in terms of the Animal Improvement Act, 1998 (Act No. 62 of 1998) on 10 April 2012, Registration No. 62/98/B-68.

2. OBJECTIVES
Subject to the provisions of the South African law, the Animal Improvement Act and this constitution, the objectives of the Society shall be:
   a) to encourage and promote the breeding and genetic improvement of the Boerboel breed worldwide;
   b) to strive for unimpaired purity of the Boerboel breed and to promote the interests and public image of the breed by all possible and suitable means;
   c) to ensure the accuracy of all records of pedigrees, performance, ownership and other particulars of all dogs registered or eligible for registration as Boerboel with the Society;
   d) to compile and maintain a minimum Breed Standard and other minimum standards as a prerequisite for the registration of Boerboels, appraisal for conformation in respect of functional efficiency and other testing and evaluation standards, as determined from time to time;
   e) to encourage the expansion of the Boerboel breed by means of information and educational and promotional programmes, and training courses;
   f) to safeguard and advance the interests of the Boerboel breed and members of the Society, and generally to give effect to the objectives contemplated by the Act.

3. BOERBOEL BREED STANDARD
3.1 Breed Standard Criteria
The Breed Standard is a guideline which describes the ideal characteristics, temperament and appearance of the breed and ensures that the breed is fit for function. The aim of this Breed

Standard is to provide guidelines to breeders, appraisers and judges, who should at all times be vigilant to avoid obvious conditions or excessiveness, that would be detrimental in any way to the health, welfare or absolute soundness of the Boerboel.

Type, conformation, functional efficiency, mentality and composure are equally important in the evaluation of the Boerboel as a whole. The protective character of the breed is evident, as well as its impressive demeanour, good temperament, controllability and mobility.

Although the Boerboel has become a popular breed internationally, the centre for breed-specific knowledge remains in South Africa, as this is where its character is embedded.

Faults: Any departure from the Breed Standard shall be considered a fault and the seriousness with which the fault shall be regarded, shall be in exact proportion to the degree and its effect on the health and welfare of the dog.

Disqualification: Any serious deviations and/or combinations of deviations from the Breed Standard that may affect the dog's health and/or performance negatively shall lead to disqualification at the discretion of the senior appraiser. (**Refer to 3.3: Disqualification**).

3.1.1 Temperament and Character
The Boerboel is:
- a) manageable, reliable, obedient, trainable and intelligent;
- b) self-confident and fearless;
- c) a dog with a strong protective instinct and loyal to members of the family;
- d) shows courage when threatened;
- e) steadfast and calm, with a balanced and confident nature when approached and
- f) a dog requiring training and firm handling from an early age.

3.1.2 General Appearance
The Boerboel is:
- a) a large dog with a strong-boned structure;
- b) perfectly balanced within the desired proportions for the breed. The main structural components of the dog should show acceptable proportions to each other. The body is approximately 10 – 15% longer than the height (at the withers) and is measured horizontally, from the prosternum (breastbone) to a vertical line at the rear of the rump;
- c) a dog with prominent and well-developed musculature;
- d) impressive and imposing in appearance, created by a combination of conformation, carriage, confidence and powerful, buoyant and unencumbered movement – notwithstanding its size.
- e) Males are distinctly masculine, larger and more heavily built with stronger bone, while females are distinctly feminine, but without weakness of substance or structure. Sexual dimorphism must be clearly evident.
- f) The ideal height of a male is 66 cm but not lower than 60 cm.
- g) The ideal height of a female is 61 cm but not lower than 55 cm.
- h) Height must always be in relation to mass (minimum of 1:1 and a maximum of about 1:1.25), overall balance and conformation of major body components.

3.1.3 Head
The shape and size of the head is a typical feature of the breed. The head
- a) is large and typically Boerboel with no signs of another breed, and in proportion with the rest of the body components;
- b) circumference equals the height to the withers (upper point of scapula);
- c) is short, broad, deep, cubed, muscular and has well-filled cheeks.

Head characteristics are quantifiable in terms of:

3.1.3.1 Skull
- a) The skull is large, well-muscled and cubed in appearance.
- b) The width of the skull is equal to the length thereof.
- c) The length of the roof of the skull (measured from the middle of the eye to the end of the occiput) must be relative to the length of the nasal bone in a relation of 1:1 to a maximum of 1:1.5.
- d) The plateau is wide and flat with prominent musculature.
- e) When the dog is alert, the upper level between the ears appears flat.

3.1.3.2 Face
- a) The face gradually blends with the scull.
- b) The face may be with or without a black mask.

3.1.3.3 Ears

The ears are defined by:
- a) Setting:
  - i. The earflaps are set high and wide.
  - ii. The earflaps are carried close to the head.
  - iii. When attentive, the top of the earflaps must form a straight line with the plateau.
- b) Shape:
  - i. Obviously V-shaped;
  - ii. no creases and
  - iii. a broad base.
- c) Size:
  - i. The earflaps are medium sized and in proportion to the head.
  - ii. The bottom edge of the earflap is in line with the dentition.

3.1.3.4 Eyes

The eyes are defined by:
- a) Size and setting:
  - i. medium sized, rounded, forward facing, and widely spaced;
  - ii. set on the same horizontal level and
  - iii. not protruding, slanted or deep set.
- b) Eyelids:
  - i. Firm, well pigmented;
  - ii. no structural deviations such as entropion, ectropion, disticiasis or signs of surgical intervention.
  - iii. The third eyelid (haw) should not be visible.
- c) Colour:
  The colour of the eye is any shade of yellow or brown, and preferably darker than the lightest shade of the pelt.

3.1.3.5 Stop
- a) The stop is visible, but not prominent/pronounced or absent.
- b) The section between the eyes is well filled.

3.1.3.6 Nasal bone (Muzzle)

The nasal bone is defined by:
- a) Shape:
  - i. Deep, broad, cubed shaped, and tapers slightly towards the front, but not snipey.
  - ii. Straight and parallel to the line of the cranial roof.
  - iii. Well attached and filled below the eyes.
  - iv. The nostrils are large and widely spaced.

    b)   Width and depth:
        i.   The width is almost equal to its length.
        ii. The depth should equal the length.
    c)   Length:
    The nasal bone is in proportion to the head, and measures approximately a third of the total length of the head, i.e. approximately 10 cm for a male of 66 cm and 8 cm for a female of 61 cm. (Refer to 3.1.3 above.)
    d)   Pigmentation:
    The nose leather is black.

3.1.3.7 Lips
    a)   The upper lip (under the nose) covers the top of the bottom lip.
    b)   The upper lip does not extend below the underline of the lower jaw.
    c)   The bottom lip is moderately tight (not too loose and fleshy), without open or excessive lip.

3.1.3.8 Teeth
    a)   Dentition is complete.
    b)   Teeth are correctly spaced.
    c)   Teeth are ideally in a scissor bite.

3.1.3.9 Jaws
The jaws are strong, deep and broad and taper slightly towards the front.

3.1.4 Neck
The neck is defined by:
    a)   Shape:
        i.   Forms a unit with the head and the shoulders;
        ii. muscular and ideally with a discernible crest.
    b)   Length:
    The neck is of medium length and in proportion to the rest of the dog. The length equals about 1/3 of the height at the withers.
    c)   Scruff and dewlap:
        i.   The scruff is loose.
        ii.   The dewlap is noticeable and loose from under the chin.
        iii. The dewlap becomes taut between the front legs.

3.1.5 Forequarter
The forequarter is well-muscled and correctly angulated from the well-sloped shoulder blade down to the elbow at an angle of 90°.
The forequarter characteristics are quantifiable in terms of:

3.1.5.1 Chest
The chest is:
    a)   strong, muscular and broad;
    b)   well pronounced and placed deep between the front legs with good volume;
    c)   the point of the prosternum is level with the point of the shoulder.

3.1.5.2 Shoulders
The shoulder blades are well attached with an approximate 70 mm space in between.

3.1.5.3 Elbows
    a)   The elbows are stable, parallel to and carried close to the body when in a stationary position and during movement, not limiting the optimal volume of the centre piece/torso.
    b)   The height of the elbows is equal to ½ of the height at the withers.

3.1.5.4 Front legs
The front legs:
    a)   have a substantive bone structure;
    b)   are thick, strong and sturdy;

c) have a well-defined musculature on the in- and outside of the upper parts and
d) are vertical, as seen from the front and the side.

3.1.5.5 Pasterns

The front pasterns are:
a) short, strong and of adequate girth as seen from the front and the side and
b) are a vertical extension of the front legs as seen from both the front and the side, but slanting forward at a slight angle.

3.1.5.6 Front paws

The front paws are defined by:
a) Size:
   The front paws are large in circumference.
b) Shape:
   i. Well padded, ball shaped and tight;
   ii. strong, curved, with dark pigmented toenails.
c) Tread:
   The front paws point and tread straight forward.

3.1.6 Centre Piece

The centre piece (torso) must be of adequate width and depth with a level, straight top line and a slight abdominal tuck-up. The length of the chest, loin and croup (rump) is approximately proportioned (2:1:1).

The centre piece characteristics are quantifiable in terms of:

3.1.6.1 Ribcage

The ribcage (the area from the first chest vertebrae to the last rib bone)
a) is well-sprung with a deep, rounded brisket;
b) must ideally have a length proportion of 2:1 to the loin;
c) the depth is equal to ½ the total height of the dog at the withers, descending slightly below the elbow;
d) is filled behind the shoulder blades.

3.1.6.2 Back

The back (from a point behind the top of the scapula to the last rib bone) is:
a) broad;
b) flat;
c) straight and
d) well-muscled.

3.1.6.3 Loin

The loin (from the last rib bone to the front of the primary thigh) is:
a) of adequate depth (slightly less than the length of the loin);
b) short (ideally • of total torso length);
c) wide and flat when seen from the top;
d) strong and muscular and
e) moderately tucked up.

3.1.6.4 Top line

a) The top line (from a point behind the top of the scapula to the beginning of the croup) is straight without any deviations.
b) A very slight, non-flexible dip just behind the shoulders is normal.

3.1.7 Hindquarter

The hindquarter is broad, of substantive depth, well-muscled, in proportion to the rest of the dog and correctly angulated.

The hindquarter characteristics are quantifiable in terms of:

3.1.7.1 Croup
The croup is:
- a) broad, strong/muscular;
- b) correctly angulated at 23° – from the ilium to the ischium and
- c) the height should not exceed the height at the withers.

3.1.7.2 Tail
- a) The tail is a natural extension of the spinal cord; therefore, it is set fairly high, of adequate girth and straight.
- b) Docked tails should ideally be docked at the third caudal vertebrae, leading to an ideal adult tail length of about 8 cm.
- c) Long tails are permissible and are sabre shaped and should reach approximately to the hocks when the dog is standing.

3.1.7.3 Primary/Upper thigh
The upper thighs are broad, deep and with well-developed muscular definition when viewed from the side and the rear.

3.1.7.4 Secondary/Lower thigh
The lower thighs are well developed and display adequate, visible musculature down to the hock.

3.1.7.5 Stifles (Knees)
- a) The stifles are strong and firm.
- b) The angulation between the femur, tibia and fibula must be approximately 110° as seen from the side.

3.1.7.6 Hocks
- a) The hock joints are strong and stable;
- b) correctly angulated (45°) as seen from the side and
- c) parallel with each other when viewed from the rear.

3.1.7.7 Pasterns
- a) The hind pasterns are relatively short, strong and of adequate girth.
- b) When viewed from behind, they are parallel with one another.
- c) When viewed from the side, they are vertical.
- d) The front of the hind pastern is in line with the back of the haunch.
- e) Dewclaws may be removed.

3.1.7.8 Hind paws
- a) The hind paws are as the front paws but should be slightly smaller than the front paws.
- b) The hind paws point and tread straight to the front.

3.1.8 Skin
The skin is:
- a) thick and loose, and
- b) should show dark eumelanin pigmentation.
- c) There are moderate wrinkles on the brow when the dog is attentive.

3.1.9 Coat
The coat is short, sleek and shiny with dense hair coverage.
The recognised colours are:
- a) All shades of brown (tan, red) or fawn.
- b) Solid black.
- c) Brindle: a colour pattern with irregular apparent vertical lines of only black hair on a brown (tan, red) or fawn base colour.
- d) Piebald: white spots on a brown (tan, red), fawn or brindle dog.
- e) Irish: a brown (tan, red), fawn or brindle dog with a white blaze, a white chest that can extend to a white collar and white feet and legs.

OF CLUBS, COMMITTEES AND ORGANISATIONS 107

- f) All the colours and associated patterns should be accompanied by good pigmentation.
- g) No other colours or colour patterns or tan markings are acceptable.
- h) Undesirable colours are:
  - i. Excessive/large white areas in all colours are undesirable and must be eliminated.
  - ii. More than a third white of the total body surface is undesirable as it may influence pigmentation.

(Definitions: 'Undesirable' means: Not recommended, but acceptable. 'Unacceptable' means: Disqualification)

3.2. Illustrated Breed Standard Terminology

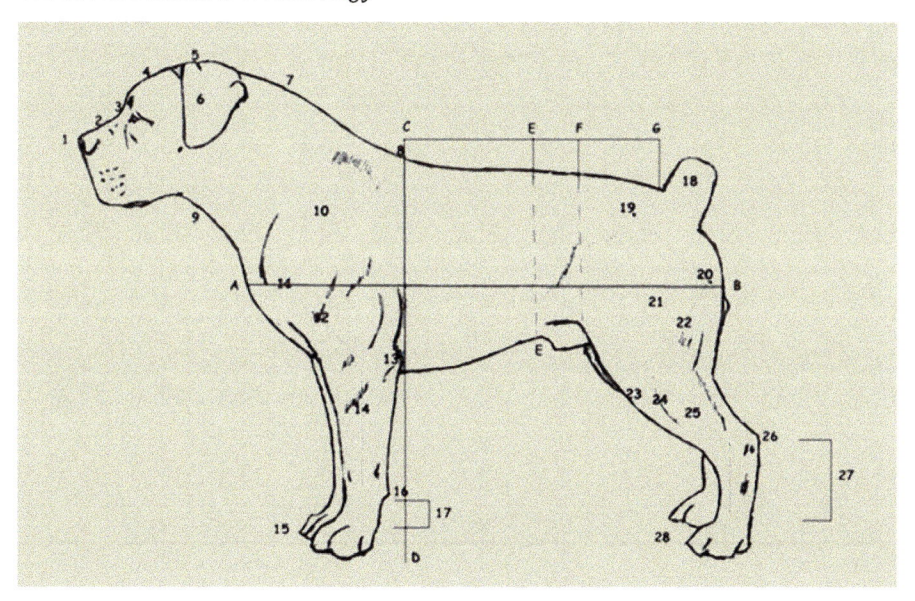

Illustration of a Boerboel in outline for the purpose of mapping the breed standard © SABBS 2018

Body length: measured from A (prosternum) – B (rear of the rump/croup)
Body height: measured from C (withers) to the ground (D)
Forequarter: A – C
Centre piece: C – F
Loin: E – F
Back: C – E
Croup/Rump: F – G (tail setting)

1. Nose leather
2. Nasal bone (muzzle)
3. Stop
4. Cranial roof
5. Plateau
6. Ear
7. Muscular arch on neck
8. Withers (top of scapula)
9. Dewlap
10. Shoulder blade (scapula)
11. Shoulder joint (point of shoulder)
12. Upper front leg (humerus)
13. Elbow
14. Lower front leg (radius and ulna)
15. Front paws
16. Pastern joint
17. Front pastern
18. Tail
19. Ilium (point of hip)
20. Ischium (point of buttock)
21. Primary thigh
22. Femur
23. Knee (stifle)
24. Secondary thigh
25. Tibula and fibula
26. Hock
27. Hind pastern
28. Hind paws

3.3 DISQUALIFICATION

3.3.1 To gain comprehensive statistical and genetic data on all Boerboels, SABBS urges members to present all dogs for appraisal. Dogs that do not meet the minimum score at an appraisal and dogs that have been disqualified (for whatever reason) shall not be registered, but shall be recorded in the PET Register. (**Refer to 3.3.3**).

3.3.2 The senior appraiser has the discretion to disqualify a dog without the appraisal process having been followed through, in which case the fees paid shall be reimbursed. He shall also notify the Office providing reasons for the disqualification.

3.3.3 A dog that is disqualified because of aggression, timidity or was not fully developed at the time of appraisal, may again be brought forward for appraisal, provided that it has improved and/or matured.

3.3.4 The Society retains the right to disqualify and/or remove a specific dog from the database of which documentation presented proves to be fraudulent and/or incorrect.

3.3.5 Any serious deviations and/or combinations of deviations from the Breed Standard that affect the dog's health/performance/functionality and/or mobility negatively are considered unacceptable and can lead to disqualification and/or the placing of breeding restrictions, at the discretion of a senior appraiser in order to retain breed integrity.

3.3.6 Traits that shall lead to disqualification are:
  a) Any indication of another dog breed
  b) Temperament
   - Any behavioural abnormalities, i.e.:
   - An overly aggressive and/or uncontrollable dog.
   - A timid or insecure dog.
   - A dog that bites its owner.
  c) Size:
   i. A dog not meeting the prescribed height.
   ii. A dog with insufficient bone structure.
   iii. A too petite dog.
   iv. A too clumsy/unbalanced dog.
   v. Unacceptable proportions of body components.
  d) Head:
   i. A head that is untypical Boerboel.
   ii. A too small or nondescript head.
   iii. Erect or semi-erect ears.
   iv. Structural deviations of the eyes.
   v. Any other colour than yellow or brown eyes.
   vi. A nose leather that is not black.
   vii. Excessive deviations of dentition.
   viii. A narrow, too long or sharply pointed muzzle.
  e) Body:
   i. A chest that is too narrow.
   ii. Bandy or crooked legs.
   iii. A top line that is too hollow.
   iv. A top line that is humpbacked.
   v. A top line that is S-curved.
   vi. Serious cow hocks.
   vii. Serious sickle hocks.
   viii. Absolute straight hind legs.
   ix. Deformed spines.
   x. Kinked, corkscrew, deformed or tightly curling tails.

f) Skin and pelt:
   i. Long and/or curly hair.
   ii. Excessive skin.
g) Colour:
   i. Unacceptable colours and patterns in respect of the breed standard:
      - Liver colour on any basic breed standard colour.
      - Ticking on any basic breed standard colour.
      - Split face on any basic breed standard colour.
      - Dilute/ powder and solid blue colour dogs.
      - Black and tan dogs.
      - Coat colour of more than one third white overall.
      - Solid black with more than a white spot on the chest and white on the toes and paws.
      - Tri-colour
      - Any colours not part of the Breed Standard, to be voted on during the 2nd General Meeting.
   ii. Insufficient pigmentation.
h) Reproductive organs:
   i. Males without two natural and well-developed testicles.
   ii. Females with signs of vaginal hyperplasia or prolapse.
i) Mobility:
   i. Clumsy or unbalanced movement.
   ii. Any visible impairment that seriously affects mobility.
   iii. Physical handicaps which are not the result of an earlier injury.

Boerboel International

This particular organisation, although based in Belgium and registered in the UK, represents to me a very high benchmark for its stringent ethics and beyond exceptional professionalism. Not swayed by the fashions and whims of modern social and political status symbols, its values in maintaining the principles of both temperament and movement in the Boerboel make it for me the number one choice for working Boerboel purists at this day of writing.

Its president and founder is Sonia Morgan, an articulate, educated and shrewd lady whose extensive knowledge of working dogs and the history of the Boerboel far exceeds the knowledge of today's Afrikaner Boerboel fanciers who have inherited the legacy of this breed. The database for this organisation is transparent and open for all to see once you are a fully paid up member or breed member; it is a highly advanced system, which insists that members have both genetic testing (mandatory) and DNA testing done on both the breeding sire and dam, together with a temperament test for breeding dogs. This makes theirs a thorough and comprehensive evaluation. With a whopping 30 per cent of the appraisal score given to temperament alone this breed registry has a huge advantage over those maintained by the more mainstream societies for working Boerboel enthusiasts and even pet owners. It has great potential and advantages, particularly for those living within the European hemisphere.

Official Breed Standard of Boerboel International

Preamble

Historically, the Boerboel developed as a general farm dog for the pioneers who settled in South Africa after the seventeenth century. These dogs often were a first line of defence against predators and were valuable in tracking and holding down wounded game. Old farmers told many a tale of the strength, agility and courage of the Boerboel. The dangers and harsh conditions of Southern Africa allowed only the fittest to survive. The protective character of the Boerboel is today still evident and is much sought after, as is the calm, stable and confident composure of the breed. It remains the guarding breed of choice among current day farmers and is very popular for the same reason in urban communities. The origin and purpose of the Boerboel should be understood in order to preserve the unique identity and qualities of the breed as a South African developed Mastiff. Type, conformation, functional efficiency and mentality are equally important in the evaluation of the Boerboel as a whole. The aim with the Breed Standard is to provide clear guidelines for breeders and judges to promote a singular vision of the ideal Boerboel.

1. **General Appearance**

The Boerboel:
- is large, with a strong-boned structure and a well-developed musculature. The profile of the head and body appears blocky;
- has an impressive demeanour created by the combination of conformation, carriage, confidence and powerful movement;
- has powerful, buoyant and unencumbered movement, notwithstanding its size;
- is symmetrical and perfectly balanced within the desired proportions for the breed; and
- has a distinct sexual dimorphism, with the bitch less prominently developed.

2. **Temperament and Character**

The Boerboel is:
- intelligent, trainable and manageable;
- has a strong protective instinct and is loyal to members of the family;
- is steadfast and calm, with a balanced and confident nature when approached;
- is fearless and shows courage when threatened; and
- requires training and firm handling from an early age.

3. **Head**

The head is impressive and a distinctive feature of the Boerboel.
It is blocky, broad, deep and in proportion to the body.
It is muscular with well-filled cheeks.
The roof of the cranium (skull) is square, flat and muscular.
The zygomatic arch (cheekbone) is well-muscled, but not too prominent.
The stop is definite, but not prominent, gradually sloping and well filled between the eyes.
It should not be steep, or an almost straight line between the nose and the occiput.
The muzzle is broad, deep, well attached, filled below the eyes and narrows slightly towards the nose.
The top line is straight and almost on a parallel plane with the cranial roof.
The muzzle measures slightly more than a third of the total length of the head (approx. 10cm for the male and 8cm for the female of ideal height).
The nostrils are large and widely spaced, with the septum (vertical line) of the nose perpendicular to the lower jaw.
The jaws are strong, deep and wide, and taper slightly to the front.

The teeth are white, strong, correctly spaced with complete dentition and a scissors bite (limited undershot discriminated against; overshot unacceptable).
The upper lip is loose and fleshy. It just covers the lower lip and teeth in the front but should not hide the underline of the lower jaw on the sides.
The lower lip is moderately tight without excessive jowls.
The eyes are medium sized, almond shaped, forward facing and widely spaced, with an intelligent expression.
It is well protected against the environment by firm and black-pigmented eyelids, showing no structural weaknesses.
The colour of the eye is preferably dark brown but all shades of brown (preferably darker than the pelt) are acceptable.
The ears are set wide and high and are carried close to the head.
They are V-shaped with a broad base tapering to a rounded point that reaches almost down to a line extending from the mouth.
When the dog is attentive, the top of the ears and the skull, in between, should form a straight line.
The facial expression should be intelligent, attentive and confident (not evasive, shy or threatening).

4. **The Neck**
The neck is powerful, of medium length, strong muscled and with a pronounced crest.
(In the female the muscles are less accentuated but should remain in balance with the head and body).
It is set medium high, flows smoothly into the sloping withers and forms a unit with the head and shoulders.
The dewlap is noticeable but disappears towards the sternum.

5. **The Body**
The body is approximately 15 per cent longer than the height and is measured horizontally, from the point of the shoulder to a vertical line at the rear of the rump.
(The length of the chest, loin and rump is approximately proportioned 2:1:1).
It is blocky, muscular, solid and has good depth and width.
The back is broad and straight, with pronounced muscles that form an imperceptible arch in the top line over the lumber region.
The brisket reaches down to the point of the elbow, which is approximately half the total height at the withers.
The transitions between the chest, loin and rump are well filled and flowing.

6. **Chest**
The chest is long, broad and deep, with well-sprung ribs and strong developed pectoral muscles.
It is filled behind the shoulder blades.
The point of the sternum is level with the point of the shoulder.
The shoulder blades should be well attached (not loose).

7. **The Lumber Region, Loin**
It is short, straight and muscular, and slightly narrower than the chest and rump.
The flanks are well filled, only moderately tucked up and the depth is slightly less than the length of the loin.

8. The Rump, Croup

The rump is broad, strong, muscular and in proportion to the rest of the dog.

Its height should not exceed the height at the withers. The top line drops slightly towards the tail.

The croup is broad and flat to provide a fulcrum (axel) towards powerful reach of the hind legs.

The tail is thick and set fairly high. It should be well covered with hair and without kink.

Tails are traditionally docked but undocked tails are acceptable. Docking takes place at the 3rd or 4th caudal vertebrae.

The natural tail should reach approximately to the hocks when the dog is standing.

9. Legs and Feet

Weak and malformed limbs jeopardise the physical functionality that is required of the Boerboel and should be discriminated against.

10. The Forelimbs

Are strong boned, with well-defined muscles and sturdy joints.

Should be correctly angulated from the well-sloped shoulder blade down to the metacarpus (pastern).

Should form a vertical line from the point of the shoulder down to the paws, with the elbows held close and parallel to the chest when viewed from the front.

Seen from the side the forearm should be vertical from the elbow to the carpus. The metacarpus is short, thick and strong and angles very slightly forward.

The forepaws point straight forward, are large, round, strongly boned and compact.

The toes are well arched, with curved black toenails and protected by hair in between. The pads are thick, tough and black.

11. The Hindlimbs

Are strong boned, sturdy and muscular.

The joints should be sound, strong and correctly angulated to support the powerful propulsion from the hindquarters during movement.

The upper thighs are broad, deep and muscular as seen from the side and the rear.

The lower thighs have well-defined muscles and show substance down to the hocks.

The metatarsus is broad, relatively short and perfectly upright. The front is in a vertical line with the rear of the rump.

From the rear the profile of the hindquarters should form an inverted U, with the stifles pointing straight forward and the hocks straight backwards.

The hind paws point straightforward, are slightly smaller than the forepaws but have the same quality.

12. Movement

The movement is strong, purposeful, buoyant and fluent, with comfortable reach in front and rear.

The legs and body should move in line front to rear. The feet move closer to a centre line as speed increases, forming a V shape in the observers mind.

While converging towards the centre line of travel, the legs should never cross.

At all gaits the top line is firm and strong, without swaying, or dipping in the middle, and without excess body roll.

Weak, unsound or plodding movement should not be tolerated.

13. The Skin
The skin is thick and loose but fits smoothly.
A small dewlap is permissible and moderate wrinkles over the forehead when the dog shows interest.

14. Pigmentation
The Boerboel is well pigmented, especially on the lips, palate, the skin and hair around the eyes, nose bulb, paw pads, toenails, the anus and the skin and hair around the genitals.
Only dogs with black eumelanin pigmentation are acceptable.

15. The Coat and Colour
The coat is short, dense, smooth and shiny.
The recognised colours / colour patterns are (with or without a mask):
- All shades of red, brown and yellow (fawn).
- Brindle: Brindle is a colour pattern with irregular vertical lines of only black hair on red, brown or yellow base.
- Piebald: Piebald is permissible to breed with, but should be discriminated against in the show ring. No more than 30 per cent white is acceptable.
- Irish Markings: Irish Markings are permissible to breed with, but should be discriminated against in the show ring.

All these colours and colour patterns should be accompanied by good pigmentation.
No other colours or colour patterns and tan markings are acceptable.

16. Size
Is determined by the ideal height at the withers and desirable ratios between the height and the measurements of the various parts of the external anatomy.
The ideal height for a dog is 66cm.
The ideal height of a bitch is 61cm.

17. Genitals
Male animals should have two apparently normal testicles fully descended into the scrotum.

FAULTS
Any departure from the foregoing points should be considered a fault and the seriousness with which the fault should be regarded should be in direct proportion to its degree.

DISQUALIFICATIONS
1. A dog that is out of balance / proportion.
2. An overly aggressive dog.
3. A too small and untypical head.
4. A lack of pigmentation.
5. Excessively undershot bite.
6. Excessively overshot bite.
7. Blue eyes.
8. Pricked ears.
9. Any dog clearly showing any physical or behavioural abnormalities or showing signs of another breed.

Historical Boerboel Association of South Africa (HBSA)

Although now a redundant organisation, HBSA was created as another splinter of SABT, and was both created and formed by the very prominent, founding father (among others) of SABT in 1983, Lukas Van De Merwe. The vision of HBSA was set in 1998 with the help of co-founder Jaanie Roodt. The objective was to enhance the original Boerboel which he felt was slowly being bred away from consequent to overseas demands.

HBSA Boerboel Breed Standard
General Appearance
The Boerboel is a big Mastiff type, a sturdy and smooth coated dog. Although the Boerboel should be strong of limb and muscular, it should also be agile and buoyant in movement. The Boerboel should on no account be leggy, nor must he be too short in the leg. A Boerboel's overall conformation should allow him to attain the highest degree of propelling power, together with the greatest length of stride that is compatible with the length of body. Weight is not a certain criterion of a Boerboel's fitness for his work – general shape, size and contour are the main points – the dog being in proportion the main requirement. Males should preferably weigh in excess of 50 kg, with the ideal weight being approximately 65 kg.
N.B. Old scars and injuries, the result of work or accident, should not be allowed to prejudice a Boerboel's evaluation, unless they interfere with its movement or with its effectiveness for work or stud.
Size, Proportion and Substance
In line with present day requirements, a full-size, well-balanced dog should ideally measure in height from the withers to the ground, 70 centimetres, but in any event should not be shorter than 60 centimetres – the bitch being proportionally shorter with an ideal height of 65 centimetres, but in any event not being shorter than 55 centimetres – height being related to weight.
Balance
This may be defined as the correct proportions of certain points, when considered in relation to certain other points. It is the keystone of a Boerboel's anatomy. The main points for consideration are the relative proportions of skull and foreface; head and back; height at withers and length of body from shoulder point to buttock – the ideal proportion being reached when the last two measurements are almost the same (9:10 ratio). It should be added that, although the head measurements can be taken with accuracy, the height at withers and length of back and coat are approximate and are inserted for the information of breeders and exhibitors rather than as a hard-and-fast rule.
Proportion
In proportion, the length of back (length from point of shoulder to tail set) is not equal to distance from withers to ground, or slightly longer than tall, in a ratio of 10:9. The Boerboel must not evolve towards a square conformation.
Head
The head is a very important feature of the Boerboel, as it represents it is total character. The head is short, broad, deep, square and muscular with well filled cheeks. The Boerboel should have an alert and intelligent expression. The top of the skull (occiput) is broad and flat, and from the side the muzzle and head are square. The skull must gradually decrease in width to the eyes and the stop should be visible but not prominent.
Eyes
Eye colour ranges in all shades of yellow and brown, but 90 per cent of dogs' eye colour is lighter than the pelt. The eyes should be horizontally and wide set and looking straight forward, with firm

well-pigmented eyelids. Eyes should not be protruding or set too deep, and haws should not show. Blue eyes must be seen as a serious fault (disqualification).
Ears
The ears should be of medium size, V-shaped and of moderate thickness. The ears are set high and wide against the skull. Ears should drop sideways close to the cheek. When the dog is interested, the ears should form a straight line with the top of the skull (occiput). The ideal length is when the lower tip of the ear is in line with the eye. Disqualification: Rose, tulip, pricked or full drop is a serious fault.
Nasal bone
The nasal bone is straight and as near to parallel as possible to the top line of the head, and should taper slightly from eye to muzzle, with or without a black mask. The nasal bone should be in proportion to the skull (approximately 8–10 cm long). The ratio between skull and nasal bone being 1/1.5:1.
Muzzle
The muzzle is black with large nostrils which are largely spaced.
Disqualification: Liver coloured, white or spotted nose.
Lips
The upper lip is loose and fleshy, and should not hang lower than the lower jaw. The upper lip (beneath the muzzle) should cover the lower lip.
Jaws
upper and lower should be strong, broad and muscular. The jaws should not be flat or snipey.
Teeth
The teeth should be white, well developed, correctly spaced, a complete set of 42 teeth and should have a scissors bite – a bite in which the outer side of the lower incisors touches the inner side of the upper incisors. Penalisation – badly overshot and badly undershot – i.e. more than 1 cm.
Neck
The neck is muscular and clean in outline, with no dewlap (the skin must be loose under the throat and stretched taut between the forelegs). The neck shows a noticeable muscle curve and gradually widens towards the shoulder. The neck must be in proportion to the rest of the dog. An over long or short neck should be considered a fault.

Body
Forequarters
Front legs are thick, strong and muscular to support overall balance of dog. The forelegs viewed from any direction must be as straight as possible and stand perfectly vertical, without knees or feet turning either in or out. The front pasterns should are short, strong and a vertical extension of the front legs and pastern joints. The distance from the knee (stifle) joint and pastern (wrist) joint must not be too long to ensure a well-balanced dog capable of fluent movement. Shoulders should be well laid back, with good muscle development. The upper arm should have good muscle development. The chest must be strong, wide and deeply set between the fore legs, with well attached and curved ribs. The ribcage should be in proportion to the chest. The front paws are big, well padded and rounded with strong, dark and short toenails. The paws should point almost straight forward. Most large breeds' front paws, however, turn slightly outward.
Top line
The top line should be straight.
Hindquarters
The back is straight, broad and in proportion, with prominent back muscles and a short loin. A straight 'table top' back is however not ideal for efficient movement, a very slight dip behind the shoulder ensuring better overall movement. The back sloping slightly towards the loin are

sometimes seen in young Boerboels. The hindquarters should be firm, strong and muscular and enhance effective propulsion. The hind quarters should be free from droop or crouch. The upper and second thigh (gaskin) should also be well developed with prominent muscles.

Knee (stifle)

The knees are strong, firm and correctly angulated. The hock joints are strong and firm with correct curving (45°), the hocks are relatively short, strong and thick. The hocks are parallel. (Dew claws, if any are generally removed.) The hind paws are slightly smaller than the front paws. They should be well padded, rounded and should point straight forward. The nails are strong, dark and short.

Tail

The tail is attached high to the body. It should be straight and is generally docked at three joints, however, long tails are also accepted.

Faults

A prominent dip behind the shoulder, a round back, or a sloping loin, is a sign of poor rib- and or back development. Loose shoulder blades are also considered a fault. A large male has a 'saddle' behind his shoulder blades, and behind this 'saddle' is a slight 'dip'. This 'saddle' consists of muscles.

Coat

The coat is thick, smooth, short and loose, with dark pigmentation on the skin under the hair. Moderate wrinkles on the forehead when the dog is interested. The belly and underside of the thighs should be bare. Long hair is a definite sign of another breed.

Colour

All colours are accepted, although poor pigmentation is penalised.

Gait / Movement

A smooth, powerful ground-covering ability must be seen. Movement is the crucial test of conformation. The principal propulsion power is furnished by hind legs. Perfection of action being found in the Boerboel possessing long thighs and muscular second thighs well bent at the stifles. When approaching, the forelegs should form a continuation of the straight line of the front, the feet being the same distance apart as the elbows. At a trot, both front and rear legs tend to converge towards the centre line of gravity. The Boerboel must show good extension both front and rear. Viewed from the side, the top line is firm and parallel to the line of motion – in other words in movement a straight top line should be maintained.

Temperament

From past history of the Boerboel, the modern dog draws its character of indominable courage, high intelligence, and tenacity. The Boerboel is also reliable, obedient and has a strong watchdog instinct. This coupled with its affection for its friends, and children in particular, its off-duty quietness and trustworthy stability, makes it a foremost all-purpose dog. The Boerboel has a quick and intelligent mind and is easily trained. He is outgoing and shows a tremendous willingness to please. He makes an excellent family dog as well as a trustworthy hunting companion.

Disqualifications / Penalisations

- A dog which is too small (D)
- A dog which is too big (D)
- An overly aggressive dog (D)
- A too small and nondescript head (D)
- A livered coloured muzzle (D)
- An under bite more than 1 cm (P)
- A noticeable overbite (P)
- A narrow, long or sharp mouth (D)
- Blue eyes (D)

- Erect ears (D)
- A narrow chest (P)
- Bandy legs (P)
- A hollow back (P)
- Cow hocks (P)
- Sickle hocks (P)
- Clumsy and unbalanced movement (D)
- Poor pigmentation (P)
- Any sign of another dog breed (D)

Additional Details:
CONFORMATION
Head
- large and strong
- short, broad and deep
- symmetrical and balanced
- flat between the ears
- the ideal nasal bone length of males is 10cm and that of bitches 8cm and must be straight with no upturn
- the stop not too prominent
- nostrils large and widely spaced

Eyes
- well formed with well pigmented lids
- no bulge – brow bone not prominent

Ears
- medium size and V-shaped and in relation to the rest of the head
- fall naturally against the head and positioned fairly high

Jaws
- strong, straight and broad well shut
- the ideal is a scissor bite
- lips must be pigmented and not too fleshy and must cover the teeth

Neck
- strong and muscled
- loose dewlap tautening between the legs
- form a well-balanced unity between head and body

Forequarters
- Chest – must be strong, well-muscled, broad and deep in relation to the dog and its body, with ample chest capacity.
- Front Legs – straight, sturdy and positioned under the body with slightly angulated but firm fetlocks.
- Shoulders – strong, muscled and supple.
- Elbows – must not stand out or bend in so that the dog has a comfortable movement.
- Body – length must be in relation to the size of the dog.
- Back – strong with a relatively straight topline.
- Loin – fairly short and well-muscled.

Hindquarters
- Must be strong, muscled and well-constructed.
- Legs – sturdy with slightly angulated bur firm fetlocks.
- Hocks – correctly angulated and under the body when moving.

- Paws – well padded, noticeably larger in front; must be in relation to the rest of the dog; must not turn out or in, pointing straight forward.
- Tail – preferably docked. (Long tails are allowed.) Forms a unity with the dog and set fairly high with no deformity.

EBBASA

Although no longer operating whether officially or unofficially, EBBASA was at one stage a very flourishing and successful organisation. I had the pleasure of spending considerable time with the very charming and eloquent Linda Swartz in 2006 and over dinner was also introduced to the international spokesman of that time Bruce Glanwyn of Glanwyn Boerboels, who many years ago had toyed with the idea of working with Boerboels in the pursuit of bitework and protection. I managed to give a large proportion of my time to visiting Bruce and his Glannwyn Kennels with Stoffel Bloom of the then Ysterberg Boerboel Kennels. I have included the words of Piet Sprinkhuizen as being valid for both his vision at that time and his thoughts on shaping the criteria set for that organisation. It has been fundamental to this book and to the fond memory of Linda Swartz and Piet Sprinkhuizen that the preamble of EBASSA be included.

This concept is the brain child of Piet Sprinkhuizen, a former member of SABT, who had worked, as I am led to believe, on this new organisation back in 1992. Although not relevant in today's political forum, this entry has been included first, as a point of reference, but secondly and most importantly, to pay homage to what for me was a huge loss to the bloodlines of the Boerboels.

After travelling throughout the country viewing as well as appraising Boerboels, he noticed that apart from a number of very good examples, there were quite a number of dogs classified as Boerboels that do the Boerboel name no justice. When visiting the European countries and breeders who had imported Boerboels he encountered the same problems and had to endure complaints as well as insults pertaining to South African breeders and puppy exporters. From the USA he was inundated by the same dissatisfaction from buyers, hence the initiation of EBBASA.

Founder members
- Mr Piet Sprinkhuizen (Avontuur Boerboele)
- Mr & Mrs Johan & Linda Swart (Linjo Boerboele)
- Elri Swanepoel (Eljara Boerboele)
- Koos Malan (Jabrina Boerboele)
- Rhona Chambers (Kromdraain Kennels)
- Lidia Ferreira (Lidiana Kennels)
- The (late) Dawie Venter (Von Marcos)

Words from the chairperson

Why was it necessary to form another association when there were already two Boerboel associations? Being an international judge, I was quite alarmed when judging the breed overseas, to find that too many resembled Great Danes, Staffies, St Bernards, Boxers, etc. Since the overseas market is an upcoming market, and South Africa, where the Boerboel originated from, the exporting country, it is of the utmost importance to export Boerboels of the highest quality. This appears not to have been the case in the past and that the financial gain far outweighed the quality of the Boerboel. This resulted in many dissatisfied customers overseas and, due to the bad behaviour of some badly bred dogs, negative publicity in the media.

On my return from such an overseas visit a few years ago I found that although a breeding standard existed in the existing two associations, too many breeders did not adhere thereto, and kept on breeding according to their personal preferences with the result that hip dysplasia, prolapses, eye entropion, skin disease, pigmentation problems, etc. have become a common problem with some breeders. No stringent measures are exercised with these breeders by their respective Boerboel associations, and in order to ensure that the Boerboel remains a healthy dog genetically, it was decided by a few serious breeders to form the Elite Boerboel Breeders Association of Southern Africa (International), who is only concerned with the Boerboel as a breed, and proud of our dog heritage.

Our main objectives are:
- Total dedication to the breed;
- Integrity;
- Honesty; and
- Determination.

For a breeder to be accepted as a member, the following would apply, and should the breeder qualify, he/she is issued with the respective certificates by EBBASA:

- Kennel inspection;
- Structure and hygiene according to our specifications;
- Proper bloodline selection to ensure qualities such as good temperament, no genetic abnormalities, robustness; and
- Tests to be performed by Onderstepoort for hip dysplasia and edysplasia accompanied by the relevant certificate from the tests for vaginal prolapse by a veterinarian at intervals, also eye ex/entropion, with the relevant certificate.

Piet Sprinkhuizen
CHAIRPERSON

Kennel Union of South African (KUSA)

KUSA is the Kennel Union of South Africa and has direct affiliation to the FCI. At this day of writing (2018) and following legal rulings KUSA has withdrawn its efforts to gain FCI status for the Boerboel. For a large constituency of individuals the loss of KUSA from the negotiation table and boardroom was a huge loss for this breed's future and its legitimacy under FCI recognition, which has no more deeper repercussions than for those of us who compete in FCI-recognised dog sports who can never compete in IPO all-breed international working dog trials now or in the near future.

PREAMBLE

Historically, the Boerboel developed as a general farm dog for the pioneers who settled in South Africa after the seventeenth century. These dogs often were a first line of defence against predators and were valuable in tracking and holding down wounded game. Old farmers told many a tale of the strength, agility and courage of the Boerboel. The dangers and harsh conditions of Southern Africa allowed only the fittest to survive.

The protective character of the Boerboel is today still evident and is much sought after, as is the calm, stable and confident composure of the breed. It remains the guarding breed of choice among current day farmers and is also very popular for the same reason in the urban communities.

The origin and purpose of the Boerboel should be understood in order to preserve the unique identity and qualities of the breed as a South African developed Mastiff. Type, conformation, functional efficiency and mentality are equally important in the evaluation of the Boerboel as a whole. The aim with the Breed Standard is to provide clear guidelines for breeders and judges to promote a singular vision of the ideal Boerboel.

BREED STANDARD

1. General Appearance

The Boerboel:
- a) is large, with a strong-boned structure and a well-developed musculature. The profile of the head and body appears blocky;
- b) has an impressive demeanour created by the combination of conformation, carriage, confidence and powerful movement;
- c) has powerful, buoyant and unencumbered movement, notwithstanding its size;
- d) is symmetrical and perfectly balanced within the desired proportions for the breed; and
- e) has a distinct sexual dimorphism, with the bitch less prominently developed.

2. Temperament and Character

The Boerboel is:
- intelligent, trainable and manageable;
- has a strong protective instinct and is loyal to members of the family;
- is steadfast and calm, with a balanced and confident nature when approached;
- is fearless and shows courage when threatened; and
- requires training and firm handling from an early age.

3. Head
- The **head** is impressive and a distinctive feature of the Boerboel.
  - It is blocky, broad, deep and in proportion to the body.
  - It is muscular with well-filled cheeks.
  - The roof of the cranium (skull) is square, flat and muscular.
  - The zygomatic arch (cheekbone) is well-muscled, but not too prominent.
- The **stop** is definite, but not prominent, gradually sloping and well filled between the eyes.
  - It should not be steep, or an almost straight line between the nose and the occiput.
- The **muzzle** is broad, deep, well attached, filled below the eyes and narrows slightly towards the nose.
  - The top line is straight and almost on a parallel plane with the cranial roof.
  - The muzzle measures slightly more than a third of the total length of the head (approx. 10cm for the male and 8cm for the female of ideal height).
- The **nostrils** are large and widely spaced, with the septum (vertical line) of the nose perpendicular to the lower jaw.
- The **jaws** are strong, deep and wide, and taper slightly to the front.
- The **teeth** are white, strong, correctly spaced with complete dentition and a scissors bite

(limited undershot discriminated against; overshot unacceptable).
- The **upper lip** is loose and fleshy. It just covers the lower lip and teeth in the front but should not hide the underline of the lower jaw on the sides.
- The **lower lip** is moderately tight without excessive jowls.
- The **eyes** are medium sized, almond shaped, forward facing and widely spaced, with an intelligent expression.
  - It is well protected against the environment by firm and black-pigmented eyelids, showing no structural weaknesses.
  - The colour of the eye is preferably dark brown but all shades of brown (preferably darker than the pelt) are acceptable.
- The **ears** are set wide and high and are carried close to the head.
  - They are V-shaped with a broad base tapering to a rounded point that reaches almost down to a line extending from the mouth.
  - When the dog is attentive, the top of the ears and the skull, in between, should form a straight line.
- The **facial expression** should be intelligent, attentive and confident (not evasive, shy or threatening).

4. *The Neck*
   - The neck is powerful, of medium length, strong muscled and with a pronounced crest.
   - (In the female the muscles are less accentuated but should remain in balance with the head and body).
   - It is set medium high, flows smoothly into the sloping withers and forms a unit with the head and shoulders.
   - The dewlap is noticeable but disappears towards the sternum.

5. *The Body*
   - The body is approximately 15 per cent longer than the height and is measured horizontally, from the point of the shoulder to a vertical line at the rear of the rump (the length of the chest, loin and rump is approximately proportioned 2:1:1).
   - It is blocky, muscular, solid and has good depth and width.
   - The back is broad and straight, with pronounced muscles that form an imperceptible arch in the top line over the lumber region.
   - The brisket reaches down to the point of the elbow, which is approximately half the total height at the withers.
   - The transitions between the chest, loin and rump are well filled and flowing.

6. *Chest*
   - The chest is long, broad and deep, with well-sprung ribs and strong developed pectoral muscles. It is filled behind the shoulder blades.
   - The point of the sternum is level with the point of the shoulder.
   - The shoulder blades should be well attached (not loose).

7. *The Lumber Region, Loin*
   - It is short, straight and muscular, and slightly narrower than the chest and rump.
   - The flanks are well filled, only moderately tucked up and the depth is slightly less than the length of the loin.

8. *The Rump, Croup*
   - The rump is broad, strong, muscular and in proportion to the rest of the dog.
   - Its height should not exceed the height at the withers. The top line drops slightly towards the tail.
   - The croup is broad and flat to provide a fulcrum (axel) towards powerful reach of the hind legs.

- The tail is thick and set fairly high. It should be well covered with hair and without kink.
- Tails are traditionally docked but undocked tails are acceptable. Docking takes place at the 3rd or 4th caudal vertebrae. The natural tail should reach approximately to the hocks when the dog is standing.

9. *Legs and Feet*
   - Weak and malformed limbs jeopardise the physical functionality that is required of the Boerboel and should be discriminated against.

10. *The Forelimbs*
    - Are strong boned, with well-defined muscles and sturdy joints.
    - Should be correctly angulated from the well-sloped shoulder blade down to the metacarpus (pastern).
    - Should form a vertical line from the point of the shoulder down to the paws, with the elbows held close and parallel to the chest when viewed from the front.
    - Seen from the side the forearm should be vertical from the elbow to the carpus. The metacarpus is short, thick and strong and angles very slightly forward.
    - The forepaws point straight forward, are large, round, strongly boned and compact. The toes are well arched, with curved black toenails and protected by hair in between. The pads are thick, tough and black.

11. *The Hindlimbs*
    - Are strong boned, sturdy and muscular.
    - The joints should be sound, strong and correctly angulated to support the powerful propulsion from the hindquarters during movement.
    - The upper thighs are broad, deep and muscular as seen from the side and the rear.
    - The lower thighs have well-defined muscles and show substance down to the hocks.
    - The metatarsus is broad, relatively short and perfectly upright. The front is in a vertical line with the rear of the rump.
    - From the rear the profile of the hindquarters should form an inverted U, with the stifles pointing straight forward and the hocks straight backwards.
    - The hind paws point straight forward, are slightly smaller than the forepaws but have the same quality.

12. *Movement*
    - The movement is strong, purposeful, buoyant and fluent, with comfortable reach in front and rear.
    - The legs and body should move in line front to rear. The feet moves closer to a centre line as speed increases, forming a V shape in the observers mind.
    - While converging towards the centre line of travel, the legs should never cross.
    - At all gaits the top line is firm and strong, without swaying, or dipping in the middle, and without excess body roll.
    - Weak, unsound or plodding movement should not be tolerated.

13. *The Skin*
    - The skin is thick and loose but fits smoothly.
    - A small dewlap is permissible and moderate wrinkles over the forehead when the dog shows interest.

14. *Pigmentation*
    - The Boerboel is well pigmented, especially on the lips, palate, the skin and hair around the eyes, nose bulb, paw pads, toenails, the anus and the skin and hair around the genitals.
    - Only dogs with black eumelanin pigmentation are acceptable.

15. *The Coat and Colour*
    - The coat is short, dense, smooth and shiny
    - The recognised colours / colour patterns are (with or without a mask):
        - Solid red, yellow (fawn)
        - Brindle (Brindle is a colour pattern with irregular vertical lines of only black hair on yellow (fawn) or red base.)
        - Very limited white patches below the carpal joints and the hocks, as well as on the Forechest is permissible, but should be discriminated against both in the show ring and in breeding stock.
    - **No other colours or colour patterns and tan markings are acceptable.**
16. *Size*
    - Is determined by the ideal height at the withers and desirable ratios between the height and the measurements of the various parts of the external anatomy.
    - The ideal height for a dog is 66 cm (lower than 60 cm is unacceptable).
    - The ideal height of a bitch is 61 cm (lower than 55 cm is unacceptable).
17. *Genitals*
    - Male animals should have two apparently normal testicles fully descended into the scrotum.

Faults
Any departure from the foregoing points should be considered a fault and the seriousness with which the fault should be regarded should be in direct proportion to its degree.

DISQUALIFICATIONS
1. A dog that is too small (Smaller than the minimum heights stipulated in the Breed Standard).
2. A dog that is too big and out of balance.
3. An overly aggressive dog.
4. A too small and untypical head.
5. A lack of pigmentation.
6. Excessively undershot bite.
7. Excessively overshot bite.
8. Blue eyes.
9. Pricked ears.
10. A piebald or black dog.
11. Any dog clearly showing any physical or behavioural abnormalities.

As approved Fedco 05/07 (Edition 4)

124 THE WORKING BOERBOEL

OF CLUBS, COMMITTEES AND ORGANISATIONS 125

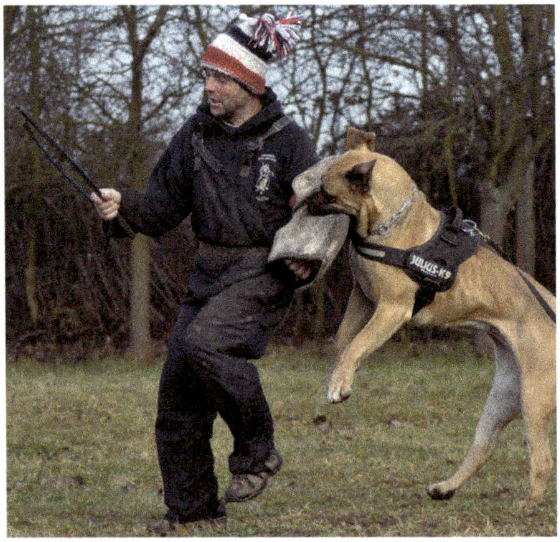
JULIUS-K9

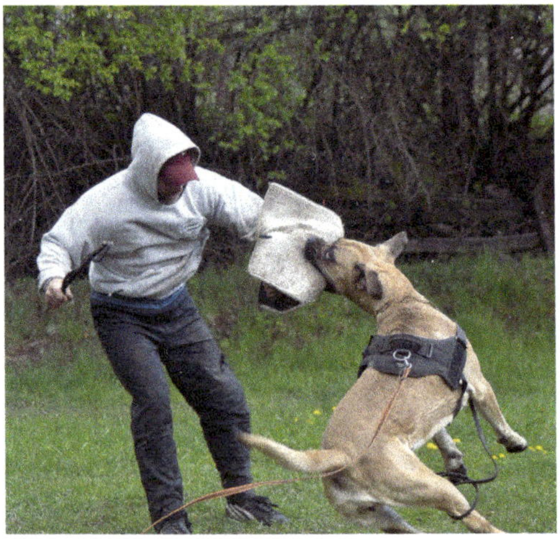

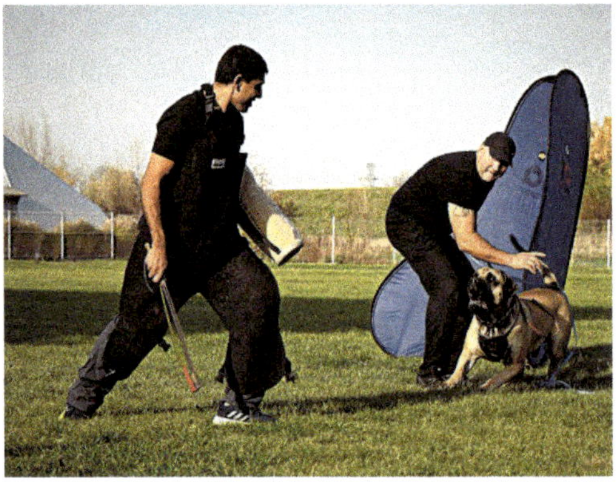

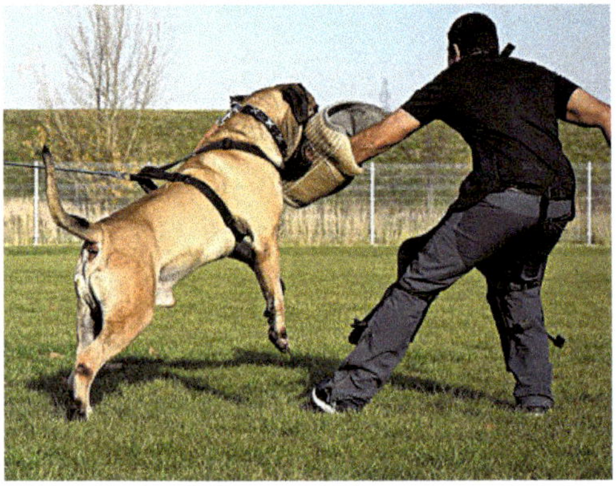

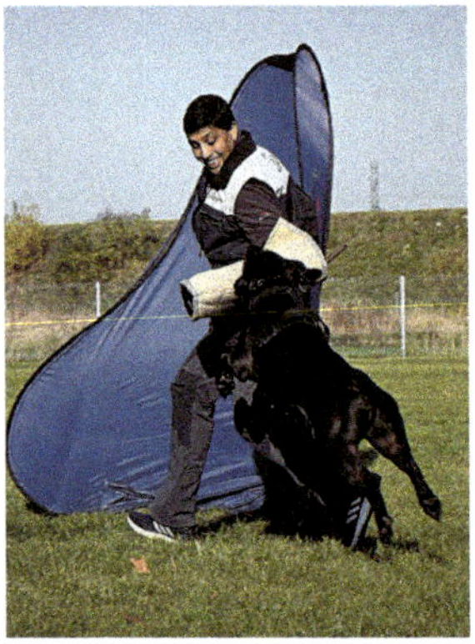

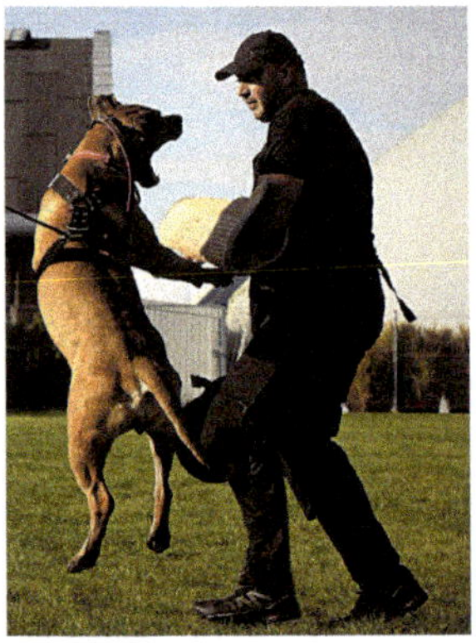

Chapter 8
The Final Curtain Call: Lessons from History

They say that if we do not learn from history then we will inevitably fall into the trap of repeating it. I have been amazed at how little the average person knows of world history – such ignorance leaves one vulnerable to powerful ideological forces that may not have one's best interests in mind. As discussed in earlier Chapters and as will be expanded upon in the last, the Boerboel breed and its community have suffered as a result of misguided ideological battles. This Chapter is a reminder to us all of the power of ideology to corrupt us. I wish to give you, the reader a brief insight into the reality of the human mind, its behaviour, and how some of its choices which have been made under the influence of politics, economics and mass hysteria have led to atrocities and suffering that in the modern twenty-first century are considered to have been acts of genocide.

Genghis Kahn – Source Public Domain.

Genghis Khan invaded and annexed many countries, and literally completely wiped some others off the map. His actions in the Middle East and China were of a genocidal magnitude. He started one of history's worst plagues, being the first to use biological warfare. His following was colossal and his allegiance of loyal followers and soldiers was huge. Today he is considered one of the greatest military strategists of all time. He wiped out over 10 per cent of the world's population in the course of his rule.

Mao_Zedong_1963
Source http-___sarbaharapath.com

Mao Zedong is known as the person who engineered modern history's worst famine, killing over 60 million Chinese in 'The Great Leap Forward', as well as a controlling dictator who ruled China with an iron fist. His actions killed about 4 per cent of the world's population.

Lord Kitchner
Source Boers.co.za

In 1902, Lord Kitchener implemented a scorched earth policy – a direct attack on food supplies to the Afrikaner Boer farmer. This resulted in the displacement of the farmers, starvation and lack of water, which caused the death of over 26 000 Boers, who were mainly children.

Adolf Hitler
Source free-largeimages.com

Adolf Hitler and his vast army brutally slaughtered 6–11 million people in the Holocaust, and directly caused the deaths of another 40 million in the second world war, as well as caused the military occupation and breakup of several countries. His actions killed around 3.5 per cent of the world's population.

Source Unknown

Joseph Stalin's rule caused the deaths of over 20 million Soviet citizens and organised a series of brutal purges sending thousands to prison camps, not to mention the invasion of over a dozen countries. His actions killed around 2.8 per cent of the world's population.

Winston Churchill
Source Public Domain

Winston Churchill and his lust to lead a colonial superpower led to the deaths of over 5 million Hindus. In his wake, wars and calamities developed in many countries. His actions killed around 1.5 per cent of the world's population.

The data above is just a very slight reminder of the more horrific examples of how humans tend to form groups and follow a leader. Each of the dictators mentioned above was promoted, glorified and worshipped as a revolutionary, a maverick. This was possible because they gave hope when there was none, they fed dreams, they were the saviours of their people. Information is an amazing tool: it creates, it manipulates, creates frenzy and hysteria, but above all, when in the wrong hands it all too readily creates a following of blinded believers.

Today, the traditional organs of the media have become social. To publish one's opinion online today does not require a qualification or experience, nor formal training or apprenticeship. To bear influence on people you simply need a large online audience: a social network. Innumerable people spend considerable amounts of time in front of a computer screen where they read information or create information. Not without concern have I noticed that these technologies of the twenty-first century offer a means to some people whose motives may not be wholesome, for it is now in this time of social media power that there is a new opportunity for the taking: one can be a leader, a visionary and an expert without ever leaving the comfort of the armchair. Armchair experts can unleash their specious arguments online and influence people and even history. The Boerboel community has been misled by inaccurate information peddled online. Your ability to critically assess information to work out whether it is reliable or not is an essential skill in this era.

On a more optimistic note, our information society offers genuinely enriching opportunities to us all. Although information technology enables the worst of us to readily alter history for our unsavoury gain, it equally enables the best of us to do so, too, hopefully for altruistic purposes. And it is not only history but also our human genome that is being shaped by how we all use or abuse information.

We must remember that the human genome is an animal genome. In the previous Chapter, 'The Importance of Aggression' we discussed the theory of dominant dogs, but we must consider that all animals – including humankind – work to improve their position for survival. Some animals use passive and submissive behaviour to get what they desire, some use violent or dominant behaviour. The river of DNA is always stronger than an individual. Your DNA was programmed to live before 'you' had developed: you the individual is but one part of your DNA. In this way, DNA gives us the desire to breed, to eat, to fight, to love and even to create economic growth, and so the selfish gene goes forth to multiply again in a new era. But it is society and the economy which have dictated the dynamics of how future human DNA will adapt to a world increasingly reliant on social media, a world where fact will be in danger of being no longer relevant, where feelings and emotions will supersede common sense, where the blind lead the blind from behind remote screens. The power button on your computer, your laptop, your mobile device or your tablet controls your power to change your direction, to follow your own goals, your own dreams, your own visions and your own reality.

We surround ourselves with like-minded people, it is human nature. But, life is a book of many chapters and it is you, the reader who defines your next Chapter, its content and its information. Truth and fact are absolute, the chromosomes and DNA you carry are fact, they are reality, the information you have been passed through thousands of years of biology's orchestrated manoeuvres; you were never born a coincidence, you were born a very physical manifestation of truth, a biological statement of fact. You are the living history of your ancestors.

In the end, your reality is dependent on your ability to discern truth over fiction. Truth does not have emotion, it cares not for feelings; truth has no prejudice, no friendships or alliances; truth is logic, it is science, and above all it is eternal.

In the 1400s in western Europe it was still believed by many physicists that the world was flat, the masses believed it, it is amazing what factual evidence and science disproves, yet at that time the masses never questioned it despite contrary evidence from the Greek times that the earth was spherical. Have we really not learned from past history.

The United Kingdom ruled that women had no right to vote from 1832 at the passing of the first bill, until 1918. It took a staggering 86 years and the deaths of over 1000 women, martyred for standing up for what they believed, for the voice of reason to be heard. Today, to ask whether a woman should have the vote would provoke utter contempt at the stupidity of the question.

The above example shows there can always be hope when a questioning thought can create seeds of change. Hope stimulates questioning and change. Through better education and the supply of reliable information we can take positive steps towards the future ennoblement of our dog breeds. Ultimately, it is up to you and I, as well as the consumers and the public, to bring about change, by questioning the validity of claims, by challenging the practices of those who feed the consumer frenzy, and by demanding standards (which for most of my working dog colleagues are considered the norm).

The ability to analyse information, to think for yourself, to rationalise, to separate emotion from reason, to yearn for truth, to demand fact, is all but gone in this modern age of mainstream and social media. It appears that the facility to think for oneself is no longer required, after all, nowadays you just need an app on your smart device to make the decisions.

It is animal nature which no doubt creates society, the same altruistic nature made by the genetically orchestrated programme that has taken thousands of years to develop and which ensures that successive versions of DNA pass safely from one generation to the next, so why would we be surprised if the coding that ensures domestic species pack together and wild species pack together does not then result in cliques? Well it does, and in humans, the cliques consist of gullible sheep who either overlook truth, fact and science or live in denial. The tendency of social creatures to want to belong to something or somebody, to establish a meaning for their existence, a sense of belonging, to not rock the apple cart, is very powerful. The importance of truth can play second fiddle at times to the needs of human emotion. Truth can hurt you, but it can also liberate you and emancipate you. They say it is easier to keep quiet then tell a fool they have been fooled.

Ever so randomly the river of DNA never flows so far from the source, it always reverts back to its cradle, a typical Bulldog look
Source Stoffel Bloom

As advanced as our own species have evolved, nature always goes back to its source, you decide its phenotype
Source Stoffel Bloom

Chapter 9
Fact or Fiction: The Awakening

Introduction

From the beginning of this book to the end, you have been thrown along many tangents, the aim of which was to seed various ideas that would be tied up in the final Chapter. To make clear sense of it all, it is both prudent and imperative to have read the book from start to finish. Now we will go through each Chapter's main points of interest and my own personal points of view to reach a conclusion.

So from the beginning of the dog's evolution to the birth of social media and identity politics as well as the importance of both aggression and the female, the significance of all the various chapters is condensed here to give you my opinion on the past, present and future of this breed. My questions and views are no more and no less different than any questions that the mainstream consumer will have when purchasing this product which we refer to as a Boerboel.

Question 1

The breed history on many websites and even more recent breed publications references the dogs of the Cynomones of Ethiopia to suggest that the Boerboel is an ancient Mastiff breed. Anemari Pretorius states in The Boerboel: South Africa's Own *that the genetic material that was used to make up the Boerboel has more pure Syrian bloodlines than any other breed in the world (Pretorius 2007, p. 5). The author as well as many other Boerboel writers then usually refer to Jan van Riebeeck's Bullenbijter as a possible link to the breed. This seems to be a common theme in all Boerboel literature in respect of the Cynomones' dogs and the Bullenbijter, can you elaborate on this?*

There is no credible reference or scientific evidence to hand that confirms if such a statement in reference to the Syrian dog is true, either in the scientific literature of modern mitochondrial evidence (which has advanced significantly in the last 20 years) or in historical sources. *The Boerboel: South Africa's Own* (Pretorius 2007) goes into no great depth or detail by which the author might have qualified or rationalised the statement. In fact, the statement is very subtle and only suggests the possibility that the dog's bloodline might be Syrian. It gives hope to those who would like to believe it, but it is not a confirmed fact.

Certainly, there existed no large Mastiff type dogs in South Africa prior to European settlement that were considered indigenous. You will also note that Anemari Pretorius refers to the African dog of the black tribes, which we most certainly now know from archaeological and scientific data was a healthy slim, medium sized animal and most certainly with pricked ears. Recent archaeological evidence of cave paintings found throughout the southern African countries and Namibia point to much smaller dogs existing within that geographical region. When compared with the documents of missionaries written from the fifteenth century to the early nineteenth, the contrary is suggested, as the documents contain paintings of dogs approaching jackal-like size.

We can also take note of the writings of Olfert Dapper (1668), Willem Ten Rhyne (1686), and George Theal (1919) which were quoted in the first Chapter, the writings of Major T. C. Hawley, E. R. Shelley's *Hunting Big Game with Dogs in Africa* (1924), and others who recounted their first-hand experience of indigenous dogs of the African tribes. They are all veritable and credible accounts of first-hand exposure to the dogs in South Africa in those times.

The dogs referred to in *The Boerboel: South Africa's Own* and various mainstream Boerboel publications and websites as having pure Syrian lines, i.e. the Cynonomes' dogs of Ethiopia, and in other accounts of the phenotype of those ancient Ethiopian dogs which allegedly date back to ancient Syria and Albania, are not what the early missionaries or the later European travellers described. The claim that the Ethiopian dogs are ancestors of ancient Western breeds cannot be scientifically validated, which makes this claim merely a biased unproven anecdote that has been used as a platform for contemporary Western romantic rhetoric about the history of the Boerboel.

Now I move swiftly onto the Bullenbijter of Jan van Reibeeck. It appears that the advent of Van Riebeeck in South Africa has become folklore. The Cape was for all intents and purposes nothing more than a stopover for traders. It was never deemed to be home. It was a form of punishment and servitude for those whom had been sent there. There is to this day absolutely no evidence that I have seen, be it photographic or written that supports the theory that Jan van Riebeeck allegedly brought over his Bullenbijter. Further theories on this have been written, but I see no correlation between accounts given in the historical texts of various writers I examined and the theories placing Jan van Riebeeck in the Cape with a Bullenbijter dog. Are we meant to assume his one so-called Bullenbijter was the Adam of all Boerboels, the prodigal son? The chosen one? And furthermore, with which dog(s) did this Bullenbijter breed with? What age did it die? And, more importantly, where are the pictures of this dog to confirm it was a Bullenbijter, and how many exactly where shipped over with the first colonists? There were three types of Bullenbijter in that era and they have three different phenotypes, so the big question becomes, which type was van Riebeeck's Bullenbijter? If anything, all we can claim to know is that Jan van Riebeeck might have brought along his dog – we cannot assume what breed or type this dog was, or if it has any relevance to the Boerboel breed. I can only conclude that this purported claim to Dutch heritage was used as marketing propaganda. And that's the true story.

But I shall further indulge you on the Bullenbijter (or Barrenbeisser) by referring you to the preamble noted by Colonel David Hancock in his book *The Mastiffs* (2000, p. 98). There, he says he sincerely hopes that the more patriotic breed fanciers do not come up with a breed history that claims the Boerboel is the direct descendant of the Bullenbijter dogs that were brought to South Africa by the Dutch in the 1700s, and then kept isolated in farms for 300 years before suddenly emerging with the characteristics of the hunting Mastiffs of Assurbanipal over 2000 years ago. Well, you the reader can figure out if his words were heeded.

And last but not least. The most critical part: the subtitle of Anemari Pretorius's book *The Boerboel: South Africa's Own*. The Boerboel is not South Africa's own, as that position is taken by the Rhodesian Ridgeback, which is the official breed of South Africa. But that is only the official story, as the real dog of South Africa is beyond doubt the Africanis. The title of her book most certainly should have read *The Boerboel: The Afrikaner's Mascot*.

Question 2
Did the dogs of the Adamant Kennels and the champion Bullmastiffs imported from the UK have significance in the make-up of the Boerboel?

As far as my sources go, which include the former president of the South African Bullmastiff Club, and drawing from the results of my research into the De Beers Mining Company and the very political and cultural separation of the Afrikaner from the British (these dynamics were occurring during the period in which the pedigree dogs were being brought over), it is absolutely beyond comprehension to imagine that breeders and breed fanciers of Bullmastiffs would have ever given, traded, or went into partnerships with the Afrikaner in the breeding of imported dogs.

The British had their own agendas, the aim of the Afrikaner was that of farming, they were aspiring landowners, their outlook was to breed according to their own needs, to create their own dogs. I am in no doubt that Bullmastiff type dogs were used, but the question should be how many? Which is why 30 years later we still see so much diversity within the Boerboel: every dog from every different geographical location within South Africa had different phenotypes, different uses.

Farmers traded and gave dogs for free, most breedings I am sure were accidental and coincidental. There was no plan, no strategy, for the majority of the Afrikaners at that time. We must note that there were breeders of fine Boerboels or frontier dogs/Boerhondes as they were also refered to from the early 1900s onwards, but they were so small in number. The Bullmastiff history is well recorded in South Africa and I am sure if we give even the benefit of the doubt to the Boerboel breed fanciers, we still do not know exactly how many Afrikaner farmers imported Bullmastiffs, and I mean ones with pedigrees, and introduced them to their stock? And even let us say they did use Bullmastiffs with pedigrees, exactly how many would have to be introduced to make a real significance? The old photos you see show the medley of concoctions owned by the Afrikaner, and guess what, they were all called Boerboels. Another important and significant point is the phenotype of the Bullmastiff in those days was very different to the modern Bullmastiff of today, and it was common practice for people to either assume or misinterpret a dog's origin. Again I draw your attention to the fact that like most information passed down by the oral tradition, it is very difficult to distinguish fact from anecdote and hearsay. Once again, we can refer to the fact that there was an abundance of dogs within the southern African part of the continent, so it would have been quite possible to produce Bullmastiff type dogs. This in my opinion is the inevitable conclusion, as opposed to one which claims the Adamant Kennels of the De Beers Mining Company Bullmastiffs were introduced methodically to a Boerboel breeding programme.

Question 3
You talk about the cross-breeding of the Boerboel, can you take us to the beginning of the formation of the Boerboel please?

The founding fathers of the breed acknowledged the Scottish Deerhound, the Bull Terrier types, and the old long-legged Bulldogs, Mastiffs with the possible inclusion of Bullmastiff type dogs as the initial strains, which most certainly corresponds to the frontier dog/Boerhonde dogs, not to be confused with the German Great Dane which also carried the same name but came from a different continent. As is recognised by most hunting journals for this period, the frontier dog and the Boerhonde were the same dog. In many historical writings and publications, writers refer to great detailed accounts of the Boerhonde being found on the frontier of nearly every military post within South Africa, and ultimately these great dogs which, as certain historical accounts note, became the foundation of Van Royen's dogs, later to be referred to as the lion dogs and finely the Rhodesian Ridgeback. The Afrikaaner Voortrekkers and their various sets of large clan families also kept these fine frontier dogs/Boerhondes and it was a common practice to trade them with British hunters. The Voortrekkers were employed in small numbers to assist both the American and British hunters as trackers and flushers of game. It is important to remember that these dogs were shipped over in their thousands for hunting purposes and for use as protection of the British on the kralls. In fact, the British paid a sum of money to its country's settlers for the purchase of dogs for protection, which contributed significantly to the frontier dog's evolvement.

The dog that most farmers will remember from the late eighteenth century and early 1900s to the 1930s will be the Steekbard, (meaning 'dirty beard', which it is sometimes called), The short-haired St Bernard was another likely factor in the make-up of the Boerboel, although only in certain regions of South Africa, such as the more mountainous regions, and evidence of this cross-breeding is clearly visible in the Boerboel today and was very common breeding practice for very old line breeders like De La Rey Schoeman as a very credible example.

The typical type Boerboel of De La Rey Schoeman
Source Die Boerboele Vol 2 (1988)

It is very difficult to get a straight answer from breeders in South Africa, in my own experience at least. It takes many trips, and most of them will accuse one another of cross-breeding. One has to be alert to the possibility that they might be sabotaging the work of each other for competitive reasons. The breeders I met are long gone now, they have quit the breed, or died.

The following breeds are commonly known to have been cross-bred with the Boerboel at much later dates in the timeline of the breed, in the early 1980s, when the Boerboel was starting to gain a following and increasingly became part of South African national identity: A desire to compete with other breeders spurned on a new form of cross breeding to enchance size and looks, the short-haired St Bernard, old English Mastiff, Pit Bull Terrier, Bull Terrier, Boxer, Bloodhound and Great Dane. I sincerely believe that most cross-breeding happened when the Boerboel became a financial commodity in the mid-eighties to late nineties and not in the time of the worldwide Great Depression as the breed history cites. And of course, this is only my humble opinion. Although, it should be noted that the De Beers Mining Company Bullmastiffs were not cross-bred with the Boerboel, there is the slim possibility that most unregistered Bullmastiff type dogs were used in the initial Boerboel breed, but we cannot confirm dates in the timeline. Another important point to make concerns the unreliability of breeding records which, up to the establishment of formal procedures with the establishment of SABT in 1983, were not robustly reviewed or verified, so it was always possible to lie about which stud was being used. There have been incidents of false pedigrees being documented when some individuals claimed that their females in heat were given to well-known stud males for breeding: later it emerged the well-known sire had died three years previously. Once official systems were in place for monitoring the breeding registry, and especially after DNA evidence had to be provided and checked, falsification of records became nearly impossible.

On this note, I would like to add that I am certain that even the black Boerboel possibly had other breeds of dogs introduced to it before black became officially accepted by the breed standard on 11 July 2015. Cross-breeding of the Boerboel has certainly been happening in the United Kingdom (as well as in other countries) from the time of the earliest records to mid-2000. Thankfully, SABBS has acknowledged these discrepancies and since 1 June 2014 DNA profiling has been mandatory. It is a great step in the right direction.

Question 4
Can you now condense the modern history of the Boerboel into a few paragraphs?

The Boerboel is a mix of, predominantly, European hunting dogs and companion dogs that managed to survive the arduous trip across the oceans to South Africa. This mix was bred with indigenous South African dogs to greatly increase their chances of survival and immunity to African diseases. This resulted in a more hardy dog that is now referred to as the frontier dog or Boerhonde. This was, in my opinion at least, the true model for the Boerboel.

Below are typically fine examples of the frontier dog or in my opinion the real hardy Boerboel dog which should be kept alive for the working Boerboel enthusiast.

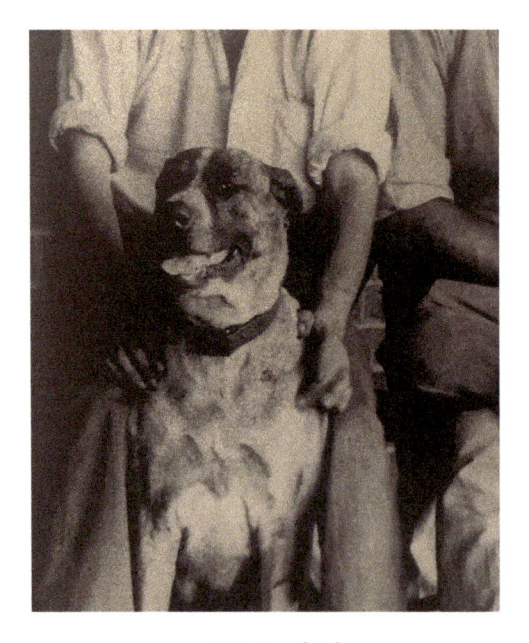

1920 Boerboel
Source Linda Costa Rhodesian Ridgeback Pioneers

1930 Typical Frontier Type Dogs Boerhondes
Source Linda Costa Rhodesian Ridgeback Pioneers

A fine example of the frontier dog Boerhonde and served with war nurses on the frontier
Source Linda Costa Rhodesian Ridgeback Pioneers

A fine example of the common frontier type dogs commonly available within the frontier and voortrekker camps, long before the breed became official.
Source Linda Costa Rhodesian Ridgeback Pioneers

FACT OR FICTION: THE AWAKENING

The same frontier dogs
Source Australian War Memorial Archives

Boerboels are often commented on with disdain and amusement by the foreign travellers in historical literature, but why this is so I cannot say. Ironically, the South African Boerboel breed registries present the Boerboel's history as hailing from an ancient classical Western civilisation, as do other Boerboel breed registries across the world. Whereas the Rhodesian Ridgeback community gives full recognition to their dog's true ancestor, the Africanis. Please bear in mind that both the Boerboel and the Rhodesian Ridgeback are from the same foundation dog: the frontier dog or Boerhonde. (Below are examples of the Rhodesian Ridgeback and the Boerboel, pictured just as described by many breed historians and on many Boerboel websites. The Boerboel photo (*right*) was supplied by Casper Labuschagne, stepson of the late Lucan Van De Merwe who was the founding father of the Boerboel breed standard. As you can see, the similarity between the Ridgeback and the Boerboel is most certainly the result of each type descending from the same frontier/Boerhonde dog type which for me is the definitive Boerboel.)

A Rhodesian Ridgeback at the Bulawayo Show 1925
Source T. C. Hawley The Rhodesian Ridgeback

The old farm utility type Boerboel of the true voortrekker
Source Casper Lausbaschagne

This fine frontier dog or Boerhonde taken and inherited by the Voortrekker has been developed into a number of types. Once any dog was considered under the ownership of an established Afrikaaner farmer it was for all intents and purposes considered a Boerbul or farmer's bull in Afrikaans. There have been the Rustervacht dogs and their northern Natal strains, which were of a pretty heavy Mastiff type, the blonde dogs of the eastern part of South Africa, and the old Retief strains over 100 years old with predominantly woolly coats (and noted to be the more aggressive variety). These latter dogs would have most certainly resembled the Vuilbaard types. Then we have the piebalds of the Vrede district in the Drakensburg foothills, and last but not least, the black Boerboels, which had been in existence long before the controversy arose over them in early 2007. The black Boerboel was confirmed and witnessed by Jan Muller, who, in 2007 was a judge of the HBSA, and believed these black dogs had predominantly Great Dane blood in them. (Once again, in no uncertain terms, I reiterate, black dogs existed within the Afrikaner community and it was common practice to consider all Boer farmers' dogs as being Boerboels, so we should assume no less for the black Boerboels.) In isolated cases, some modern-day Boerboels can be found with ridges on their backs, hearkening back to their shared ancestry with their cousin, the Ridgeback.

In 1983 we finally saw some form of recognition and establishment for the breed formerly known as farmers' dogs, or, as some called it, farmers' bulls. Today they still can be found in different colours, shapes sizes, and coat textures – even different breed names, one of which being the Mouzer Mastiff. Interestingly, as recently as 2016 a movement of people tried to resurrect the Boerboel under the new name of the Plasboel.

The Boerboel was a product of the Afrikaner farming community. Its phenotype, uses and functions were determined by the farmers, who in turn were compelled by the demands of their work, be it hunting, accompanying the famer on the veldt, working as flock guardians, watchdogs, guard dogs, pulling sleeper logs or bull carts. Or sitting on the porch at home. The end of the apartheid era, which was finally phased out between 1991 and 1996, saw an explosion in the sales of Boerboels. The *Farmers Weekly* advertised the Boerboel as a so-called 'racist watchdog bred especially for South African needs'. The advertising was paid for by the Herstigte National Party, an ultra-right-wing Nationalist movement. Jaap Maarais was at that time the leader of the party and was an avid enthusiast of the Boerboel breed, as its significance in the old Dutch Calvinist tradition of white superiority was of huge importance to Maarais. Apartheid is a very old word. For those wishing to understand, in Afrikaans it means separateness, or the state of being apart, i.e. apart-hood.

The Boerboel earned its name through its infamous reputation in prisons across the US and Europe, as well as in the fringes of society. In prison institutions it is quite common to find inmates discussing which dogs are the real phenomenon. (This notorious criminal culture was one of the factors which culminated in the ban of this breed from France, which many people are not even aware about.) As a direct result of its increasing popularity among prisoners, the Boerboel quickly gained huge momentum within the mainstream pet community as well, spurred on by this new form of economy for the disenfranchised white classes. Suddenly, neighbours, aunties, cousins and everyone in sight were becoming breeders of Boerboels, expanding a market which, in South Africa, had pretty much been a cottage industry. It is certainly at this stage that marketing activity promoting the Boerboel took a leap forward, which created a surge of new followers who were unaware that they were buying into a false, mythologised western idea that imagined the Boerboel was an ancient, purely Syrian-blooded

Mastiff breed, bred to guard and catch hares for children, able to kill wild animals; an exotic Mastiff that was bred in the environment of the formidable frontier.

But the reality is that the present-day Boerboel has probably spent at least three to five generations living like sheep or cattle, in some cases like battery chickens, in kennel facilities. They had probably spent the previous two generations only ever sleeping on the porch. The unfortunate reality is that there is just no data or working evidence to support the claim of the putative protagonist, the 'Working Boerboel'.

By the time of the mid-2000s in the US and afar, for those with limited knowledge of the Boerboel or who had invested so much in this marketing propaganda, there was simply no turning back, too much money had passed hands, too many dreams were involved, too much hope had been invested. It was easier to perpetuate the false propaganda than go against the established status quo. Today, the way people celebrate the history of the Boerboel reminds one of those who once sang and waved flags in ceremony to celebrate Hitler; they all reaffirmed each other's belief in a charade.

The history of the Boerboel as it is presented in current marketing propaganda, as I see it, is an unfortunate, absolute myth.

Question 5
You mention the work of both Bert Grabbe and Johan Du Preez and challenge their historical rhetoric. Please explain your point of view.

Johan Du Preez wrote a highly detailed and informative reflection of the Boerboel. However, although on the face of it he seems to be correct in his assumption on the frontier dog – he states that the frontier dog had little Boel blood in it, which he explains by the dog's longer legs and pricked ears – by referring to the photographic evidence available now we can easily see that this assumption is completely innacurate.

One has to bear in mind that it was (and still is) common for the Afrikaner farmer to project his own definition onto the Boerboel and other dogs from his own region to suit his uses. It is certainly the case that the frontier dog is the dog referred to in the campsite stories of old and is where the Boerboel became a legend. There is a certain phenotype and aesthetic as well as psychological make-up required for a dog to withstand and survive the sometimes minus temperatures of Africa in the nights, the scorching heat of the day and the long prolonged periods running along the caravans, all of which takes its toll. The dog's coat and density, the dog's ability to breathe and – more importantly – to dispel body heat as well as resist the tsetse fly, yellow fever and other parasites indigenous to Africa, all require hardiness. The frontier dog of both the British and the Afrikaner in the early period was both naturally and part-artificially selected; it was a common choice for both Afrikaner and British settlers. It was a longer legged dog than today's Boerboel and had a narrower chest, came in different colours (black, white, brindle, red and piebald), but still had the predominantly wide skull and deep muzzle (varying in size to a lesser extent than today's dog). In my opinion, Johan Du Preez missed a vital link in that he did not comment on the fact that the same foundation dog was used to create two breeds.

The emphasis of the Bullmastiff over the frontier type in Boerboel breeding selections would have been consistent with a period when political and social life became sedentary and the Afrikaner moved to the cities. But in 1983 when SABBS was established, the founding fathers of the Boerboel made what I consider to be a catastrophic decision by choosing a breed standard that conformed to aesthetics and not function. The frontier dog was not conformed to. The formulation of a breed standard that did not enhance the frontier dog, despite its remarkable place in Boer history, was a tragedy in respect of the tradition of the Afrikaner farmer and the immigrants who toiled on the farmland for over four centuries. Certainly, when it was established in 1983 the choice was made to set a uniform, structured breed standard that selected for the more Mastiff type dogs. Nonetheless, the river of DNA does not lie, it is a living history of our ancestors, a carefully coded sequence of probabilities that are reinforced by nature and environment. The reality is that, despite the rigidity of a breed standard set in 1983 and enforced from 1988, many fine examples of this fine frontier or Boerhonde dog can yet be found today. A most typical example can be seen in the Boerboels with defined ridges on their backs, necks and shoulders, and fine, high-scoring crowns, while the tight-skinned and tight-lipped running type of large hound pup that is born from heavy, loose-skinned, jowly Mastiff type Boerboel is another example.

Like Du Preez, Bert Grabbe spoke with authority in his history of the Boerboel, but he too showed signs of promoting a formulated marketing strategy that distorts the history of the Boerboel. In my conversations with the various founders of the SABT (Johan De Jager, Dr Andre Du Toit, Lucas Van De Merwe, Johan Du Preez, and Mrs Owen Read) on that day at the Senekal school, a prescribed Afrikaner viewpoint of the history of the breed was formalised, with the help of Dr Daan Marais from Louis Trichardt and later Dr P. L. Milstein. The idea was simply to stick to a prescribed historical theory. In time, this prescribed historical rhetoric gained in both credibility and momentum to become considered the holy grail of historical fact regarding the Boerboel from the mid-1980s to this day of writing.

In both the Rhodesian Ridgeback fancier community and Boerboel fancier community there seems to exist a staunch militant defence of their complete independent autonomy, even a prejudice or xenophobia against each other's identities, despite both belonging to the same land and soil. They find very little common ground in rationalising their co-existence although both are connected via the dog that, in a manner of speaking, gave birth to the two breeds. However, we can also see by the writings of Sandra Swart in her article 'Dogs and Dogma' (2003), published in *South African Historical Journal*, that the breeds of dogs are usually a reflective of the communities and is always a stand for national heritage and social identity. So, it is safe to conclude that the 'official' Boerboel breed history we are given is biased towards the dog's Dutch and Afrikaner heritage.

Question 6
In Chapter 3 you mentioned the many splits that were frequent within the Afrikaner community. Is that a cultural issue?

Yes, the fractious splits are most certainly a cultural issue. We can see that by looking at the writings of Frank Welsh and Major T. C. Hawley, where they report certain patterns of behaviour repeating in the Afrikaner community, and unfortunately, I imagine that solidarity does not sit well in their blood. Perhaps this might not be convincing enough for the reader, so let me break it down. The formation of SABT was followed very quickly by a new splinter group, the HBSA, which in turn was followed by EBASSA. From thereon in, further splinter groups broke off, such as Boerboel International, to name just one example, and from these even more splinters continue to occur. Even today at this time of writing we have BEU, BBA, IBBF, and a further multitude cropping up in the USA. It is the culmination of top-down management practices whereby the management dictates the behaviour of its employees at ground level.

For me the 'multitude of cooks' situation as described by Major T. C. Hawley – over 27 years prior to the formation of the first breed registry for the Boerboel – provides, among other data, a huge window into the problematic internal fighting of Afrikaner society and its mindset. That was discussed decades ago, well before the formation of the first initial breed establishment. The unfortunate reality is that while both KUSA, BI and FCI have made every attempt at negotiating with the current registry and the other registries, there has still been no clear dialogue nor a conclusion on the matter of how to unify and become one sole organisation. This situation is most certainly the result of there being too many cooks in the proverbial kitchen.

The Afrikaner, as noted by Frank Welsh, has displayed an historic pattern of internal dispute and fighting within its own society. Whether this is entirely cultural or not remains to be seen. The only way one might determine this would be to allow another country or another continent to lead the way for this breed. I sincerely hope that progress can be allowed, and the breed gain its rightful place under the watchful eye of the FCI and the international arena. At the time of writing, there is another organisation forming, while both Namibia and Russia have recently made attempts to secure legitimate status for this breed.

Question 7
Do you believe that the current breed registry SABBS has no legitimacy?

On the contrary, let me make my position very clear. First, I am a working dog enthusiast. Secondly, I am affectionate towards this given breed, and thirdly, last but not least, I am a consumer of this product. There is a very clear legal position as to the registration and appraisal procedures for the Boerboel. SABBS is the only active legal organisation operating in South Africa allowed to give registration (or an entry in the SA studbook) to a Boerboel. I might not be a huge fan of the organisation, but that's not relevant. My only interest is to work my dog, appraise it and be happy. If I was a breeder, I would comply with the criteria of the legitimate registry, breed my dogs and raise my puppies according to best practice. This sounds very simple – and that is because it really is.

Had there not been a multitude of cooks directing a herd of sheep then we would have had some form of FCI recognition by now. As of this day, outside South Africa the Boerboel breed is technically nothing more than a farm dog and increasing numbers of breeders and individuals are becoming disillusioned and are simply not registering their Boerboels. But as far as I am concerned, there is no legitimate avenue to pursue other than subscribe to the only legal entity and organisation for this breed, and I pray these internal fights and political alliances become redundant. From a personal perspective, I would only register my dogs with the legal and official organisation, which, at the time of writing, is SABBS. This does not reflect the fact that BI is not valid, it is still a breed registry and both professional and diligent. Please bear in mind that I am neither promoting or condoning SABBS. I am simply respecting their official status and complying with the procedures required to have my dog appraised legitimately with the more mainstream registry, it is really that simple. Consider a human parallel: there is a legitimate avenue to becoming a brain surgeon or a lawyer, usually it is called university and there is no shortcut.

If we want solidarity for this breed community then we simply need to comply with the governing legal body, otherwise the superfluous number of cooks will always be a problem and the host of differing, bickering organisations will provide nothing more than a range of different appraisal scores for the same dogs. At some point, a person decides to buy a Boerboel and then they might take it upon themselves to show and appraise their dog. At which point in this process did they feel that the only legal registry was not good enough for them? We now have a group of individuals, as described in Chapter 8 'Final Curtain Call', who then create new dissident groups. At what time was the influence of others within this breed community more important than the legitimate relationship you have with your dog? I believe that at some point within this breed community, the unique relationship that your dog was intended to give you becomes insignificant the minute that your dog exposes you to a new social circle of illusory and, at best, superficial friends.

Another perspective providing insight is that of the UK, where there are two main working dog registries and both give out working dog books (although both have pretty much the same resources). There is a clear distinction between the two clubs. The club of my choice for the period of 2009 to 2016 is certainly the club that had the most difficult judges and more militant and diligent working clubs. The other organisation seemed to display an amateur and cavalier attitude to the intense commitment and work ethic required in this industry, and the standards it accepted fell below the industry average. If I were to make comparisons between the current breed registries in the Boerboel world today I would only endorse the two principal, current breed registries: one, SABBS, for displaying the most professional attitude and maintaining the most meticulous registry to date as well as for the fact that it is the only major breeding registry that has been recognised by South Africa's government authority, the AIA to preserve the ennoblement of this breed and maintain it into the future; and two, Boerboel International (BI), which has risen like a phoenix above the ashes, has been defiant of the muses of superficial fashion, and has stood steadfast in holding onto its status quo in the face of the bickering masses. I sincerely wish that the founding president of BI could have taken the helm at SABBS, so as to apply their leadership qualities to SABBS to help emancipate the world's breed fanciers and Boerboel community alike. On a personal accord, I feel BI deserves especial recognition and respect for its leadership qualities, which put it in a much higher league than the multitude of other registries that, in my humble opinion, operate like chancers and opportunists. At this time of writing there appears to be in 2018 a new person involved in the leadership of Boerboel International and we wish him success; however, we hope that with any

Question 8

You discuss the super kennel syndrome and the breeding of Boerboels today. Can you elaborate on these issues?

The socio-economic dynamics at play in the Boerboel breeding industry in South Africa since the 1990s have spawned a multitude of super kennels, along with endless puppy mills where breeders produce over 20 litters a year. I have witnessed kennels where Boerboels were kept in little chicken wire cages – over 200 of them. Sure, some of these modern, liberal breeders' kennels look prim and proper, but it is what is within them that is of significance.

I visited over 47 breeders during my month in South Africa in 2006–2007. Many of these Boerboels had poor movement, were overfed to look big on internet photos and were of a very timid and fearful nature, while yet some dogs displayed heightened sensations, which stems from very inadequate socialisation and management. It is most certain that a large majority have had no character evaluation and no formal testing of the innate breed qualities that the original founders had talked of in their romantic literature.

A young female fattened up to look impressive for a westernised market in 2006
Source Author

The same female after quarantine, 1 months later stripped and built back up in the UK
Source Author

I am sure you will agree that the above picture I have painted, while not a reflection of every breeder in South Africa (undoubtedly, some are conscientious), is reason enough for those with ethical values to boycott the poor practices described above, and to help make breeders conform to a much higher international standard of breeding born from a market demand dictated by the consumer, i.e. health evaluations, temperament testing evaluations and a more grown-up approach to the mother and pups' whelping process, which in my opinion should include far greater socialisation for the pups along with other novel stimulations, the importance of which we discussed in previous chapters.

Here is a classic example of a Whelping Box, containing material such as wood, metal and plastic for the pups to bite, as well as bottles of stones, wind chimes and various novelties.
Source Author.

Open outdoor spaces contain many environmental novelties, helping expand the wiring to the brain and nervous system.
Source Author.

Question 9
You mention the validity of the prey drive in the Chapter, 'The Importance of Aggression', can you elaborate?

Displaying huge prey drive
Source Author.

Prey drive captured in poetry, sadly loosing fashion –
Source Author

In early 2000 to the end of 2010 there was a very prominent Presa Canario breeder in the UK, he was well known and well respected, not just in the UK, but across the whole world. In my time in Russia and the USA when his name was mentioned it was clear to me that he was both well respected and well known. His dogs were considered serious, the definition of which means they would not back down from a threat and would be able to handle decoy pressure. Of course, this is a double-edged sword to the owner, and is an anomaly suffered by Boerboel breeders the world over. Although serious, these dogs had no real working motivation or desire. There was a movement of individuals within Germany who had already been working Presa Canarios from quite some time, they were more militant and disciplined in their goals, they had more ambitious demands for the working Presa Canario, for what they found was that selecting for a more hunting type of Presa culminated in a much more balanced and rounded dog, more motivated, healthier, faster and more agile, and more motivated in particular to work and bite. But, more importantly, they displayed the required amount of prey drive: the dog was in general a lot more flexible in its ability to work consistently. So, everything that people considered to be correct selection practice previously was all of a sudden proven to be incorrect.

Source Satty Gill

Source Satty Gill

At this point I must make it clear that these Presa Canario breeders in Germany did not discover this new selection theory over the internet – it was discovered by trial and error, through blood, sweat and tears, and over many years after many mistakes. Subsequently, the breeder of these lesser prey-driven dogs is no longer breeding Pressas today. Well, why is that, you might ask? This very famous Presa breeder had selected dogs on thin nerve, the result of which was a heightened defensive-protective instinct, which, as discussed previously, comes from the same place as fear. It reminds us, of course, of the Flat Earthers described in Chapter 8 'Final Curtain Call'.

But let us now put the Boerboel into context. In my own experience, the majority of Boerboel puppies have been very flat in terms of the hunting/prey drive, which in the course of natural selection would have meant the puppy going without food and subsequently dying. However, selecting for and choosing for an enhanced prey drive will lead to a change in phenotype, i.e. longer muzzle length, less droopy skin, longer legs for running, and a slightly sharper temperament, it also can make for a little flightiness which is not a problem for those of us whom train more advanced behaviours. The Mallinois is an extreme example of an incredibly flighty dog and yet it is the most sought-after working dog in the world. Selecting for the hunting type that displays more prey drive will lead to a more balanced Mastiff in the Boerboel breed and a more versatile and useful dog.

Source Satty Gill

Source Satty Gill

The archetypal working Pressa, notice the tinn bone density and non exagerated chest size.
Source Satty Gill

Archetypal working Pressa type, again both athletic and workable size.
Source Satty Gill

More importantly, proper selection will ensure that the Boerboel's ability to hunt, run and bite, and kill will lead to the creation of Boerboels with well-defined predatory behaviour. And, in my opinion, enhancing this with ultra-dominance will create the perfect working type specimens. To achieve this, you will certainly need a huge contingent of like-minded individuals to follow this same goal, and to extract such material from the mother source in South Africa where you will find more isolated examples of these types in greater abundance. We can see from the many social media marketing campaigns online depicting colossal, wide-chested and small-legged types of Boerboel that most commercial breeders are not selecting for the predatory working type I outlined above.

And, of course, this leads us to the more significant point to consider, which concerns the breeders' market. In order for us to give the Boerboel the name of 'Working Boerboel', the international working dog community must be given a market to choose from, offering an abundance of quality puppies from breeders and from proven stock. The fact that this market is not readily available indicates a lack of participant breeders. The disorganised state of the Boerboel breed industry makes it almost impossible to fathom how any working dog person is able to independently research the vast multitude of breeders and potential matings, as well as every single dog's temperament, not to mention how they gauge the degree of prey drive for the purposes of work that any one dog displays.

After taking into consideration all of the above challenges, we next have to think of the working dog people from the US, the British Isles and Europe having to either travel to South Africa or source dogs over the internet (a resource which, in my own experience, is never comprehensive). In addition, we must think of the financial costs, the training costs, the time that is required to invest in this pursuit, the travel expenses, and the huge risk factors relating to the unknowability of the dog's eventual health and possible temperament after the probationary training phases. One does not have to be a rocket scientist to realise there seem to be a number of vital issues to address.

Question 10
In the Chapter 'The Importance of Aggression', you mention the value and merits of the defence drive. Can you please elaborate on this?

Boerboels, like most Bull breeds, have a very high defence drive and I have seen first-hand that Boerboels with a high strong defence drive tend to be bully types. In my experience of Bull breed people and their training methods, the defensive form of training tends to be favoured. But, as with the prey drive, a strong defence drive carries with it potentially problematic behaviour. The defence drive comes from the same place as fear or concern and is easily tapped into, requiring very little effort from helper trainers and decoys to stimulate it. In the working dog world it is well known that the defence drive can be troubling and highly stressful for dogs when it is activated for prolonged periods. The effect is observable in the dog's behaviour during the latter part of training, or during intense testing, in that the bite of the Boerboel starts to falter, and chewing behaviours and retargeting lower down or higher up the arm tend to occur. Those behaviours are the inevitable side effects of a conflict between the selection for neoteny, biddability, and passive characteristics and a drive state that is inherent in nearly every species of animal. It is easy work at best to get Boerboels to bite under this pretext, however, the results are not the most desirable for consistency and reliability.

This dog displays clear signs of neoteny. Source Author.

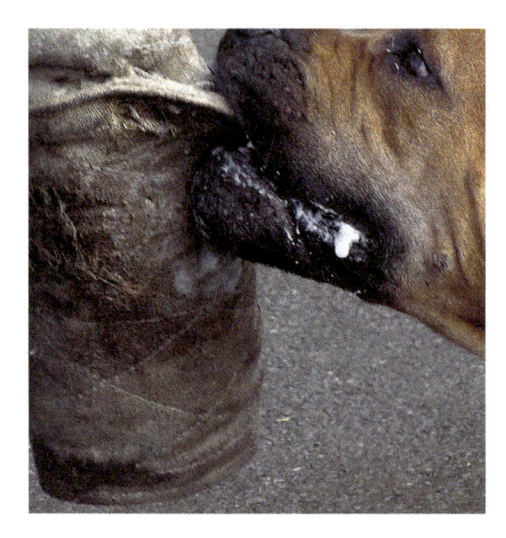

A clear case of conflict in the dog caused by neoteny. Source Author.

Another issue tends to occur with the more heavy, Mastiff-type of Boerboels kept as pets in households that do not practice sound dog management, which working, service, sport and work enthusiasts recommend. These dogs tend to be larger in size than other Boerboels, and they know they are big, so if they are raised in home environments where they are not given boundaries then it can lead to the dogs displaying problematic behaviour whereby they display authority over its owners, which is a behaviour not necessarily associated with natural, true ultra-dominance. In order for future evaluation to be effective in such cases, there needs to be various trials and tests that are able to identify true dominance and prey drive and defence drive alike. In common breed tests the current method of protection of handler suffices for the pet market, but it is insufficient for the mainstream international working dog consumer. The merits of the defence drive are that it can manipulate healthy, strong aggression to create a natural guard and watchdog, but there is also, alas, a price to pay, which is why the prey drive is critical to any balanced training programme. Defence drive has merits that provide longevity in the protection of itself and its handler, defence drive has value for selecting and testing for the forward element of this drive, which when tested with ultra-dominant examples displays huge fight drive and the ability to extinguish the concern with good strong violent attitude.

Question 11

Can you please explain the value of temperament testing criteria?

A temperament test will consist of around 10-12 assesment stations, this one will show a heavy can of stones dropped to measure recovery time.
Source Author

During the early foundation stages of the breed's history (certainly prior to the formation of SABBS), we can be sure that most farmers bred and traded dogs for themselves; the dogs' monetary value was of no significance. The moment the financial aspect became important, an authority became necessary: to regulate dog breeding practices and rubber stamp the claims made by breeders about the dogs they were trading and breeding. Just like every other industry needs a regulatory body, so too does the Boerboel breed industry, to define and uphold a set of objective breeding ideals that are based on fact and not hearsay. At the time of writing, I know of only one organisation in the world that does temperament testing in the Boerboel. And that is BI.

Although I do not prescribe to the style of the BI's temperament test, I strongly support its efforts at making a sincere attempt at it. That is not to say that their testing is especially different to the mainstream temperament tests available for other breeds, but for the purposes of evaluation on an international working dog platform which would no doubt involve stringent requirements, I feel the BI test is not exhaustive. (There is another organisation at the small scale European stage level which has toyed with the idea of a temperament test, but unfortunately it does not appear to be making any formal commitment to developing one.)

The Boerboel in the historical preamble of its breed standards must be courageous and self-assured, it must be able to protect its territory and people. These are not my words. So it is safe to assume that in addition to tests that look at the movement, nerves and general disposition of the dog, there should be a temperament test assessing the dog's ability to show courage, protective behaviour and a solid, sociable, confident character around people and crowds. Such a test should be mandatory and constitute one of the qualifying criteria for the breeding of the Boerboel. The test must be independently performed, and independently judged by a non-breed judge or international judge of non-breed affiliation to ensure transparency and prevent judges currying favour from friends or being biased for or against specific breeders. (In the world of German Shepherd evaluation, i.e. IPO it is common for competitors to trial their dogs when their friends are the judges. This practice should not be copied.)

Unfortunately, mandatory temperament testing for the Boerboel is not the case now nor has it ever been the case, since the creation of SABT in 1983 to the present day. In fact, ironically, bite work – which is part of any temperament test – was banned by SABT not so long ago, in early 2000, simultaneous to the ban of the Boerboel in France, which was in response to underground drug racketeers using the Boerboel. The popularity of the Boerboel in criminal society made the breed infamous internationally and catapulted much of its overseas sales. As we can see in the image below, which appeared in *Die Boerboel* (1988 Vol. 2 p. 9), bite work was seen to promote the Boerboel as a protector of Afrikaner heritage and adversary to any would-be trespassers.

Source Die Boerboele Vol 2 (1988)

The Boerboel's reputation as protector of Afrikaner heritage has been noted by the well-regarded scholar, Sandra Swart, who also describes the Boerboel as a mascot for Afrikaner cultural identity. In her article 'Dogs and Dogma' (Swart 2003, p. 24) she states that the Boerboel was purportedly first promoted by the Herstige National Party (a staunchly right-wing party, discussed in Chapter 3) as a protector of white homes. The HNP is proud of its late leader Jaap Marais' knowledge of the Boerboel. In the Mail and Guardian on 27 June 1997 the Boerboel appears advertised as a 'rascist watchdog', bred specifically for 'South African circumstances'. One can only imagine that economic pressures effected a change to the breed's image, from that of protector of Afrikaner (farmer's) heritage to that of a consumer pet industry commodity just a few years later.

The board of SABT finally deemed it fit to lift the ban on bite work however, with a clause stating that only in a professional capacity and only those in the service industry could bite work training with the Boerboel breed be considered acceptable. And despite all this, in over 34 years we have seen absolutely no constructive formation of a working test to evaluate the Boerboel. And that, for me, shows how very short-sighted are the goals, if there are any, of the breed's ambassadors. The situation also reflects what the consumer in general really wants, which perhaps is not a working breed.

Question 12
You discussed the importance of pack-keeping. Why, exactly?

In the days of the treks and kralls, and certainly in the 50s, 60s, and 70s, it was quite a common practice for the Boer farmer to keep his dogs in packs, as he was able to evaluate and assess his dogs on their own merit and without prejudice, and of course there was always an element of natural selection at play. The farmer's choice of pack-keeping and the process of natural selection worked primarily hand-in-hand, and this combination was a prerequisite to developing stable, non-aggressive dogs. The farmer's role was crucial; he assessed and evaluated what he was breeding, he was both judge and executioner, culling bad-tempered pack members, or those with shy, nervous, fearful, or skittish work temperaments. He was able to monitor the pack's dynamics and see how dominance plays an integral and critical role in the breeding of both high ranking male and female dogs, however, of course this is not always the case as most dominant males should and would breed with every female in heat. (This is a phenomenon that can only be controlled in humans by social and religious codes of conduct, but it would require a separate book to explain such complexities.) Natural selection is a process involving both sexual opportunity and a high sex drive and is absolutely critical for any species. The ability to replicate one's own coded sequence of genes many times over is what our very fabric was designed to do. Those pack-keeping days have almost completely disappeared in the modern era of 2015 onwards, with very few breeders across the world supporting this practice. It has also disappeared consequent to the advent of an overseas market that is mostly driven by an interest in owning single dogs for purposes unrelated to farm work.

Source James Brennan

We have discussed the importance of the dog's neurological and sensory development, which are fundamental to breed development. In pack-keeping this development is always maximised. The ability of trusted, educated breeders to assess their pack members' innate natural behaviours is crucial for ensuring the best development of this breed's working characteristics, which should hark back to the frontier or Boerhonde dog stage it once was. This does not hold in the case of sport work, where, perhaps, we are wanting to develop individual characters; for a working Boerboel, pack-keeping is about breeding, which is an entirely different matter. The Boerboel, the frontier dogs and the foundation Ridgeback were all raised as pack dogs, as watchdogs and as visual as well as frontline defence. The culture of buying South African dogs has been shaped by the promotion of pack-keeping and dominance by some farmers, well before the lure of potentially lucrative international sales bore any effect, and by the hard processes these dogs had to go through when they were working farm dogs. It is true that these dogs went through incredibly tough experiences when they worked on farms, defending the farms from large predators, and this is why they became known as legendary working dogs.

Question 13

We hear a lot of talk and read a lot of discussions about the amazing ability of this breed's threat perception instinct. Can you explain it, please?

The threat perception instinct, as it is described in numerous articles and writings (and has been eloquently discussed by numerous breeders with me, in person) is far from the reality, in my opinion. The concept is that the Boerboel instinctively knows when its owner is threatened and will immediately assess the threat and take action to neutralise the danger. In fact, all dogs have the ability to feel or sense danger, and all dogs, or at least most breeds of dogs, have the ability to read the physical body language of an owner or handler. In the working dog world, we call this non-verbal communication and it is the first form of language that dogs learn, but the fact that it has been ascribed exclusively to the Boerboel and is now marketed as one of the

Boerboel's best qualities does a disservice to all dogs. The Boerboel has no exclusive right to this status and in fact, the Boerboel's ability to act on perceived threats is still a cause of debate, as unfortunately, there is no authority to conduct tests for or evaluate working ability and courage. Without such tests, it is very difficult to establish the level of working ability and courage in a Boerboel, even if we give the benefit of the doubt to those claiming that the modern South African Boerboel will take the correct action for the appropriate threat, i.e. engage, bite and commit.

Now I would like to bring to your attention a 2007 article titled 'Boerboel Temperament' written by Craig Bloom from Ataraxia Kennels in Australia. The article has been published on various internet breed fancier forums and sites. In the paragraph subheaded 'Threat Perception Instinct', Bloom argues that the best Boerboel should rely on its threat perception instinct, and our failure to identify this is a failure to recognise what makes a Boerboel unique. He further adds that there are much better dogs suited to bite work than the Boerboel and that if one wanted to select for this attribute within this breed, it would be best to cross-breed the Boerboel with another breed, i.e. Pitbulls, bandogs, Pressas, Rottweilers etc. Bloom also narrates an anecdotal tale of a young female Boerboel (offspring of his dog Napoleon) who chased a local thief and drug addict out of the store, but did not physically stop or engage with the threat. Bloom also discusses his dog Napoleon whom he said would always stick by his leg; he believed this should be the selection process for this breed. He goes as far as to say there is no dog that he could cross-breed with the Boerboel that would enhance its threat perception instinct. He claims that his dog Napoleon was the most impressive and serious dog ever encountered in the 30-year career of a two-time world champion trainer and behaviour expert. There are several issues I will take to task with Bloom's article.

Let me start by exposing how this article was legitimised to the wider novice community. First, there is no such thing as a two-time world champion trainer. Secondly, a champion trainer in what, exactly? Thirdly, in the twenty-first century, there can be no such thing as a qualified dog trainer, since there is no formal qualification offered by a reputable, recognised university or school of higher education. There is a leading herding breed trainer, who is one of the most accomplished dog trainers in the world: a seven-time world qualifier and five-time national US qualifier, who in total entered 24 world championships. He states that he is not a qualified trainer. The US has one of the highest numbers of dog trainers and online trainers in the world, but again, these trainers are not qualified in a mainstream, conventional sense, that is to say, holding a degree from a leading university resulting in a BA, BSc, MA, MSc, or PhD. These trainers are only qualified by their own merits and what they have achieved for themselves and their clients. It is their experience and past results which merit their status of being 'qualified'. Caution must be taken in drawing any conclusions from prevailing opinions and unverified articles.

The most suitable types of dog in the world today for staying close to you, never leaving your side and perceiving threat (like no other breed I have ever seen), which have been genetically selected for these purposes, are the flock guardian breeds of central and eastern Asia, i.e. the Ovcharka and the Kangal (the latter does not even need to be trained for protecting). Due to their intimidating size and vocal gestures, flock guardian breeds create a definite deterrent to potential threats, but studies looking at the predatory motor patterns of these dogs have found those patterns to be weak (Coppinger & Coppinger, 2001). Such dogs may be the best instinctive, personal protection dogs in the world, but they are better at deterring threat through their intimidating appearance than by engaging directly with the threat. A methodical approach to choosing selection criteria has been taken in breeding these dogs, based firstly on the necessity to keep the sheep or flock safe from the flock dogs' predatory behaviours, and secondly on the high number of sedentary hours at work required in the pastoral regions where they are put to work. These requirements would not be fulfilled by, say, a Mallinois or a German Shepherd very easily.

In comparison to the herding breeds, the Boerboel is readily acknowledged as one of the most reliable personal protection dogs, simply by design by current mainstream pet industry consumers when we go back and look at the history of the frontier dog we are quite clearly able to ascertain that nearly all its predatory motor patterns would have most certainly have been bred and selected for at least in part by natural selection. This very statement about Boerboels sticking close supports the ideology that we should now select for everything against what the Boer dog was selected for if at all this is a true statement, to which there is no factual evidence about the selection criteria for this breed in either pre-SABT days, or post-SABT days and promoted in past oral history. One should also consider the submissive nature of this breed and the current selection preference for this attribute, as well as neoteny, in breeding programmes, which seeks to make the Boerboel totally reliant upon and in submission to its master. Submissiveness is a trait that can give the illusion that this breed is loyal or is protecting you. A dog might stick to its owner's side because it wants to feel safe and protected, or simply more secure. In the world of working dogs, we learn that every animal (this applies to humans, too) always chooses an action which will benefit its position in life; ensuring safety for itself is a dog's principal priority. Bloom's analysis on cross-breeding the Boerboel for improving its bite work abilities, because he deems it not inherently suitable to do bite work, is contradicted by my own findings, which have been made in the real world, on the field and on the streets across the world.

There is one point I will agree with Bloom on. If the current market demand breeds and selects for overly heavy, loose-skinned and wrinkly faced dogs, then I agree that they are not suitable for bite work. However, one has to take into consideration the fact that the original frontier dogs displayed a far different phenotype to the current breed fashion has created today. Evidence against Bloom's hypothesis that the Boerboel will not independently engage with a threat can be found in the articles and adverts in the *Farmers Weekly* that marketed the Boerboel for the purpose of family frontline defence, and in historical accounts (discussed in Chapters 1–3) that give accounts of these dogs performing amazing courageous acts of bravery.

If we listen to the marketing propaganda of a few isolated individuals then than we are forgetting the hardships, pain, suffering and blood spilt by the Afrikaner pioneers of the breed, and the propaganda does very little to promote the very sound principles of breeding that the Boer farmers and trekkers practised, which were to develop mentally stable, fast, healthy, agile, low-maintenance dogs.

Completely untested and a natural strong very deep bite, most certainly innate
Source Author

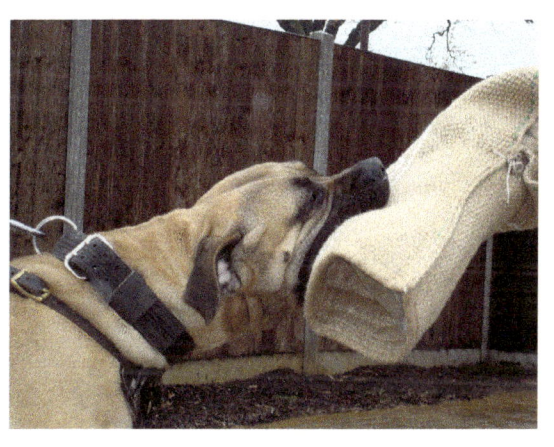

Deep strong and very commited
Source J. Sheldon

Question 14
You discussed the importance of dominance for the Boerboel breed and its significance in selection practices. Can you elaborate further on these points?

Nothing will bring me more pleasure, this subject is close to my heart. We have read about the controlled experiments of Belyayev, the writings of Konrad Lorenz, the detailed works of established ethologists, scientists, academics and behaviourists, and we have discussed breeding for neoteny, which means the retaining of juvenile behaviours. In the old days of the real Boer dog or frontier dog, my sources of historical information in South Africa recall that their dogs were loyal, but confident, self-assured and most importantly self-sufficient. These traits are the opposite of those created by neoteny, such as neediness, sickliness, self-doubt and a need of constant reassurance.

For a farmer, a working service man, a dog sport competitor, a military operative or any other individual who requires dogs for work or protection, neoteny (or what others describe as biddability) in a Boerboel is the mother of all destruction for this breed. Dogs bred for neoteny are sickly and puppy like long into adulthood, they are unsure of themselves and constantly look to the handler for reassurance. They break down and fold under handler pressure. The practice of breeders selecting for neoteny has grown over the last 20 years. Why do we constantly talk of breeding biddable dogs, as if this is the pinnacle of progress? The truth is that selection for neoteny presents certain moral and ethical dilemmas.

A large number of breeders will view the dogs they have from an emotional perspective.

Despite all intents and purposes, they will project their more gentle emotions onto their dogs expecting their dogs to become subservient and manageable in response, for they call this behaviour controlled. They evaluate their dogs according to their set of preconceived, westernised, middle class ideals, which favour docility and juvenile characteristics, and then they rationalise such behaviours as representing the correct temperament. I view biddability as a weakness, a fundamental flaw of nature, and it results in an animal that has no legitimate right to be alive in the interests of evolution or defining a working specimen. They are the genetic freaks outside of nature's carefully orchestrated plan, and by creating these types of dog the breeders do a huge disservice and display a lack of respect to those pioneers who created a dog to serve a legitimate survival need for humans living at the frontier. Breeding for neoteny or biddability can wreak destruction on a breed.

The Boerboel community now needs to work together and respect each other's opinions so as to formulate methodical working breeding practices that ensure the future longevity of the Boerboel. By being more clinical and constructive in our thought processes, we can understand that if a Boerboel is easy to train, it will not be of any use to real working dog people or trainers.

An easy, manageable Boerboel is a welcome addition for the middle class American family or the suburban home counties of the UK and Europe, where it will be perceived as an exotic breed, a powerful status symbol, with links to the gladiators and colosseums of ancient history. But such a dog can only ever be a symbol, and not a true Boerboel.

Question 15

Is the Boerboel a working dog or not?

During the days following the formation of SABBS (or SABT, as it was called), we were drawing from old lines of Boerboels and we were not sure exactly what they would produce or how they performed. In Russia the old Avontuur lines predominated. In Europe there were various other lines from Dopper, to Baden, to Yserberg etc. The US had yet other diverse lines such as Mizpah, Piona, Waakasam, Egoli, African dogs (a recent addition in the last decade and a half), and other lines as well as all the above.

Testing, bite and prey drive

Conducting a temp test for the first time for a new breed registry, unfortunately with this breed we have to compromise greatly in standards to gain participation from breed enthusiasts – Source Author

From 2003 onwards, few people were testing Boerboels for bite work and protective capabilities, but of those who were a large proportion were in the US. David Harris from Harris Boerboels was one of the first, an old school farmer and former racing greyhound man. John Blackwell was a formidable and well-respected breeder of the American Bulldog previous to working with Boerboels. Then there were other individuals who produced satisfactory dogs through testing. There was one lady who tested and bred good dogs initially. There were Russians who both worked and tested their dogs long before any of us in the West did. In the world of sport was Norman Epstein and his dog Gordo, who managed to put the Boerboel on the international working agenda within the Boerboel breed fanciers' radar. Norman Epstein has done a huge service to the Boerboel breed, he was an avid opponent of selection and promoted work-tested evaluation. Then of course Brandon Wilson and his dog Zeb became the highest titled working Boerboel in the world, with an amazing score of IPO3, AWD3, FH2, and BH, and the only man in the US to propel the Boerboel to international working dog status. Brandon is a humble and sincere man and his resignation from the Boerboel world was a huge loss.

Zebulun the highest working titled Boerboel in the world to date, attaining a major AWD3, IPO3, FH2 and BH.
Owned, trained and handled by the very talented Brandon Wilson USA
Source Brandon Wilson

In South Africa, no-one tested Boerboels, albeit from one or two individuals who did so for their own satisfaction, but did not go to the lengths of using their testing as selection criteria.

There is a recently formed club in the Western Cape doing protection work with Boerboels, but I have seen only a marginal contribution from them regarding a temperament test or involvement in formulating a breeding programme. To date they have completed several tests, so theirs is a work in progress. They must take a more assertive approach and redesign their temperament test according to their own standards – as working dog people – and not to the criteria set by current mainstream breed societies. There is a window of opportunity for them, which they have not yet taken advantage of particularly considering their geographical location and their access to a readily available source of potential Boerboels to work, test and train. Elsewhere, in Namibia and Kenya there are individuals using Boerboels as anti-poaching dogs. I am not aware of how effective their selection process or their training procedures and methods are. In South Africa in 2005 I was made aware of an individual called Shaamil Majiet who wrote an article in 2003 for the SABT publication *Die Boerboel*, in which he discusses the pros and cons of the Boerboel from a security perspective. In 2017 I had the huge privilege of meeting Shaamil Majiet and although he no longer keeps or owns Boerboels he does still train and work them for individual clients. He also assists with temperament tests for the Western Cape Boerboel Club and used Boerboels quite prolifically in the late 1990s for his own security business and breeding programmes.

In western Europe no-one tested Boerboels. Initially, when I first started out with this breed I gained a bad reputation. Along with my brother I was considered a thug, as crazy. Even today, people's views might not have changed, but if that is the case then it could only be a result of misunderstanding our goals. It was not until my trip to South Africa 15 years later that people started to warm to the idea of testing their dog's protective capabilities, and together we ended up creating a movement which is now considered acceptable and not deviant or underground. So that is certainly a positive aspect of having worked hard to promote the value of testing.

After you read the previous answers to the questions and the previous chapters of the book you will understand that the Boerboel was a hardy farm dog. A multi-purpose versatile utility dog born of a need to ensure the survival of farmers. Natural selection in the Boerboel played a greater part in its history than in nearly any other Bull breed in the history of Mastiffs, partly due to the trade embargos in force during the apartheid regime.

If we are to examine whether the Boerboel is a working dog today, we need to define the meaning of work. Then we would need to work a significant number of dogs in a prescribed breed working test, over a period of years, if we are to approach this scientifically and be able to draw clear conclusions from the results. In over 34 years we have seen no progress towards achieving this; we are challenged by being but a small number of individuals across the world. The numbers are so insignificant in comparison to the whole Boerboel population, and the titles of many of those dogs so basic, i.e. companion dog titles, that they can hardly be considered. The working Boerboel population probably constitutes 1 per cent of the entire Boerboel population.

Compare, for example, the Perro de Presa Canario which has its own form of breed test that provides as accurate a measure as is possible of that breed's ability to to do service duties and protection work. The Presa Canario people, or the Alano Verein Deutschland e.V. (eingetragener Verein), have a character test called the ZWP (1, 2, and 3) comprised of assessments for bite work as well as social and environmental ability. Participation levels in the ZWP tests are higher than in most Bull breed tests, and are increasing, which is a strong indication of the work ethic and philosophy of the AVD. In my opinion, this is probably one of the hardest and most demanding Bull breed tests in the world to date. One more point worth mentioning about the Presa Canario community concerns its consensus on the identity of the Presa dog. Earlier, I discussed the significance of the identity of specific breeds (that is to say their purpose, like herding), and I found that the various Presa Canario communities around the world strongly agreed on the working dog identity of the Presa. In contrast, there are more pet Boerboels in the world then working, so the working identity of the Boerboel is under serious threat. Work, be it protection, sport or personal security work are viewed from the rest of the breed fanciers with a very voyeuristic approach.

I can only speak from experience in dealing with the Boerboels I have worked, trained and tested across the world (over 287), but I can assure you that across the world, the working Boerboel population makes up less than 1 per cent of the total Boerboel population.

The majority of green Boerboels I tested did not display a real ability to either bite well or commit, which I felt was mostly down to a lack of courage and desire. The fundamentally important finding in my research was that the dog's desire to engage its mouth in a natural, predatory fashion can only be assigned to a genetic flaw, which, as the Coppingers had quite rightly pointed out, reflects a lack of predatory motor patterns. In the case of the Boerboel, a lack of predatory motor patterns signals that they either have not been selected for or have been aggressively pursued in dog breeding selection criteria.

Another major component contributing to the dog's inability to bite well or even bite at all, is the fact that these dogs are part of a pet industry that does not promote predatory behaviours in Boerboels. The pet community does not encourage the use of the teeth from an early age with this breed, and a commonly and widely accepted belief is that tactile use of the mouth, and teeth expression, in young puppies should be firmly suppressed. Another example of an obvious genetic flaw is seen in overly exaggerated lips, which can significantly hinder the dog's bite development and can cause fanging, where the front canines go straight through the cheeks. In my early days, I had such a female Boerboel; she had an amazing desire and drive to bite, however, I constantly had to pull her teeth out of her cheeks. On the same topic, in my years of training I observed a surprisingly small number of Boerboels who did bite very deeply, and strong and hard. This gives our community great hope and I believe that the working aspect of the Boerboel can succeed if we promote aggressive selection criteria based on working dog criteria, and also promote breed testing evaluations. I cannot help wondering what endless possibilities there could be for these Boerboels, if we practised consistent, clever training. Such dogs would achieve great heights in mainstream dog sports and prove themselves excellent choices for service and security work.

A young 18 month-old male, completely green and showed very strong forward aggression and fight
Source Author

A very high-hunt drive male, displaying real genetical deep bite and incredible strength
Source Author

A very deep and natural bite
Source Dapo Ojaro, Lagos

A deep and natural bite pictured in Brooklyn, New York
Source Author

The modern-day Boerboel in general has very little prey drive in adulthood. However, we must state that there is a small minority of Boerboels still displaying this hunting drive behaviour, and if every effort is not made to preserve this behaviour (which is one of the foundational functions of this breed) then we will lose a major genetic ingredient of the working dog. The prey drive is a behaviour that drops out of the dog's repertoire very quickly during the puppyhood stages, for both the bully type as well as the hunting type of Boerboel, which comprise a very small percentage of the total Boerboel population. Nearly all of the Boerboels we trained and tested had social play behaviours in abundance, especially with their owners, but the dogs had no ball, prey or hunting drive that would make them useful as a consistent working dog in adulthood.

The absence of a prey drive is the result of juvenile traits having been selected for over the last 20 years. The dog's ability to work in its defence mode lasts momentarily. However, in theory, when a threat is magnified the defensive response should actually be prolonged and should not wane as easily as the prey drive, but the lack of selection for strong dominance has created a very weak and submissive behavioural trait (not usually considered the norm for Bullbreeds or Mastiffs) that has diminished its defence drive. From the perspective of green dogs, the Boerboel's intention to neutralise threat through violence is significantly small, and what strikes me as even more alarming than that is that even in those dogs which did display forward, strong, defensive aggression, the use of the canines was almost completely inhibited. When we compare the Boerboel with, say, the American Bulldog or the Presa Canario then it is clear that we have a daunting future ahead to make this breed a working breed.

In today's world, myself and my colleagues select overly dominant dogs which show the genetic ability to remain in the fight and will be more likely to keep up a high defensive momentum. The modern new age Boerboel has the tendency to not stick in the fight if victory requires too much effort.

The author in Russia 2007 here testing very true natural dominance – Source Author

This flighty characteristic belongs to the same group of behaviours that defensive aggression stems from, i.e. fear. Fight or flight are the by-products of this selected trait and inevitably flight will manifest when fight cannot secure victory, by the same token we must point out that, as explained in Chapter 6 The Importance of Aggression', the more that dominance is selected for in breeding requirements then the greater the chance this selection criteria can bring a lot more determination and fight to the dog's ability to stay in the fight and neutralise the defensive threat. The reasoning behind a watered down and weakened defensive drive within this breed is primarily due to the modern breeder selecting males and females for neoteny, submissive or passive qualities and to produce a dog that is very easy to manage.

A prime example of neoteny this is only one of many examples of this breed's lack of fight drive Source Author.

Another example of submissiveness, this is why temperment testing is so vital – Source Author

Even without conflict this dog shows very passive behaviours – Source Author

When tested for defensive qualities during breed suitability tests, most Boerboels look to their handler or owner for help or reassurance. The fundamental flaws in a dog bred for neoteny are its biddability and its sensitivity to its handler's verbal or physical correction. People are aghast, but, yes in the working dog world we really do use negative as well as positive correction. Alas, only a minority of Boerboels have a huge prey drive and prey drive traits are rarely selected for by mainstream breeders. The prey drive is one of the Boerboel's biggest assets but it is overlooked and neglected during assessments of breeding potential.

The sole purpose of the Boerboel should always be to overcome correction to get its trophy or prize. It is a purpose that stems from the survival impulse. To survive in the wilds of Africa, dogs had to work with what nature had given them and altruism was one of nature's many gifts. In Chapter 7 'The Importance of Aggression', I discussed the importance of pack-keeping and showed how a dog's altruism enables teamwork in a pack, and these characteristics become part of predatory behaviour. A 2017 scientific study carried out by Marshall-Pescini et al at the veterinary department of the University of Vienna looked at cooperative skills in wolves and dogs. The results showed the inability of pet dogs to work together to pull a string in order to release food, while wolves were able to not only work together but to also wait for each other's partner to get there before they pulled the string. This experiment was also done with parrots and had the same effect. The loss of cooperative skills demonstrates the huge price we pay for breeding for neoteny or what some people refer to as biddability. This is the very opposite of what we need to select for. Neoteny results in a Boerboel that is nothing like the true frontier dog.

In the days of the Great Trek when the dogs were roaming free and running alongside the caravans of the trekkers, they were susceptible to danger and the indifference of the Voortrekker to the plight of the dogs forced the dogs to think as part of a pack (with the other dogs) to solve survival challenges (predators, hunger, thirst, exhaustion etc.). Without human intervention, under these conditions, most of the pups would inevitably die, thus ensuring that only the most intelligent or strongest would survive. The attitudes of the Voortrekkers towards their dogs suggests they believed in what we would call today a Darwinian view of natural selection. The trekkers in those days respected nature and let it take its course. The dogs would survive through an assertion of dominance, and the females had to cope with fluctuating hormonal secretion levels in conditions of environmental uncertainty where protection was not afforded by humans, and the female would go to great lengths to ensure the survival of her puppies. Remember the discussion on the river of DNA and how it is programmed to live and multiply despite huge external conflict.

Now back to the working Boerboel, the vast majority that I tested and trained showed an almost non-existent prey drive after the age of 12 months. The defence drive was initially strong, although not committed or convincing enough. When pushed, at least 90 percent of the dogs would run, with their tail tucked. Dogs know their size, they really do, and big dogs have the ability to try and show dominance when it is not really dominance, but a bluff. It is posturing and mostly an avoidance behaviour. In terms of the actual bite a Boerboel will deliver, a lot depends on its training. In general, based on my own experience, if a Boerboel is openly encouraged and promoted to bite from a very young age, or if it is worked at in defence at a more mature age and allowed to gain quick wins, then the bite will be a powerful, deep and convincing bite. However, this would be the result of nurture not nature. The Boerboel has an innate ability to bite well only when the phenotype presents an appropriately shaped head and lack of excess skin folds, but even still the influence of breeding for neoteny will cause problems. The dog will be conflicted in its commitment to the bite and during the latter part of fight development. This poses a serious obstacle to the cultivation of a working Boerboel type. And, of course, the breed's overly hanging jowls will be a detriment to such progress.

Overly large and floppy hanging jowls, an example of the Alpine Mastiff curse
Source Author

Now, do not think I am shooting the Boerboel down. This book is about truth, fact, and not fiction or romance, so here are some positive snippets.

In terms of training Boerboels for work, one must raise them from a very early age, they must be imprinted in the whelping box from three to ten weeks, they must be stressed to create adaptation to the secretion of stress hormones, they must be treated very much like a working dog is raised. They have become a breed of comfort, not through their choice, but by their breeder's selection process, fuelled by market demands.

The puppies must be well socialised, and constantly reassured through positive reward and experience. The young pups need your constant promotion of biting behaviour, chasing and shaking etc., in fact all the predatory motor patterns discussed in the previous chapters should be diligently promoted. This should be done from five weeks onwards with care, due diligence and a fanatic's zeal. They must be shown how to hunt, smell and search for their food. They must be exposed to rain, cold weather and other elements, in fact everything that the breeder took away from them in indiscriminate thoughtless breeding practices must now become the responsibility of the consumer.

The author preparing this young female for a client, prey development is vital for this breed and helps with motivation later in the training programme
Source Author

Promoting grip development with this young pup bred by the author and prepared for a client in 2010
Source Author

Prison service

The author with the commited and diligent dog unit of the Western Cape Correctional Facillity
Source Drakenstein Correctional Facility Dog Unit

Once mature and when the predatory patterns of behaviour are established, the dog's confidence and self-assurance will be apparent, although remember that it is not genetic, it is manufactured. Even if diligently manufactured, throughout the course of this dog's working life one has to monitor it, assess it, adjust it and even back chain it. The Boerboel can perform a jump two and maybe four times, but then on the fifth attempt decide no, it will not work to repetition, and for working dogs, repetition is required. Before you disagree, there was once talk of this dog being used in the prison service, so let us give an example, sniffing for narcotics in the prison service might require a dog to search 30 cells, well, that is working to repetition. (Although, this is not a breed-specific task, and a cocker spaniel would be much more suited to this task, but the Boerboel has become a multi-purpose utility dog.) So other than being a sentry dog – which is a role any dog from the pound can fill – the modern consumer's pet Boerboel has no real merit for working in the prison service. There are three to five Boerboels currently working within the prison service in South Africa, in the Cape Province. These numbers are growing, as the current South African government's financial restraints are forcing local government authorities to search out the dogs from local pounds.

This phenomenon is not new and certainly not unique to South Africa. In the US, in the deep South, the shortage of good police dogs led to a new concept of training from the renowned and talented Gene England. England was the man responsible for table training, which took the world by storm and became a highly formalised system of training weaker and unconfident dogs. His method was fashioned from his experience in training up the dogs that had not been strong enough and lacked the requisite courage and confidence to be useful for local US service authorities. As discussed in earlier chapters, thanks to the internet Gene England's table training concept was used the world over by what we refer to as YouTube dog trainers. Watching videos on YouTube and then applying the concept to every dog in a generic sense without understanding the concept, philosophy and application does not work and this practice destroyed a lot of good dogs. The same concept was seen in the electric collar which, again, was used by internet trainers and destroyed many good dogs. Yet the concept of electrical stimulation from my own perspective is a highly effective and desirable training aid and is probably the kindest and most effective communication for dogs in modern dog training in the twenty-first century.

Whether the Boerboel continues to be used in the present day South African prison service, and possibly also the police service in the future, will inevitably boil down to whether there is a shortage of other credible herding breeds, or whether it is chosen as a cost effective measure, or is chosen as the result of a concerted political manoeuvre. But since only three to ten Boerboels have been used so far, from a population of millions, it will be difficult to properly and fairly evaluate the Boerboel's working potential and suitability as a prison service dog. Huge credit must be given to the South African prison staff of the Drakenstein Correctional Facility, Western Cape for their diligence and skill in turning around many of these Boerboels and utilising them in a positive and effective manner. From my observations the whole team had commitment and passion for the training and their dogs, it is a very positive reflection of their attitudes and desire to succeed with such a breed that has seen no working selection criteria imposed.

Classical training for most service dogs here being carried out at the Drakenstein Correctional Facility
Source Drakenstein Correctional Facility

Efficient and diligent use of a very well-conditioned and working-type Boerboel
Source Drakenstein Correctional Facility

Source Drakenstein Correctional Facility

Source Drakenstein Correctional Facility

Tracking

Source Author

Source Author

The author in Brooklyn accompanying his good friend preparing his dog for IPO tracking portion
Source Author

In terms of tracking, the natural ability of the modern Boerboel is difficult to gauge as the participation of Boerboels in this arena is limited. The breed is becoming increasingly short muzzled, which has implications for both breathing and sense of smell. There is, after all, in the region of around 150–200 million receptor cells in the muzzle of a Boerboel, and as we read in the previous chapters, the ability of those cells to form links with neurological development at an early stage are so vital. Imprinting for this work should be done early and from puppy stage. I can safely say that the sport dogs I have trained for tracking, which all had a sufficiently good length of muzzle, performed above satisfactory levels in tracking, and Boerboels in general make excellent tracking dogs, but longevity and motivation in their work are always the key challenges.

A major point to make which is of fundamental importance is that, at one point, under the then chairman of SABT many years ago, the decision was toyed with to introduce a shorter muzzle length for this breed. This tragic controversy then led to the formation of EBBASA, a new organisation set up by Piet Sprinkhuizen to preserve the phenotype of the old Avontuur dogs which had longer muzzles than the then chairman of SABT thought beneficial to the breed. When Sprinkhuizen (the breeder of Avontuur Boerboels) closed his kennels most of these dogs were spread across the world from Europe to Russia to the USA. The single most destructive act done to the Working Boerboel was the decision by SABT to demand a shorter muzzle length but also detrimental was Sprinkhuizen's decision to form his own registries. Some of the finest examples of green tested dogs I have seen from Russia to Europe have been the old Avontuur line Boerboels.

A Boerboel's agility, its movement and fluid gait, is influenced by the selection process of the breeder. The current trend in today's Boerboels is to show a much deeper and wider chest, shorter legs and body, and larger bones with denser bone mass. This greatly hinders the fluidity of movement and causes elbow, hip and joint problems during the course of training and limits the operational service life for any working dog. From a sporting perspective, the current trend of short and stocky does not permit freedom of movement or expression and harmony in the heelwork but resembles instead an awkward and unpoetic gait

I have bred Boerboels that have been light in frame. With one dog in particular, even though it had low bone density and great angulation, the broad width of its chest resulted in the dog being euthanised at seven years old for elbow dysplasia. This was a tragic course of events and is indicative of the problems arising from the selection for temperament as against seeking a balance of healthy mind and healthy body. Rarely do we find both joining together hand-in-hand. Again this is purely down to the consumer demand or lack of it.

Source Author   *Source Author*

Conclusion on the Working Boerboel question

To conclude, the modern consumer Boerboel is not designed for work, and note my choice of words, i.e. The Modern Consumer Boerboel. A working test of international stature will require rigorous trials, tests and even more tests from puppyhood to adult age, to determine the dog's ability to cope with stress, to form the ability to withstand pressure and recover, to breed and produce consistently healthy viable progeny. Any breed of dog that aims to be the prototype working dog must undergo a breed-specific test to monitor, maintain, develop and progress its breed further. A working test and the definition of work are not burning topics on social media. This lack of interest in taking work and working tests seriously is reflected in today's marketplace where we find Boerboels biting sleeves for 30 or so seconds. A working evaluation is thorough and demanding and has evolved to put the dog through rigid and difficult training to complete the tests or trials. The ability of a Boerboel to protect the handler in an enclosed sterile trial environment is simply not sufficient for this breed's development.

Once the Boerboel is selected for attributes designed for work it will outperform any other Mastiff breed. If trained with diligence I firmly believe that the durability of the Boerboel is on a par with (if not higher than) the Rottweilers of today. There are prerequisites for this. They must be highly dominant, have impeccable fluidity of movement, lightness of bone, a healthy leg length, strong and profound angulation of the rear legs, proper depth and length of muzzle, brought up in a manner that prepares them for work, and have rigid and consistent boundaries set for them.

I can only speak from my experience and that of my colleagues within this breed. There are some formidable and exemplary specimens of this breed, some being utter flukes that were not selected for or perhaps considered as possible examples of a working Boerboel. They have been completely green and shown absolute composure during stress, attack on handler, and under heavy pressure training. I have seen Boerboels with ultra-high dominance which was real and innate, I have seen and experienced fine specimens of a very highly dominant fabric cause severe damage to their owners, I have been privy to information and first-hand accounts of some of these fine dominant specimens being shot by the police, but unfortunately people do not select for this quality. Many years ago I participated in intense debates (at times these were incredibly heated discussions) over the lack of understanding that people had of the importance of selecting for ultra-high dominance for this breed to be considered a working dog. So, I know from experience that there is an abundance of Boerboels that have potential for the international working dog arena. But as there is no authoritative selection process, or formal evaluation, and no governing body to regulate the breeding of working Boerboels (mainly a consequence of overseas consumer demand), it is with regret – and I mean sincere regret – that I have to admit that this breed cannot under present circumstances be recognised as a working breed. The archetype Working Boerboel is sadly a myth.

Below is a very few small examples of how the river of DNA flows like a perfectly orchestrated symphony, at times fighting through human error and reproducing itself in its glory of a time before consumer vulgarity, when the need for purpose was the staple foundation for every good dog man and woman .

FACT OR FICTION: THE AWAKENING

A female recently acquired from South Africa by the author. Huge difficulties were faced in finding the right kind of high dominance together with tight skin, thin bone and good, tight front legs and length of leg
Source Author

A fine example of the frontier dog, the real Boerboel, and sadly out of fashion
Source Stoffel Bloom

A modern example of what the true frontier dog is and was
Source Sascha Jirsak

A prime specimen of the frontier dog, deceased due to dominance issues, a huge loss to the breed
Source Author

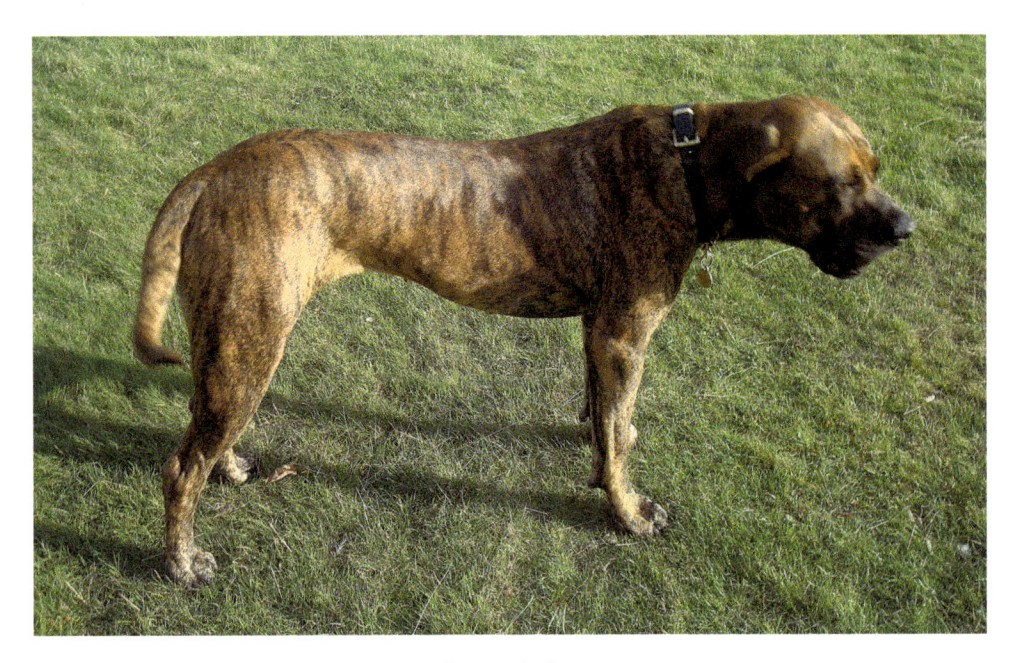

Source Author

Question 16

Currently, there are numerous people around the world working Boerboels, and also some who tout the Boerboel as a personal protection dog and working Boerboel. What do you think about this?

The Boerboel is being used around the world as a proper working Boerboel, but the numbers, as discussed above, amount to a mere fraction of the total Boerboel population. For those of us who work Boerboels, whether that work is weight pull, sled racing, personal protection work, sport work, IPO, Mondeo or KNPV, hunting, herding or guard dogs, the fact that we are working our dogs is not relevant when such an enormous number of Boerboels are not being worked. If individuals will claim to market their Boerboels as working dogs, then the working Boerboel should be considered a product, a brand even. But where are the stringent tests that have been compiled to determine the validity of that product? Where are the consistent results for that product over at least five generations? Which robust data will reassure me that the puppies are consistent products of that brand and attain the high standard that any quality brand offers? The reality is, as we have clarified, there is no such a thing as a working Boerboel.

Based on my own experience I estimate that of the 1 per cent of people who actively do work with Boerboels, only 0.5 percent will be training and working their dogs on a daily basis. Of those who profess to use the Boerboel for personal protection dogs, they may do bite work once or twice a week, if that. I can only say this from my own observations of such people. There is a reason why nearly every sport field and working dog club in the world takes a cautious approach to the Bull breed people and I fundamentally agree with this cautious attitude. Bull breed people in general only want to do bite work with their dogs, they only prescribe to this, they believe this defines a working dog. The sad reality is that in the Boerboel world the less of this false marketing we have the better the development of this breed will be. Bite work is a very small part of working a dog and over many years I have seen numerous people all rushing to legitimise their dogs as working Boerboels through bite work.

In order to ascertain what defines a working dog we have to give credit to its design, its ability to use its muzzle, its ability to withstand hard handler correction, its ability to work under heavy adverse weather conditions, its ability to jump, to run, to bite with intention, and its ability to comply with obedience orders out of desire and motivation. Today, what you see on the internet are snippets of video or photos showing dogs biting a sleeve, and for this we give credit to those who profess to elevate their ordinary status as the new Working Boerboel Breeders. We have already clarified that to tout the Boerboel as a working dog then we must take a far more grown up approach to this phenomenon and come together as a collective group and comply with a formulae and set standard of both testing and evaluation. But the multitude of egos and financial attractions influence people to sidestep a commitment to progress and culminates in splinter groups, even within the 1 per cent of working dog people. So, certainly, any cooperation towards achieving some progress is not going to materialise out of thin air, at least not in the near future.

Furthermore, we can readily see that today's Boerboel is not the original form, which makes us question this new, short, stocky, wide-chested and large-boned design's place within the working Boerboel type. From an international perspective, for those who might wish to buy a working breed, we already have numerous dogs that spring to mind, such as the Mallinois, German Shepherd, or Rottweiler, to name but a few. If we are looking to find a working Boerboel we face a dilemma, for although there are dogs within the Boerboel breed that would make exceptionally great working specimens by design, we would have to spend innumerable hours trawling and sifting through contradictions, lies, dishonesty and false accounts to find one. Poignantly, some of the most titled Boerboels in FCI-approved working tests have unproven parentage; this means that diligent training and the skills of trainers can override average or unsuitable working material. And this is a fact. It is evident that for the international arena of working dogs some regulatory body qualified to assess this breed's inherited values has to be established, and until then, the statements of individual breeders and of those who do limited work with this breed must be taken with the greatest of caution. Particularly so in the arena of the personal protection enthusiast who simply is not able to quantify exactly what makes their breedings stand out. A working line Boerboel is by definition a dog of proven parentage over many generations and is assessed not by just one dog in a given litter but by all of the siblings within that litter.

Another concern is that most of the dogs touted as personal protection dogs simply have no place in developed countries in the twenty-first century. In most of Europe, the US and the northern hemisphere there are more than adequate police forces, with relatively effective response times. The laws and regulations of many countries across the world frown severely upon so-called personal protection dogs. The reality is that the average member of the public does not need a dog to protect them, in our society our personal safety is rarely in any danger. If we now take into consideration the exhaustive time required to research the purchase of a Boerboel suitable for protection and bite work, and the innumerable hours genuinely required for training these Bull breeds for this work, then we can clearly see that protection and bite work are a breed fancier's choice and have nothing to do with the Boerboel's supposed genetic suitability for that work. And on that basis, it is safe to conclude that claims of a Boerboel being a naturally effective personal protection dog are simply false, dishonest marketing propaganda.

Recently, I was involved in one of the many volatile debates that have erupted over the years on a forum designed specifically for working Boerboel fanatics, where one member from the US, a self-proclaimed Working Breeder, made the statement 'I am breeding for handler soft dogs, but my dogs are civil aggressive'. If not challenged or questioned such statements will lead others to blindly accept this ludicrous dribble. That statement demonstrates exactly what a hard task we have ahead of us in giving this breed true clarity and a chance to be recognised at an international level for working dogs. In the world of the Presa Canario or American Bulldog people I rarely if ever hear them talk about or try to tout their dogs as personal protection dogs. Any claim that the Boerboel is a working line or personal protection dog is unfortunately either a deliberate lie or at best an ignorant mistake.

Question 17

Is the Boerboel, in your experience, a suitable candidate for a family guardian dog?

In my years of involvement with the Boerboel and its training I have been exposed to the mainstream pet world, pet dog market and pet dog breeders. During my childhood our family's dogs were our companions and friends, but never elevated to the importance that I give to my own species. The pet dog world has a penchant for liberal, leftist anthropocentric moral values and ethics, and projects that onto dogs. In my time training problem dogs and human owners alike, the majority of the problem dogs have been males aged between nine months and three years. Mainstream teachings of certain celebrity dog trainers based in the US which are widely publicised on mainstream television have caused dog owners to strip out their dogs self-esteem and self-confidence. Their methods take away self-confidence and self-esteem and are tailored to subjugate the dog and demoralise it. In effect, this modern pet dog training philosophy demoralises a dog's motivation and takes away the main component of good training, i.e. hope and anticipation. If we remove heavy socialisation, add testosterone, add a sharp dose of defensive reaction and ensure there are no negative consequences for unwanted behaviour, we will inevitably nurture a disaster in the making. It is not a case of if but more a case of when the disaster will strike.

As covered in the chapter on the importance of aggression, dominant examples of the Boerboel which have been subconsciously bribed (known in the pet dog world as positive reward), their egos inadvertently stroked then grow to magnanimous proportions and combine with a surge in testosterone and instable human ownership to create a dangerous dog who will lack complete control. The inadvertent outcome of this is that the dog that was purchased to bring comfort and companionship to the human now becomes excluded from the activities of modern life that it was designed to participate in. Humans stop taking their dogs out, they walk across the road, avoid other humans and dogs, and at this point the dog will find its own advantage, the ability to control you.

At the other extreme, as discussed in the chapter on the importance of aggression, there can be sometimes sanguinary repercussions of allowing ultra-dominance to develop in a dog. The abusive anthropomorphising ethics and moral values of the pet dog world can lead to disastrous results and have culminated in some fine examples of very workable Boerboels being euthanised.

But let us take this further and look at the pet industry which has financial stakes in this new, liberal, fluffy pet dog world: the dry dog food kibble that is filled with additives and preservatives; the dry dog food snacks that cannot be digested and easily wrap around the stomach linings; the shampoos that give rise to allergies and skin issues; the fluffy beds and blankets that cause irritation to the dog's skin; and the fillings within the beds that when ripped by intention or accident can cause dogs to choke; all of these are designed for precisely such purposes. It is convenient that manufacturers who pay large sums of money to veterinary schools and practices to promote their foods, products and medications, create products that cause lots of pet dogs to get sick and be taken to vet clinics.

Nowhere in the world other than the affluent societies of western Europe and North America does one see this almost perverse dog obsession, which borders on insanity with its irrational projection of emotions upon an animal who did not ask for this abusive set of values imposed upon it.

The repercussions I have seen include growling, biting, lunging and complete emotion shutdown. And then the pet industry markets itself as a pet lover. It is shameful that in a society of educated individuals we have reached a point where humans spend more money on keeping their 12-year-old two-legged old dog alive for their own selfish reasons than on helping their own species. In fact, the most striking and sanguinary point I noticed in my flirtation with the pet dog world is how they would rather spend money in rescuing dogs then perhaps helping a small child get an education from a poorer, less developed country. We call this liberal progressiveness. I call it insanity.

The Boerboel is a very accommodating breed. Some Boerboels for sure can be very clingy dogs, but not all of them. It is sensitive in general and is highly affectionate and good around children. I find the Boerboel to have what I consider an eerie emotional intelligence, but I can say that quite confidently about the Rhodesian Ridgeback as well, it might be an African thing. (I must say it fascinates me and endears me to these dogs tremendously.) The Boerboel in general is a well-balanced and loyal breed and thrives on tactile affection. It is alert, watchful when on guard, territorial and protective of family if trained or nurtured correctly . It is vital to note that a dog of any breed requires you to train it for a desired or specific task. It is highly unfair to expect a Boerboel to be both reliable and effective without giving it prior training.

Special care must be taken with adult males as they reach maturity, testosterone kicks in and bullying and a bad attitude can and in most instances do start to manifest. Females tend to be more diligent as guard and watchdogs, and a lot more manageable. Once males or females establish negative behaviours, if they are not quickly corrected then the risk is that these behaviours become self-satisfying behaviours, and like all animals the dogs will quickly exploit their opportunities. They will find a way to improve their situation.

Adult male being sent to the author for intense nervous aggression issues, here finding heart and soul in the London Underground
Source Author

Another male dog sent for residential intense work, this dog had good drive, was starting to learn clarity, leading to its emancipation
Source Author

A male for 28-day residential with no food drive or ball drive, in addition to a surge in testosterone and a natural nervous sharp temperament, these were challenging times
Source Author

Here the author is in Germany. Socialising our working dogs is vital; service work inevitably includes working in public, built-up spaces
Source Author

The general rule of thumb in urban areas is to practice excessive socialisation and consistent and fair handling. And the application of both negative feeling and positive feeling during this process will help the male dogs through the initial period that their testosterone kicks in.

As a dog for the home and family I am more than confident in recommending a Boerboel, and promoting it as a welcome addition to a family environment, especially with children. Over the years, I have experienced highly dominant males and females which I would without any uncertainty allow to accompany my child to the shop. And if I needed to leave the house for brief periods I could always be assured that the particular Boerboels I had would dependably act as both a visual and violent deterrent to any intruder. In saying this I must point out that training and the process of rearing working dogs improves both one's judgement and clarity of thought. However, like any other breed of dog, certain Boerboels can be nervous, sharp, or fearful, but it is a consumer's market and it is your job to research breeders and visit them to obtain reassurances to inform your choice. As a consumer I urge you to go out there and make demands from Boerboel breeders, raise your expectations and demands and do not settle for second best. There is a small band of individuals who believe that, because of the size of this breed, taking an alpha role and subjugating this dog into submissive behaviour is necessary. I find this deplorable and abusive. The individuals who believe a very firm hand is necessary for this breed will have great difficulty managing any breed or size of dog. Do not believe the hype. Good luck and enjoy this breed for what it is: a wonderful family companion dog.

Question 18

You mention in the 'Final Curtain Call' your disdain for marketing propaganda, can you elaborate on this?

Over the course of the past 15 years, I have come across a number of online platforms dedicated to sharing information on the Boerboel. The website www.boerboel.co.za (created by Casper Lausbaghne), was one of the best early resources, although it is redundant now. A large number of chatrooms and chat forums have contributed to the Boerboel community and I have seen many individuals on there come and go. Moderators of such forums do not vet the chatroom members' curriculum vitae, and some of the advice shared on these sites was undoubtedly unreliable, written by non-specialists. This problem is now widespread across the web. We read studies of genetics by so-called experts who do not have qualifications, we read the work of historians who lack a basic grasp of grammar or cannot rationalise arguments, we read the advice of dog training experts who have never trained a dog, and we read about breeders who have never bred dogs. What these putative authorities all have in common is the ability to convince an audience of strangers that they are credible and speaking from experience. In this modern society of instant information the question we must ask is the information reliable? It does not follow that an individual who is eloquent and emotionally intelligent is also an expert in any subject that they feel passionate about – let us say, in the field of training or working dogs, or genetics. Although Lenin is credited with having said 'a lie told often enough becomes truth', in this era of fake news it has become a commonplace; with careful manipulation and repetition an utter mistruth can slowly be incorporated to mainstream fact, eventually.

Based on my observations of Boerboel social media groups there is very little intelligent debate going on. It seems to me that there are large numbers of people who must have an abundance of free time on their hands; their online debates, if heated, can lead to censorship of some of the individuals (banned from the forums), which is probably the most insidious of actions, although censoring an individual's point on the basis that it might offend or hurt the feelings of someone else seems to be the accepted norm in modern society. I have observed on many occasions so-called experts in these various groups across the world (but in particular the USA) claim that the Boerboel breed would fight off baboons and keep away lions. The reality is such rhetoric perpetuates the myths about the Boerboel and further sustains a marketing propaganda that, since 1983, has increasingly fooled the world into believing that thousands of dollars spent on this working dog is imperative if you want a baboon-hunting, lion-fighting, South African defender of homes.

While we have touched upon the subject, it would be opportune to elaborate on the cost of this breed, which, to all intents and purposes can reach tens of thousands of dollars. Setting aside such astronomical amounts of money for a Boerboel might be justified if it is a popular sire, belongs to a favoured breeder, and is a high-scoring show champion. For the working dog purist and those seeking functional dogs (but excluding breed fanatics), we can put the cost into perspective by comparing the cost of a Boerboel with other similar breeds. For example, a fifth generation working German Shepherd pup can readily be attained for no more than 1000 USD and that could include five generations of health testing and working FCI titles to the pup's credit. Also consider the working Mallinois, the Dutch herder, with over ten generations of KNPV titles which can sell for only 1000 USD and under.

One might ask just why do Boerboels cost so much? The position of Boerboel breeders is clear – keep the price inflated by promoting the dog as a mystical mind-reading exotic Mastiff. The market for Boerboels is saturated with ill-informed buyers who often believe such romantic rhetoric. Many breeders in the UK and Europe believed that by keeping the price high for this breed it would somehow protect it from the unscrupulous fringes of society in the dog world. In effect, it enabled the pond life of society to get rich quick and cut corners without ever needing to prove the credibility of the product to the mainstream consumer market.

Why did the herding breeds not similarly fall into the hands of a fringe society? The answer lies in numbers and collective cooperation. If the community of working Boerboel enthusiasts and professional trainers, breeders, testers etc. works together to drive down the price of Boerboels, more dogs will be available to us to breed and train properly for working purposes, more dogs will be available to test and evaluate, which will allow genuine, working dog people the opportunity to work and train these dogs. Dogs that take a minimum of two years to attain a thorough evaluation of both health and temperament through exhaustive breed testing will inevitably need trainers and competitors, and if we wish to increase the numbers of dogs being trained and put into competitions the price has to be reasonably accessible. It is then inevitably the best performing dogs that will reflect the due diligence and hard work of the breeder. The result will be that only the breeders whose dogs are the absolute best will be able to demand the highest prices.

A working dog should be produced for a working market, not a fluffy middle class consumer market. The current price of the Boerboel is simply unattainable for the mainstream working dog purist, and that price tag has nothing to do with social status, despite what many Boerboel breeders would like you to believe. They charge astronomical prices because they can get away with it: so long as the public believes the Boerboel is an exotic, mythical, gladiator 'superdog'.

Alternatively, some breeders will cite their costs as being the reason for their high prices. When we factor in the time, petrol, helpers and equipment as well as special diets, it costs tens of thousands of pounds for owners to title their working dogs. By contrast, the cost for pet breeders consists only of vet fees and food. But their high spending on vet fees has become necessary as a result of their choices: the modern Boerboel is nearly always bred by artificial insemination. Caesarean section has become the commonplace method of birthing and natural birth, like organic fruit and veg, is marketed as a privilege. It reminds me of the Chelsea mums in London who are too posh to push.

I hope we can now see the problems faced by the Boerboel market as a result of society having been misled by false information that online platforms and mainstream media have exposed it to, and as a result of society having inadvertently participated in perpetuating the idea that this veritable breed has a place within the pet market. The last bastion of working Mastiff that was born from a process of natural selection has been bastardised to become so deformed it cannot even perform the role afforded to every living species, that is to say, of natural reproduction.

The beauty of the genuine working dog world is that while we can type all we want, as fast as our stubbly little fingers can move, to convince the world we are the best and our dogs are the best, at some point in time we know that the truth will out, because to win titles and qualify a dog to working status one has to perform on the field. Like the seasoned pro boxer before the fight can talk and talk, inevitably, he must face his own confidence in that ring where, no doubt, sceptics and fans alike will be the judges of what they see, whether he himself knew it or not. My message to newcomers to this breed is to go and meet people in person, never assume that someone's online fancy words and convincing rhetoric are authoritative, the person on the other side of that screen is most likely not the person you imagined. But, above all, ask for evidence, ask for factual proof. Do not accept as fact the rhetoric you may hear from breed fanciers and so-called breed experts. Base your viewpoints on information that can be examined on a much higher platform – from an international level dog perspective as opposed to a breed fancier's, for only then we will truly understand the information out there and rationalise it properly, as independent, freethinking individuals should.

Question 19

What do you think will be the future of this breed especially concerning its progression as a working breed?

In 2002–2003 under the main breed registry kept by SABBS (who at that time were called SABT) there were 1000 listed Boerboel breeders in South Africa. However, it is fair to say that most of those people were registered as breeders despite not having bred this particular dog. At that time there were no more than 11 or 12 line breeders of Boerboels, each had their own set type. The same can be said of both mainland Europe and parts of North America at the time. Given that South Africa was the cradle of the Boerboel and its natural motherland it was deeply regrettable that the 12 or so line breeders in South Africa represented less than 1.5 per cent of the entire breeding community. My visit to South Africa in 2006–2007 took me to over 49 Boerboel breeders. The array of dogs available and the kennel setups including the variation of types was promising but certainly left room for improvement. My last visit before the printing of this book took me back to the cradle of the Boerboel in 2017. The picture I saw was both harrowing and troubling. Nearly all the major large breeders and, yes, the super kennels, (which, although I certainly do not agree with, did at the very least contribute some genetic variation and outcrossing possibilities) have nearly all but disappeared.

Today, the South African motherland has literally no line breeders left. Every year, what was once a plenitude of experienced breeders and knowledgeable Boerboel people is diminished, as individuals die or decide to quit the Boerboel world after realising that the financial gains are not good enough. What was the golden age of the Boerboel between the late 1990s and mid-2000s has been subsiding now year by year. Similarly, the Rhodesian Ridgeback, which was once the famous mascot of British heritage in South Africa, is slowly declining.

The departure of line breeders and the inevitable situation to come whereby the Boerboel will have to be bred within the strict confines of its current breed standard will together create a catastrophe. The breeders I visited in 2017 in South Africa represented dog dealers and peddlers, not breeders or line breeders. The aims, visions and goals of many of them were lacking and this indicated that they were milking the last of the money out of the Boerboel industry. Most breeders I spoke to in 2017 stated they were only doing it for financial gain and the breeding of bigger, wider, stockier dogs was purely for the American and European markets.

We can thank the ignorance of a minority of Americans and Europeans for fuelling this demand and driving a stake deep into the heart of what was once the last bastion of pure unadulterated Bull breed. These sentiments are not exclusively mine nor typical of those of an outsider looking in. The Historical Boerboel Association of South Africa newsletter in July 2004 points out:

> Harsh words have been said about the breed standard and the appraisal system commonly in use. If it can be manipulated like it is commonly experienced, then it serves no purpose and it will not prevent the degradation and misrepresentation of the breed. Old and established breeders are busy disappearing from the scene and their heritage is visibly following the same path as a result of a defective structure to preserve the qualities of the breed in South Africa. The assiduous scramble of almost uncontrolled exports underlines the short-sighted view with regard to the interests of the Boerboel locally.

When I first started with this breed I was rigid in my belief system. Today, in 2018 a new political struggle is stirring in South Africa, the seizure of land from the Afrikaner, in the previous chapter 'The Final Curtain Call' I emphasised that if we do not learn from the past then history will repeat itself. The dynamics of a politically evolving South Africa will play out (we hope its lessons will be learned from the Zimbabwe crisis) and if they don't, we will see a huge exodus of Afrikaners from the African continent and the legacy of this fine frontier dog/Boerboel will be erased from its mothers cradle.

The breed might be catapulted to the one place I feel will inherit this legacy, the country – or as many consider it the corporate entity – that is the US, for there they will no doubt remarket and restrategise the Boerboel to evolve into a more lucrative commodity. History shows us the demise of veritable working Bull breeds like the Neapolitan Mastiff, the Bullmastiff, and the Dogue de Bordeaux to name a few, while at the other end of the spectrum we can also argue that the working line German Shepherd and the Mallinois, excessively selected for high-pointing, yapping, prey-driven dogs, have gone to another extreme. Again, we forget to learn from history.

Now that I have reached the end of this book, with all honesty I feel I have reached nirvana. So, my final words will remain true to the forefathers of this breed. The real Boerboel was born out of adversity. From both man-made and natural selection, occupying inhospitable lands, it developed by pure necessity. The true Boerboel was never sold as a commodity. The real Boerboel is like religion, it is like economy, it is ever evolving. Its temperament is neither defined by me or you the consumer. The only true curators, the only true masters of its design were its forefathers, its African breeders and its African heritage – its use designed by the farmers purely to meet the challenges of a geographical area, who bred it to work with them. The worth of this magnificent frontier dog, the Boerboel, was its capacity and desire for work.

The Boerboel ceased to be a true representative of its breed, of its heritage and its hardened design, the minute it became an official breed. Once it became a breed standard its use was redefined. From that point onwards it became the Boerboel by superficial design. In that little schoolhouse in 1983 the creation of a new phenomenon occurred. The last bastions of that design are still present in isolated pockets today. The new modern Boerboel breed of post-2000 is not a working breed, because the work is not defined and the role of the breed is not clarified. Its goals are too diverse, there are far too many grey areas.

In this last chapter, I can state with clarity that **the real Boerboel was the frontier dog**. It has evolved into a new type of dog, providing a use, which has been influenced by economy and commerce, that is nothing more than that of a breeding cow or sheep for the privileged in a culture separated from reality, and far removed from all that the Boerboel stood for. I refer to you, the consumer: the new money, the vulgarity, without class, the get rich quick dreamers, the Kim Kardashian generation of the dog world, obsessed by photos of big, thick boned dogs, huge bone mass and hanging jowls, the superficial generation which has fuelled the demand for creating a new use for the Boerboel. Its new identity, its new phenotype, is not its history, it is a phenomenon spurred on by the power of economy and commerce. But is this new use, this new breed really a Boerboel? In South Africa there will always be good genetic material for breeders, whether a cross Ridgeback-Boerboel, or Boerboel-Pitbull, its use and ability to withstand heat, to run and walk without needing to seek shade, its ability to gather its own food, to be able to withstand pain and overcome injury, to survive as scavenger or predator, its ability to show civil disobedience to me, is what I seek. And in return for this, I ask not for beauty, I ask not for admiration, I ask not for recognition – but for function and dominance, as its will to succeed will always stands first and always has since 1652. The westernised viewpoint of and use for this breed is not important, because it was not designed for you or me, it was designed out of hardship by farmers, pioneers and hunters alike. This use stopped in 1983 when commerce dictated a new era.

Yann Martel's *Life of Pi* (2001) was an amazing book. It told the story of a boy stranded on a boat with a tiger and of their adventures. Many years later a publisher wished to produce the story, only the boy had grown up and in this new reality he had created came the tale of the boat with two different stories, one false and one true. After both stories were acted out for the publisher, he was asked which story he believed. The end of this book asks you, the reader to decide. Do we choose the romantic adventurous fiction or plain, boring non-fiction? Which story do you really want to buy into? I can take a wild guess. For history has clearly showed me the answer.

Appendix

SANCTUARY KENNEL'S 'APOLLO'

Sanctuary Kennels

In a book about the Boerboel it would be prudent to include a passage on the wonderfully honest and progressive Shaamil Majiet, who runs Sanctuary Kennels. He first started training and competing with German Shepherds in the early 1980s in FCI (KUSA) working trials, while providing trained dogs to the service industry. I came across Shaamil's publication in *Die Boerboel* (discussed below) on the working Boerboel in early 2005 and duly took note of his advice to rectify the problems that were developing within the breed all those years ago.

What adds infinite weight to his words are the facts that first, he is first and foremost a working dog man; secondly, he has no vested interest in breeding or in procuring any financial interests from the Boerboel breed; and thirdly, the work ethic and structures of training that Shaamil lays down in his initial foundation work for all service and working dogs is at a standard I consider to be on a par with my fellow IPO sport competitors at international levels.

Shaamil purchased his first Boerboel in 1998 and later that year was to purchase a second Boerboel called GroenvleI Clyde. He said to me that these two dogs had good prey and defence drives, and were not big or overly built. The third dog he purchased was a Piona dog which had a Great Dane type head. The dogs of the Piona lines, he told me, were much leaner with good stamina; however, a majority tended to display excessive, very loose skin, a problem we can still see inherited today within the Boerboel breed. The dog he purchased was Piona Lara, a dog which he states had strong and real aggression. He then went on to breed three litters for his own use, which was in the security and service industries.

He comments on the modern Boerboel to say it although its general appearance in terms of consistency and type has improved, he yet finds its ability to work sharply declined and they tend to lack prey or hunt drives.

Today, Shaamil still trains Boerboels on an individual basis and has assisted the Western Cape Boerboel Club in two temperament tests to date. His background in German Shepherds and KUSA working trials gives him a huge advantage over those in South Africa who currently provide and train dogs for the service and security industries.

Shaamil has granted permission for his article in the November 1999 edition of *Die Boerboel* to be reproduced here:

'The Boerbeol As A Working Dog'
by Shaamil Majiet

For the past few years I have been training guard dogs for personal protection as well as commercial security purposes, we used mainly German Shepherds and Rottweilers. When we acquired our first Boerboel Bitch not much was known about the breed. It was especially in its working ability that I was interested in. I then proceeded to train it and place it with our commercial working dogs. We supply many of the larger companies in Cape Town and our dogs therefore have to work under varying conditions. They sometimes have to work among crowds and other times alone guarding premises in dangerous areas.

For commercial purposes dogs have to be alert and aggressive but at the same time, have a steady temperament as they often have to work with different handlers. They have to be obedient to that handler but firm enough to attack and protect when called upon. Size is important, as a big dog can be good deterrent to criminals. They also have to be agile enough when chasing a person. Not only must they have a good bark but be able to bite hard when needed.

The bitch proved to train well and be obedient and with the protection work did very well. We later added a male, GroenvleI Clyde, to our collection and these two were mated. The pups were placed in different homes so as to draw a development comparison.

The Boerboel proved to be a good working dog. The two we own are used all over Cape Town to promote the breed as a working dog. Many questions were asked, and people were impressed; the working Boerboel had come to Cape Town.

Recently they were used at the university of the Western Cape to guard the hostels in an effort to recover millions in unpaid fees. Even in crowd control situations they were indispensable on the technical side; the following can be noted.

It is fairly obedient and trains well. It is intelligent enough to understand you. It is agile and strong enough to master most of the agility jumps. It has a loud enough bark to deter any persons at a distance. Its natural guarding ability makes it an excellent sentry dog. But it is the power that is really impressive. It has almost twice the power of the average Rottweiler, it bites very hard and conventional attack suits prove almost useless, so extra padding has to be added. Yet its good temperament makes it an easily controllable dog. Recently, our third male Boelie saved a guard's life when he was attacked by four men. After being ordered away the first time, the thieves had returned a second time, apparently with firearms. Boelie was then released and he chased all four of them away biting two of them in the chase. On the down side it eats more than other guard breeds, it also develops slower and reaches maturity later than other breeds. It sometimes is playful, which can be irritating to a trainer.

To other breeders out there, please breed so that we do not lose the working ability of the breed (as has happened to many other breeds). The standard calls for a workable size – breed towards that. Too heavy and too large a dog will tire easily. Do not neglect its guarding ability at the expense of the temperament. Do not breed for looks alone. Remember we are breeding a guard breed, which should be practical dogs. Let us work together to promote our breed. It is time that our own guard breed took its rightful place.

Conclusion

Pictured with the author – Source Author

The article was written over 20 years ago and highlights the dogs used by Sanctuary Kennels and their ability to work; it is revealing that the author warned all those years ago that the Boerboel would start to increase in size. Please remember that all animals are designed to conserve energy and the greater the mass of an animal the greater the likelihood of lethargy. Another interesting note the author made was on the playfulness of the Boerboel, which is an absolute disadvantage for working dogs and is suggestive of the retention of juvenile behaviours i.e. neoteny.

Another striking and poignant comment was made about the strength of the dogs used by the author, and yet they were of an average working size and not overly large or cumbersome, they were, in his words, athletic and prey-driven. The biggest and most common mistake in the worlds of the pet dog enthusiasts and working dog people is the inability to differentiate between size and strength. In Chapter 6 'The Importance of the Female' we discussed the roles of the female athlete and the cross-sectional muscle coverage. The same might be quite easily said of size. I have seen a 40 kg female Boerboel dominate and flip over 70 kg male dogs and almost choke them out. I have handled 80 kg male Boerboels that have flipped out on me and spun to bite my face. It was quite easy to control them with just one hand leaving my right hand free to finish my coffee. Yet I have seen 50 kg male dogs that are thin and stripped that will drag me straight down to the floor with an internal power and use of muscle that you could not have imagined.

Quo Vadis Commander a highly strong dog with ability to use his body so rare in this breed.
Source Author

The secret is not in the size but the movement of the body, which is what generates the strength. Simply put, big dogs have very little ability to move with fluidity and generate strength from particular muscle groups. Recently, I worked a medium sized male Boerboel in the United Kingdom on a bite sleeve, his strength for me was one of the most powerful I have come across, with the exception of an Avontuur dog based in the UK.

Avontur Clive, a genetically deep and hard bite, and I was fortunate to have been the first ever to have tested this dog when he first arrived in the UK
Source Mark Beesley

Reviewing video footage over and over, I noticed this dog had an amazing ability to understand his body – his muscles would ripple from the jaw all the way down to his rear thigh muscles. Very few dogs have this ability in the Bull breed world. It once again serves as a reminder of the fact that the trait which created this poetic and elaborate display stems from the hunting type, of which he most certainly belonged.

Shaamil is one of the few Boerboel people I have met that has both a knowledge of the bloodlines that were available in the mid-1990s in South Africa as well as a knowledge of the working ability of those bloodlines. This together with his classic foundation methods of training, which still remain to this day the blanket foundation of championship trainers the world over, puts Shaamil Majiet in a highly prominent position in the working Boerboel world and in the industry of trainers within South Africa.

The men behind the curtain

Source Brandon Wilson

A special dedication goes out to a good friend and mentor, a highly humble and dignified gentleman, Mr Brandon Wilson of Kentucky, USA whose help in advising me, and supporting me has been both charitable and gracious. A highly talented trainer and the only man in the world to have achieved recognition for the Boerboel breed from an international perspective, attaining with his dog Zeb the illustrious IPO3, AWD3, FH2, BH working titles. Zeb was featured in the illustrious Scutzhund USA magazine and gave the Boerboel immediate international recognition from the fellow sport dog and protection dog enthusiasts the world over. As owner, handler and trainer this gentleman for me is one of the most accomplished working dog purists in the world to-date for this breed. I thank Brandon for his contribution to my works.

A special dedication goes out to a very dear friend and fellow working dog enthusiast, Dapo Ojaro from Lagos Nigeria, it's amazing how small the dog world really is. Dapo was instrumental in chairing and bringing together the whole world community of working Boerboel enthusiasts. His endeavours for this breed make him for me a true ambassador of the working type Boerboel. A committed dog trainer and highly talented, he has worked with great results and accomplishments with his dogs. We owe him greatly, as his vision and predictions for the inevitable decline this breed might inevitably face and his call of duty to fight against such changes was fought by him many years before we knew the conclusion of show dogs vs working dogs ethos within this breed.

A special dedication goes to Shameel Majeet who gave me so much information regarding the early days of training Boerboels for his security company and his hard stance on the ability and use of Boerboels for work and utility dog purpose. Again, another humble person who toiled tirelessly behind the scenes with diligence and integrity. Such ambassadors are lost in the world of superficial appraisal scores and the shallow world of show dogs.

The author with John Greyvenstein Snr
Source Author

Huge respect must also go to John Greyvenstein from Braveheart in Pretoria, South Africa for his invaluable information regarding the very formation of the Boerboel breed in the late 80s and early 90s. With probably the largest most advanced dog training academy in South Africa, John is also incredibly specialized in Scent work and detection dogs and teaches both military and police academies. John's resilience in not compromising the qualities required for a working Boerboel in the formation period of this breed led inevitably to John removing himself from the founding fathers of this breed. It's a shame that in 1983, had the founding fathers followed John's prototype working standard for this breed, we would never have had to compile works of this magnitude.

A picture can speak a thousand words

During my 15 years of working and testing, and training Boerboels across the world, I have been invited and entertained by many wonderful people along this journey. Here is a list of photos compiled along my journey and for those whom helped to arrange the many working sessions in order for me to put my works together.

Special thanks to Adelina Makunina in Russia, the most gracious and wonderful host and her diligence in promoting the breed in her native Russia. Alla Freidman for her gracious hospitality and interesting discussions and debates.

The author with Alexey Breykin in Russia 2008
Source Author

Alex Breykin for his exceptional talents as a trainer and helper, a true seasoned dog sport competitor and team captain, and his hard and diligent work helping during my stay in Russia.

My American friends, Ernest Momo Chambers who was one of the first men to IPO title Cane Corsos in the USA at both national championship and club levels, amassing many first-time titles in sport work, to my good buddies Raymonde and Gavin Hercules for helping me to organise my schedules in Brooklyn and showing me their dedicated and passionate work. My US friends have worked hard for many years, never stepping into the limelight, but rather working diligently behind the scenes, for it is their passion that makes them toil the many hours required in order to compete this breed amongst many Bull breeds in the world of sporting/protection dogs.

The Author and Shawn and Earl
Source Author

To Earl and his owner Shawn of the UK for being only the 2nd Boerboel in the world to have passed in my opinion the hardest Bull breed test in the world, the ZWP 11 or the Presa Canario breed test of the AVD, and for allowing me to test this dog's immense desire.

A special gratitude goes out to Kevin Hartzenburg and the guys of the Western Cape Boerboel Club whose determined enthusiasm to embrace a temperament evaluation and assessment, working hard to improve the breed's working ability.

To my many friends in Europe who train hard and quietly without fanfare, without seeking adulation or economic improvements.

The ability of the Boerboel to pursue work – the last bastion of its heritage, is slowly and inevitably going to diminish unless we make every conceivable effort to preserve and test for its inherited genes in a more advanced and thorough testing procedure.

- For you the reader, the consumer, the hobby breeder of the future, go out and challenge the myths, ask for evidence and never settle for second best.
- Respect is earned in the world of working dogs and it is your job to break down the arrogance of dog breeders by insisting on evaluation of temperament.
- The health of the sire and dam, the ability to perform under severe pressure, the fluidity of movement and running, jumping and climbing are the fundamental assets of any farm utility dog from whichever geographical location it might hail.
- The ability to be stable under busy social distractions, the puppy whelping procedures and preparation designed for working puppies going to new homes, insist and demand, and demand again, it is your right as a consumer of a product to demand from the supplier a quality of goods.

Only you the public can change the course of this breed's future. And, inevitably, with the demand for a physical need to work we will start to rekindle the embers of the real Boerboel or as we can now say the real frontier dog.

Bibliography

Articles

Agricultural Journal of the Cape of Good Hope, Vol. 34, Issue 2, Feb 1909, pp. 186–188. Available at: http://journals.co.za/content/ajcgh/34/2/AJA0000018_1086?fromSearch=true Accessed: 1 August 2018.

Bloom, Craig, 'Boerboel Temperament' (2007) http://oz.dogs.net.au/sirrek/uploads/documents/Boerboel-Temperament.pdf [accessed 16 July 2018].

Die Boerboel Vol. 1, November 1986.

Die Boerboel Vol. 2, March 1988.

Ekvall, Robert B. (1963) 'Role of the Dog in Tibetan Nomadic Society' *Central Asiatic Journal*, Vol. 111. https://doi.org/10.1210/jcem.84.3.5565

Joan C. Lo, Valerie M. Schwitzgebel, J. Blake Tyrrell et al., 'Normal Female Infants Born of Mothers with Classic Congenital Adrenal Hyperplasia due to 21-Hydroxylase Deficiency', *The Journal of Clinical Endocrinology & Metabolism*, Vol. 84, Issue 3, 1 March 1999, Pages 930–936,

Majiet, Shaamil. 'The Boerboel as a Working Dog', Sanctuary Kennels, Die Boerboel, November 1999.

Swart, Sandra. *The South African Historical Journal*, Vol. 48 (2003)

Books

Abrantes, Roger. *The Evolution of Canine Social Behaviour* (Wakan Tanka Publishers, 2005).

Altbecker, Anthony. *A Country at War with Itself: South Africa's Crisis of Crime* (Jeppestown: Jonathan Ball Publishers, 2007).

Armitrage, George C. *Thirty Years with Fighting Dogs* (Jack Jones, 1939).

Arsensis, Mylda. L. *Ridged Dogs in Africa* (M. Arsenis, 1981).

Baines, Thomas. *Explorations in South West Africa, Being an Account of the Journey in the Years 1861/1862* (London: Longman, Green, Longman, Roberts & Green, 1864).

Baldwin, William Charles. *African Hunting and Adventure from Natal to the ZambesI from 1852 to 1860* (2nd edn, London: Richard Bentley Publisher in Ordinary to Her Majesty, 1863).

Canon, Walter Bradford. *Bodily Changes in Pain, Hunger, Fear and Rage* (New York: D. Appleton and Company, 1922, c1920, 1929a).

Coppinger, R. & Coppinger L. *Dogs: A Startling New Understanding of Canine Origin,*

Behaviour & Evolution (1st edn, Prentice Hall & IBD, 2001).

Costa, Linda M. *Rhodesian Ridgeback Pioneers* (1st edn, Kantara Investments, 2004).

Cumming, Roualyn Gordon. *Five Years of a Hunters Life in The Far Interior of South Africa*, Vol. 2 (New York: Harper Brothers, Franklin Square, 1874).

Du Preez (SOURCE UNKNOWN)

Grabbe, Bert. *The Boerboels of Southern Africa* (South Africa: SABT, 1995).

Green, Lawrence G. *Lords of the Last Frontier* (Howard B. Timmins, 1952).

Guibault, Andre. *The Tibetan Venture* (London: John Murray, 1947).

Hall, Sian. *Dogs of Africa* (Alpine Books, 2003).

Hancock, David. *The Mastiffs: The Big Game Hunters, their History, Development and Future* (Charwynne Dog Features, 2000).

Hawley, T. C. *The Rhodesian Ridgeback* (Pretoria: Major Craft Press, 1957).

Helgesen, David, H. *The Definitive Rhodesian Ridgeback* (1982).

Homan, Mike. *A Complete History of Fighting Dogs* (Ringpress Books, 1999).

Hubbard, Clifford, L. B. *Working Dogs of the World* (London: Sidgwicks and Jacksons, 1947).

Hutchinson's Popular and Illustrated Dog Encyclopedia, Vols. 1–3 (1st edn, Walter Hutchinson, 1930).

Kastil, Pavel. *The Degeneration of the Dog Family* (2006).

Lucius Junius Moderatus Columella. trs. Harrison Boyd Ash, E.S. Forster, and Edward H. Heffner (London: William Heinemann, 1968).

McCrindle's Ancient India as Described by Ptolemy (1st edn, Calcutta: Chuckervertty, Chatterjee and Co.,1927).

Murray, J. N. *The Rhodesian Ridgeback: 1924–1974* (1st edn, privately published, 1976).

Oliff, Douglas. (ed.) *The Ultimate Book of Mastiff Breeds* (Ringpress Books, 1999).

Pretorius, Anemari. *The Boerboel South Africa's Own* (2007 in conjunction with SABBA).

Raiser, Helmut. *Der Schutzhund (The Protection Dog)*, tr. Arman Winkler (1st edn, Sooke Printing: 1996).

Rohrer, Ann & Flamholtz, Cathy J. *The Tibetan Mastiff Legendary Guardian of the Himalayas* (1st edn, OTR Publications, 1989).

Rosenthal, William, S. *The Black and Tan Rhodesian Ridgeback Genetic Issues and Possible Solutions* (2005). Available at: http://class.csueastbay.edu/COMMSCI/Black%20and%20Tan%20RR%20Genetics.htm. Accessed: 1 August 2018.

Selous, Frederick Courteney. *A Hunters Wanderings in Africa: Being a Narrative of Nine Years Spent Among the Game of the Far Interior of South Africa*, (Alexandar Books: 2001) [original: London: Richard Bentley & Son, 1881]

Semenic, Carl. *Gladiator Dogs* (TFH Publications, 1998).

Serpell, James. *The Domestic Dog: Its Evolution, Behaviour and Interactions with People* (Cambridge University Press, 1995).

Shelley, E. R. M. *Hunting Big Game with Dogs In Africa* (Becktold Printing, 1924).

Soman, W. V. *The Indian Dog* (Popular Prakashan, 1963). Reprinted online: http://indianpariahdog.blogspot.com/2017/07/weve-brought-back-classic-indian-dog-by_2.html. Accessed 1 August 2018.

Theal, George McCall. *Ethnography and Condition of South Africa before A.D. 1505* (Allen and Unwin, 1919).

von Flemming, Hans Friedrich. *The Complete Sportsman* (1719).

Wagner, John P. *The Boxer* (Orange Judd, 1939).

Wynn, M. B. *The History of The Mastiff* (Vintage Dog Books, 2006).

Historical, Socio-ethological Books

Anthony Altbecker. *A Country at War with Itself: South Africa's Crisis of Crime* (Johannesburg & Cape Town: Jonathan Ball, 2007).

Cook, Michael. *A Brief History of the Human Race* (Granta Publications, 2003).

Cultural Theory: The Key Concepts (Routledge Publishers, 2002).

Darwin, Charles. *On Natural Selection* (Penguin Books, 2004).

Darwin, Charles. *On the Origin of the Species* (Harvard University Press, 2003).

Dawkins, Richard. *A Pilgrimage to the Dawn of Life*: *The Ancestors Tale* (Phoenix Books, 2004).

Dawkins, Richard. *River Out of Eden: A Darwinian View of Life* (Phoenix Books, 2004).

George, McCall Theal. *Ethnography and Condition of South Africa Before 1505* (George Allen and Unwin, 1919).

Heunis, Jan. *The Inner Circle: Reflections on the Last Days of White Rule* (Johannesburg & Cape Town: Jonathan Ball, 2007).

Lorenz, K. *Man Meets Dog* (Routledge Classics, 2002).

Lorenz, K. *On Agression* (Routledge Classics, 2002).

Pakenham, Thomas. *The Boer War* (Abacus Books, 2006).

The Early Cape Hottentots Described in The Writings of Olfert Dapper (1668), Willem Ten Rhyne (1686), and Johannes Gulielmus De Grevenbroek (1695) (Cape Town: The Van Riebeck Society, 1933).

Welsh, Frank. A History of South Africa (Harper Collins, 1998).

Scientific Data

Cannon, Walter Braford. Bodily Changes in Pain, Hunger, Fear, and Rage. (New York: Appleton-Century-Crofts, 1929).

Grandin, Temple & Deesing, Mark J. 'Genetics and the Behavior of Domestic Animals' in: *Behavioural Genetics and Animal Science* (San Diego, California: Academic Press, 1998).

Jordana, J., Manteca X., and Ribo, O. 'Comparative Analysis of Morphological and Behavioural Characters in The Domestic Dog and Their Importance in The Reconstruction of Phylogenetic Relationships in Canids'. *Genetics and Molecular Biology*. Vol. 22 No. 1 March 1999.

Sandra Swart (2003) 'Dogs and Dogma: A Discussion of the Socio-Political Construction of Southern African Dog Breeds as a Window on Social History', *South African Historical Journal*, Vol. 48, No. 1, pp. 190–206, DOI: 10.1080/02582470308671931

Schultz, D. *Sensory Restriction* (New York: Academic Press, 1965).

Scott, J. P. 'Critical periods in the development of social behavior in puppies', *Psychosomatic Medicine*, January 1958.

Skinner, B. F. *Behaviour of Organisms* (New York: Appleton-Century-Crofts, 1958).

Tinbergen. N. *The Study of Instinct* (New York: Oxford University Press, 1951).

Trut, Lyudmila, N. 'Early Canid Domestication: The Farm-Fox Experiment' *American Scientist*, Vol. 87. No. 2, March–April 1999.